SPORTS COACHING
A Practical Guide

Effective
SPORTS COACHING
A Practical Guide

Alan Lynn

THE CROWOOD PRESS

First published in 2010 by
The Crowood Press Ltd
Ramsbury, Marlborough
Wiltshire SN8 2HR

www.crowood.com

British Library Cataloguing-in-Publication Data
A catalogue record for this book is available from the British Library.

ISBN 978 1 84797 194 4

Disclaimer
Please note that the author and the publisher of this book do not accept any responsibility whatsoever for any error or omission, nor any loss, injury, damage, adverse outcome, or liability suffered as a result of the use of the information contained in this book, or reliance upon it. Readers are reminded that sports can involve activities that are too strenuous for some individuals to engage in safely. Accordingly, it is essential that readers consult a doctor before undertaking any form of training or participation in any sport.

Dedication
To Mum, Jackie and Cameron without whom I wouldn't be inspired to keep writing.

Typeset by S R Nova Pvt Ltd, Bangalore, India

Printed and bound in Singapore by Craft Print International Ltd

Contents

Preface

This book is something of a departure for me. Up until now I have written (in books at least) exclusively about my sport of swimming. My professional life now includes as much time dealing with generic coaching issues as it does with sport-specific ones, so it is logical to put some of that experience down on paper. The book is intended to be something of a 'cookbook', that is, it is a how-to book, although there are no patented 'success' recipes, coaching is too complex for that. It is a book giving advice on how to become a more effective sports coach and there are lots of questions, exercises and practical hints on how to improve your coaching practice. I have mostly used the generic term 'athletes' to cover all of the possible descriptions of the people you coach – young or old, individual or team sport, novices or advanced performers.

It is not an academic book in the sense that it is written for an audience of coaches, not researchers in coaching, but everything contained here is grounded in research evidence (where it exists) and many years of experience as a coach and coach educator. There is a reference section at the end of the book, which gives you guidance on where to find out more. It is also not a book for coaches at the high-performance end of sport (the possible subject of another volume?), but I do illustrate the context of elite sport in a case study. It is hoped, however, that the book will help you to become a high-performing coach in whatever domain you operate (more of which later).

But without hesitation, it is a book for coaches who want to improve, who probably are not full-time – that is almost 1 million people in the United Kingdom at the most recent estimate and who are looking for some assistance with the practicalities of their chosen vocation. I have tried to use examples from a range of sports, with not too many from swimming and the images and diagrams serve to represent the written descriptions of coaching practice.

Please do not forget that coaching is a complex 'people business'. By that, I mean that all your interactions, your hopes and ambitions will be governed by the vagaries of what is frequently called 'the human condition'. I hope that you enjoy the book, that it provokes as many questions as answers and that you gain some insight, which will benefit your invaluable work with your athletes.

Throughout there are a number of quotations, some intended to be inspirational, some to emphasize a point being made. In the spirit of that trend, let me end with an apposite quotation from Elbert Hubbard, American philosopher, biographer and essayist:

> If I can supply you with a thought,
> You may remember it or you may not.
> But if I can make you think a thought for yourself,
> I have indeed added to your stature.

Alan Lynn
December 2009

Happy coach.

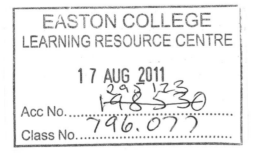

PART 1: SPORTS COACHING

1

Coaching Ethics

> Our children are watching us live, and what we ARE shouts louder than anything we can say.
>
> *Wilfred A. Peterson*

All books on coaching should start with a section on ethics, because, without a positive set of ethical values, the rest of coaching is irrelevant. 'Integrity has no rules' should be the maxim by which all coaches conduct their practice. Unfortunately, a lack of ethical and moral standards seems to pervade much of society these days (just scan the newspapers for stories to back this up), and sport is no different. This is in total contrast to the principles on which many sports were historically founded. Characteristics such as fair play, sportsmanship and honour were enshrined in the development of rules and regulations in almost all sports from their inception, although many people today would question whether these factors are apparent at all in some professional sports and their participants. There are beacons of hope amid the moral mess and I discuss these later in the book, but for now let's look at some common issues in coaching ethics: (i) ethical standards; (ii) ethical dilemmas and (iii) ethical conduct.

Figure 1 Football coach.

ETHICAL STANDARDS

In modern sport the role of the coach is commonly considered to be one of facilitation and guidance in the realization of athletes' sporting talent. In the public sphere the dialogue about the coaching role is dominated by influential attitudes; for example, how much credence is to be given to football managers in the United Kingdom. If athletes' results are less than were expected, coaching expertise and competence are often questioned and the coach is given responsibility for failures. If the outcome is sporting success, athletes and teams are usually given the primary responsibility. What does this mean for the coach attempting to 'do his best'? Where does innovative strategy end and cheating begin?

Ethical behaviour on the part of a coach involves not only his observing the rules of a particular game, but also, and more importantly, behaving according to the true spirit of the game, or according to the unwritten rules that are an integral part of every sport. These rules are concerned with the conduct of a coach or athlete and have been established and observed through the years under the generic terms sportsmanship or fair play. Violating the spirit of a game is often referred to as gamesmanship – doing something simply to upset or psych out an opponent in order to win. For example, in golf it is not against the written rules to make a noise or accidentally, on purpose, develop a coughing fit when your opponent is putting. However, everyone (players and spectators) is expected to remain quiet at this time because it is in the spirit of the game to do so. This does not stop some mindless idiots shouting encouragement the millisecond after the ball leaves the club, but the vast majority just behave 'properly' because it is expected of them. Likewise, the culture of 'sledging' in cricket or 'trash-talking' in basketball have no real basis in rules transgressions, but players see it as a perverted 'badge of honour' both to dish it out and to cope it with it themselves. The biggest irony is that it does not take rule changes to alter this behaviour and eliminate such unethical conduct – coaches could stop things instantly if they made it clear that such practices were completely unacceptable. Officials implement and monitor adherence to the written rules, but coaches and athletes are the true guardians of the sport through their deeds and actions.

Since sport began there have been claims that it builds character and integrity – claims that were unchallenged for many years. However, this is not so in today's media-crazed and highly forensic world of public scrutiny. It is hard to argue that professional fouls in football (soccer) are character-building, or that diving in the penalty box is acceptable and honest endeavour. Yet, players and pundits alike are adamant that they are 'just part of the game'. Managers and coaches are no less culpable, especially since success and failure in professional sport are closely linked to such tactics. Television advertisements may poke fun at such approaches, but the serious fact remains that coaches and players consciously adopt cheating strategies to gain an unfair advantage.

One of the difficulties coaches encounter in youth sports in attempting to teach or expect ethical conduct is the fact that the players come from differing backgrounds and with differing experiences as to what is right and wrong, fair and unfair, and acceptable or unacceptable behaviour. Nevertheless, the fact remains that it does not matter whether you are a coach or an athlete, expert or novice performer; there is no excuse for cheating, stealing, lying or deliberately harming another person. These attitudes and actions should not be tolerated in a civilized society and they should not be part of sport.

Ethical behaviour is not innate. As parents and adults, we teach children right from wrong every day, and in sport it is the responsibility of the coach to continue teaching right from wrong. Sport can be a significant factor in developing young people's ethical values. It depends on the coaches displaying exemplary conduct and behaviour to opponents, officials and participants. It is about setting ethical standards by word and by deed. An interesting piece of research in this area was conducted by the Institute of Youth Sports at Michigan State University on high school American football coaches. They concluded that the coaches did not see the coaching of 'life skills' as separate from general coaching strategies for performance enhancement, and, while highly motivated to win, the personal development of their players was a top priority. The research is particularly interesting because high school sports in the US are a hotbed of competition and where many lifelong attitudes and behaviours are formed. Plato once said, 'You can discover more about a person in an hour of play than in a year of conversation.' Moreover, this is never more true than in the highly charged, emotional world of adolescent sport. Competition can bring out the best and the worst in people. On a recent trip to the States, I attended on one day, a high school football game, a university rugby match and an NBA contest. At each of these events the coaches and players were in intense competition with each other and it showed in their conduct. The high school football saw profanity and physical contact between a coach and his quarterback as the game drew to a close and their team was losing by a point; the rugby illustrated both camaraderie and fist-fighting in a real contrast of behaviours, and the professional basketball contest was as much about the players talking 'smack' to each other as it was their winning the game. Wanting to win is natural, but when winning becomes the most important thing the temptation to cut corners becomes all too great and many coaches, and athletes, cannot resist.

Can ethical behaviour be learned through sport? The answer is obviously yes, but the lesson is not automatic and it will not happen through osmosis. Ethical behaviour must be taught and modelled by the coach. Everything you do and everything you teach must be from a strong ethical standpoint and then your athletes will get the message that cheating is unacceptable. Coaches often say that they break the rules only because

Figure 2 American football coach.

their opponents do, therefore to keep things 'fair' they cheat too. This is flawed logic and only an excuse by weak coaches to justify their actions. Mostly, coaches cheat because (i) they want to prove that they are 'winners' and move on to better jobs; (ii) they don't want to lose their current job; or (iii) they are dishonest in the first place. Whatever the reason, such conduct is unethical and unacceptable. It makes a mockery of the claims made for sport to teach life skills, build character and develop integrity.

ETHICAL DILEMMAS

Many situations in sport demand that coaches or athletes react to or make decisions involving honesty and ethics. You need to recognize these situations because they become important lessons for you and should not be ignored. The following ethical 'dilemmas' (Fig. 3) are examples of those I use in teaching courses with coaches and university students. There may be 'right answers' in some cases, but rather than assuming that such outcomes exist, consider them in the context of you, your sport and, most importantly, your coaching philosophy; these are all 'real' situations which I have come across or heard first-hand accounts of.

ETHICAL CONDUCT – A CODE OF ETHICS FOR COACHING?

A code of ethics defines what is considered good and appropriate behaviour. It reflects the values held by a group. These values are usually organized into a series of core principles that contain standards of behaviour expected of members while they perform their duties. It can also be used as a benchmark to assess whether certain behaviours are acceptable. Why

---

Coaching – 'A Kingdom of Ends?' Or How Might Kant Apply to Sports?

Examine the following situations and try to give a reasoned, and reasonable, explanation for possible outcomes from both your own perspective and that of the children being coached. There may not be any 'correct' answers, although one would expect that certain principles of 'morality' would be approached.

- You have eleven basketball players and need to select two teams of five to play a game with small teams. How could this be organized in such a way that the players actually understand your reasons? How do you think an eight-year-old might follow your reasoning? Discuss all the potential issues and solutions you might consider.
- You are the head coach to a large volleyball club. The coach to an under-sixteen team is attracted to one of the players and feels that this is reciprocated. The coach's friendship with this player is becoming more intense and, as the player's sixteenth birthday approaches, he is concerned about the 'morality' of what they are doing. What questions does such a relationship pose for you? Would it be any different if it were a male or a female coach? How would you take action?
- As coach to a regional youth rugby team you have become aware that some of the players are being actively encouraged to take drugs to enhance their performance by their club coaches. What sort of stance would you take on this issue, given that the parents of the players do not seem too bothered as long are their children are successful?
- You have a policy for your football team that, when you lose the ball to the opposition and they have the opportunity of making a serious breakaway you encourage your players to stop play deliberately through either foul play or by feigning injury. A new, exceptionally talented player arrives who does not agree with the policy and refuses to implement it in a match. This player could help you to win the league/cup and the team is much poorer without him. Should you make an exception? Does it matter as long as you win?
- As coach to a local tennis club with excellent junior players, you have decided that parents are not allowed to make vocal contributions, positive or negative, during matches. The sanction for doing so is that children will be expelled from the club if this happens. Should a child be made to suffer for the adult's behaviour? What other rules or sanctions might you impose?

Do not simply take the path of least resistance in these discussions, 'Well, I wouldn't do that', is not a reasoned or acceptable response. Think the issue through in as much depth as possible and try to get what lies behind it from a perspective of sports ethics and morality. If necessary, have someone play devil's advocate to stimulate debate.

Figure 3 Ethical dilemmas in coaching.

a code of ethics in coaching? Sports organizations across the world have long established practices of setting out the moral framework for their sport. For example, global organizations such as the WADA (World Anti-Doping Agency) have the responsibility for ensuring fair play and robust policies with regard to drugs in sport (Fig. 4 is the WADA Coaches' Pledge and Fig. 5 is the WADA Coaches' Checklist). One of the most celebrated approaches to coaching comprises the core values expressed as a series of principles in the Canadian National Coach Certification Programme (NCCP) Code of Ethics. These can be thought of as a set of behavioural expectations regarding participation in sport, the coaching of athletes or teams and the administration of sports. This code helps coaches to evaluate issues arising within sport because it represents a reference for what constitutes both the good and the right thing to do. For example, the NCCP Code of

The following passage suggests a way for you, as a coach, to make a statement about your commitment to doping-free sport. You are invited to take a few moments to reflect on your role as a coach towards protecting the integrity of your sport. Afterwards, you may decide to sign this pledge as it is, add elements in your own words or even write your own pledge. You can also decide to keep your pledge as a commitment to yourself or use it to make a public statement by sharing it with your athletes and fellow coaches.

> *Because I believe in doping-free sport and fair competition, I hereby declare that:*
> *I will coach within the spirit and letter of the rules of my sport.*
> *I will provide my athletes with the support needed to train and compete doping-free.*
> *I will not cover up nor lie for others if they break anti-doping rules.*
> *I will display honourable behaviour to set a positive example for my athletes and for younger coaches who may follow in my footsteps.*
> *If I fail to respect this pledge, I will take responsibility for my actions.*

Name:

Signature:

Date:

Figure 4 WADA coaches' pledge.

Checklist for All Coaches

Clearly state your expectation that no one on your team will use prohibited substances or methods; have everyone sign a pledge.

Ensure that you and everyone on your staff set a good example.

Enforce your team rules objectively and consistently.

Let your athletes know that they can talk to you about their fears and concerns regarding doping.

Encourage athletes to set personal goals that are realistic and assist them in making gradual progress toward those goals.

Help your athletes to develop appropriate decision-making skills.

Be sensitive to changes in mood, attitude or behaviour among your athletes.

Never ignore the signs that one or more of your athletes may be doping or considering it. Never avoid making tough decisions.

Give a presentation, invite a guest speaker or lead group discussions on doping issues.

Take advantage of increased media attention on a doping issue to express and reinforce your commitment to doping-free sport.

For Coaches of Athletes Likely to Be Tested [See checklist for all coaches above]

Find out the schedule for submitting whereabouts and remind your athletes a few days before, every time.

Provide your athletes with all available information on upcoming team activities (such as dates and locations) long enough ahead of time for them to fulfil their responsibilities with respect to submitting information on their whereabouts.

Inform your athletes who are not currently in a testing pool of upcoming competitions where there may be testing so that they shall have sufficient time to apply for therapeutic use exemptions if necessary.

In October every year, obtain the new Prohibited List issued by the World Anti-Doping Agency, which will take effect on 1 January of the next year and remind your athletes to consult it.

If you take a medication containing a prohibited substance for a personal health condition, carry your medication in its original packaging accompanied by a copy of your prescription.

Figure 5 Coaches checklist.

Ethics helps coaches to make balanced decisions about achieving personal or team goals and the means by which these goals are attained. There are many variations of the NCCP Code in existence throughout the world, a British version of which is shown in Fig. 6.

These ethical principles are being piloted in an initiative called Positive Coaching Scotland (PCS). Based on the hugely successful Positive Coaching Alliance initiated at Stanford University by Professor Jim Thomson in 1988, PCS has the aim of 'Transforming Scottish youth sport so sport can transform youth.' Through a series of workshops, the programme reinforces the concept of a Double-Goal Coach.

Double-Goal Coach

The first goal is winning. Learning to compete effectively is a necessity in today's society. We want to win – not at all costs, but through concerted effort.

The second, more important goal is teaching young people vital, character-building life skills through sport that will equip them for the future.

Life skills such as leadership, handling adversity, teamwork, persistence and compassion mirror the aims of the Scottish government's flagship education policy – *A Curriculum for Excellence*. By including the whole community – parents, coaches, teachers and local sports leaders – and tailoring the message to each audience, PCS provides the tools and framework for a positive sporting experience that can also be character building. PCS also sets out to empower parents, coaches, teachers and sports leaders to help to create a more positive sporting environment. Sport can educate young people about winning, losing and cooperation, while at the same time encouraging them to learn and develop new skills.

As part of the Positive Coaching Alliance's strategy to transform youth sports, a Positive Coach Mental Model has been developed. There are three major elements to the job description of a Positive Coach: a positive coach: (i) redefines the concept of a 'winner'; (ii) fills athletes' emotional tanks; and (iii) honours the sport.

Redefines 'Winner'

A Positive Coach helps athletes to redefine what it means to be a winner through mastery, rather than a scoreboard orientation. He sees victory as a by-product of the pursuit of excellence. He focuses on effort rather than outcome and on learning rather than on comparison with others. He recognizes that mistakes are an important and inevitable part of learning and fosters an environment in which athletes do not fear to make mistakes. While not ignoring the teaching opportunities that mistakes present, he teaches athletes that a key to success is how one responds to mistakes. He sets standards of continuous improvement for himself and his athletes. He encourages his athletes, whatever their level of ability, to strive to

Coaches' Code of Ethics and Conduct

- Respect the rights, dignity and worth of every individual athlete as a human being.
- Treat everyone equally regardless of sex, any disability, ethnic origin or religion.
- Respect the talent, developmental stage and goals of each athlete in order to help each one to reach his or her full potential.
- Operate within the rules of your sport and in the spirit of fair play, while encouraging your athletes to do the same.
- Advocate a sporting environment free of drugs and other performance-enhancing substances within the guidelines of the World Anti-Doping Code.
- Do not disclose any confidential information relating to athletes without their prior written consent.
- Be a positive role model for your sport and athletes and act in a way that projects a positive image of coaching
- All athletes are deserving of equal attention and opportunities.
- Ensure the athlete's time spent with you is a positive experience.
- Be fair, considerate and honest with athletes.
- Encourage and promote a healthy lifestyle, refrain from smoking and drinking alcohol around athletes.

Professional Responsibilities

- Display high standards in your language, manner, punctuality, preparation and presentation.
- Display control, courtesy, respect, honesty, dignity and professionalism to all involved within the sphere of sport; this includes opponents, coaches, officials, administrators, the media, parents and spectators and encourage your athletes to demonstrate the same qualities.
- Be professional and accept responsibility for your actions; you should not only refrain from initiating a sexual relationship with an athlete, but should also discourage any attempt by an athlete to initiate a sexual relationship with you, explaining the ethical basis of your refusal.
- Accurately represent personal coaching qualifications, experience, competence and affiliations; refrain from criticism of other coaches and athletes.
- Seek continual improvement through on-going coach education and other personal and professional development opportunities.
- Provide athletes with planned and structured training programmes appropriate to their needs and goals.
- Seek advice and assistance from professionals when additional expertise is required.
- Adopt appropriate risk management strategies to ensure that the training and/or competition environment is safe.
- Ensure that equipment, rules, training and the environment are appropriate for the age, physical and emotional maturity, experience and ability of the athletes.
- Encourage athletes to seek medical advice when required.
- Provide a modified training programme where appropriate.
- Maintain the same interest and support toward sick and injured athletes as you would to healthy athletes.
- Protect your athletes from any form of personal abuse.
- Refrain from any form of verbal, physical or emotional abuse of your athletes.
- Do not harass, abuse or discriminate against athletes on the basis of their sex, marital status, sexual orientation, religious or ethical beliefs, race, colour, ethnic origins, employment status, disability or any distinguishing characteristics.
- Any physical contact with athletes should be appropriate to the situation and necessary for the athlete's skill development.
- Be alert to any forms of abuse directed towards athletes from other sources while they are in your care.

Figure 6 Coaches code of ethics and conduct.

Figure 7 Positive coaching.

Figure 8 Children's coach.

become the best athletes and people that they can. He teaches athletes that a winner is someone who makes maximum effort, continues to learn and improve, and does not let mistakes (or the fear of mistakes) stop them.

Fills Players' Emotional Tanks

A Positive Coach is a positive motivator who refuses to motivate through fear, intimidation or shame. She recognizes that every athlete has an 'emotional tank', like the gas tank of a car. Just as a car with an empty tank cannot go very far, so an athlete with an empty emotional tank does not have the energy to do her best. A Positive Coach understands that compliments, praise and positive recognition fill emotional tanks. She understands the importance of giving truthful and specific feedback and resists the temptation to give praise that is not warranted. When correction is necessary, a Positive Coach communicates criticism to athletes in ways that do not undermine their sense of self-worth.

A Positive Coach establishes order and maintains discipline in a positive manner. She listens to athletes and involves them in decisions that affect the team. She works to remain positive even when things are not going well. She recognizes that it is often when things do go wrong that a coach can have the most lasting impact and can teach the most important lessons. Even when facing adversity, she refuses to demean herself, her athletes or the environment. She always treats athletes with respect, regardless of how well they perform.

Honours the Game

A Positive Coach feels an obligation to his sport. He understands that honouring the game means getting to the *ROOTS* of the matter, where ROOTS stands for respect for:

R: rules allow us to keep the game fair; if we win by ignoring or violating the rules, what is the value of our victory? Honouring the letter and the spirit of the rule is important.

O: is for our opponents, without an opponent, there would be no competition; rather than demean strong opponents, we need to honour them because they challenge us to do our best; athletes can be both fierce and friendly during the same competition (in one moment giving everything to get to a loose ball, and in the next moment helping an opponent up), coaches showing respect for their opposing coaches and players set the tone for the rest of the team.

O: is for also for officials; to respect officials, even when we disagree with their calls, may be the toughest part of honouring the game; we must remember that officials are not perfect (just like coaches, athletes and parents); take time to think about how best to approach an official when you want to discuss a call; what strategies do you have to keep yourself in control when you start to get upset with officials' calls? We must remember that the loss of officials (and finding enough in the first place) is a major problem in most youth sports organizations, and we can confront this problem by consistently respecting officials.

T: is for teammates; it is easy for young athletes to think solely about their own performance, but we want athletes to realize that being part of a team requires one to think about and respect one's teammates; this respect needs to carry beyond the field/gym/track/pool into the classroom and social settings; athletes need to be reminded that their conduct away from practices and games will reflect back on their teammates and the league, club or school.

S: is for self; athletes should be encouraged to live up to their own highest personal standard of honouring the game, even when their opponents do not; athletes' respect for themselves and their own standards must come first and having this definition of honouring the game is a start.

To make honouring the game the youth sports standard, coaches, leaders and parents need to discuss this concept with their athletes. Coaches need to practise it with their athletes (that is, have the players officiate at practice). Moreover, and perhaps most importantly, all adults in the youth sports setting (coaches, leaders, parents, officials and fans) need to model it. If these adults honour the game, the athletes will too.

A Positive Coach teaches his players to honour the game. He loves his sport and upholds the spirit, as well as the letter, of its rules. He respects opponents, recognizing that a worthy opponent will push his athletes to do their best. He understands the important role that officials play and shows them respect, even when he disagrees with their calls. He encourages players to make a commitment to each other and to encourage one another on and off the field. He values the rich tradition of his sport and feels privileged to participate. A Positive Coach realizes that one of the most difficult times to honour the game is when the opponent does not, and he reminds his players to live up to their own highest standard (respect for self). Ultimately, a Positive Coach demonstrates integrity and would rather lose than win by dishonouring the game.

As a final thought, this unattributed verse should be on the door of every self-respecting (and ethical) coach:

> I have to live with myself, and so
> I want to be fit for myself to know.
> I want to be able, as days go by,
> Always to look myself straight in the eye.
> I don't want to stand with the setting sun,
> And hate myself for the things I've done.
> I can never hide myself from me;
> I see what others may never see,
> I know what others may never know,
> I can never fool myself and so –
> Whatever happens, I want to be
> Self-respecting and conscience-free.

2

Sports Coaching in the United Kingdom: A Brief Historical Context

A lawyer without history or literature is a mechanic, a mere working mason; if he possesses some knowledge of these, he may venture to call himself an architect.

Sir Walter Scott

The status of sport in a society is the product of historical processes. Accordingly, the individuals involved in sport are influenced in many ways by the cultural standing sport has. This chapter examines briefly the history and development of sports coaching alongside the history and development of sport in the United Kingdom. After this, the concept of the coaching process is introduced as a framework for analysing coaches and coaching. Finally, we look at how to develop a coaching philosophy, with examples provided by practising coaches.

In medieval times, the practices that we would recognise as sports or leisure-related were more often based on military or economic activities, for example, jousting tournaments. This began to change after the seventeenth-century Restoration in this country that influenced the aristocracy to revel in their recently rediscovered leisure diversions. The newly fashionable and overt consumption of leisure by the upper echelons of British society contributed to the formalizing of sports and arguably to the emergence of the first sports coaches. The first wave of this process included the sports of horseracing, cricket, boxing and golf. The potential financial gains resulting from betting on these sports meant that the aristocrats who organized these activities were willing to pay for expert performance and/or tuition, while those involved as instructors and performers were of a lower social status than their wealthy patrons. These conditions resulted in a public perception of the coach as little more than a semi-skilled artisan – something that observers of sport today might still accord with?

What Is the Current Status and Profile of Coaches and Coaching in Your Sport?

THE NINETEENTH CENTURY

During the nineteenth century, the growth of the British middle class, with its moral code of respectability, led to a shift in leisure patterning and to a further cultural denigration of the sports coach. An important element in the supremacy of the aristocracy and its upper-class allies was a masculine and exclusive public school supremacy. In this environment, sporting activity was dominated by disorganized games. Two nineteenth-century socio-economic developments brought about major changes in the public school system, with associated changes in the emerging world of organized sport. First, the rapid industrialization that began in Britain in the mid-eighteenth century had created a growing and increasingly affluent, socially ambitious, middle class. Parts of this new class saw access for their sons to the public school system as a way to enhance and secure their social status. This hardnosed, pushy and energetic capitalist class included a large element that prioritized and expected discipline and value for money. In the second development, these expectations coincided with those of a new group of public school headmasters who shared the view that the better management of all aspects of school life would improve the moral, spiritual and academic development of their charges, thus endorsing the Latin phrase *mens sana in copore sano* (a healthy mind in a healthy body). The fanaticism of these headmasters, plus the demands and concerns of the fee-paying middle class, led to the regeneration of the public school system. From there it became permeated with value-laden moral and ethical imperatives, many of which were subsequently embodied in team games and their rules and values.

As various groups of public-school old boys sought to continue competition, there emerged another taxonomy of sports during the second half of the century. The moral imperative of these middle-class groups merged into the new classification of sports and undermined formal instruction. Here, the value system within public-school sports demanded both a strict adherence to an amateur ethos, and, despite the seriousness with which these activities were regarded, a relaxed, devil-may-care attitude and a desire not to be seen to be trying too hard. Within this prevailing landscape, the practice, the training and the consistent advice from non-participants both contradicted the British notion of sport and were labelled dishonourable and unpatriotic. Thus sports coaches were labelled as socially undesirable and organized coaching structures were undermined in Britain for almost a hundred years.

During this time many working-class athletes were still willing, or needed, to earn additional monies from activities outside of work. In their sport this clashed with the middle-class, amateur ethos. Once Association

Football became professional in 1888, and after the rugby rift of 1895 when the Union–League split occurred, the middle-class bureaucrats of sport withdrew to their amateur fortresses and maintained their own sports, with strict policies concerning the appropriate gentlemanly standards. Apart from the payments received for participation, Association Football remained amateur and resisted organized training until well after the Second World War. The middle-class aversion to professionalism meant that most football clubs were financed by wealthy industrialists and merchants from Britain's expanding towns and cities (compare this with today's clubs run by oligarchs instead of home-grown industrialists). Their capitalist outlook ensured that they were willing to support limited professionalism (such as player payments), but, as upwardly mobile, aspirational and patriotic members of the community, their cultural dissent was limited. In most cases, Association Football clubs maintained a management and coaching structure based upon and rooted in amateur ideals: they employed an administrator-secretary, but formalized skill learning was ad hoc, unorganized and remained the responsibility of the senior players.

This restricted the opportunities to coach even for those who wanted to do so. The legendary Arsenal coach Herbert Chapman and others like him began to change this situation in the 1930s, but recognized coaches in any sport did not appear until after the Second World War. Even then, Walter Winterbottom, who became English football's first national coach in 1946, was both team manager and FA Director of Coaching into the 1960s without ever selecting any of the players in his teams. In the amateur world of middle-class sports, resistance to any form of team management, coaching or tactical development, beyond that provided by the team captain and senior players, remained embedded until much later. In support of this fact, the rugby coach Ian McGeechan in his recent autobiography described the role of the national rugby 'coach' as that of 'Captain's Adviser' well into the mid-1970s.

These difficulties with organized coaching were not the same across the world. Whereas in Britain, training and coaching during the later nineteenth and the early twentieth century were associated with working-class sports, in North America a more complex relationship emerged. In both the United States and Canada there was also a class-based rejection of coaching similar to that seen in Britain. However, the commercial imperative of financial advantage in a franchise system of organized sports leagues saw to it that coaching was a much sought after commodity. The status of coaches and coaching seen in the US and Canada today stems from this desire to seek out the best to improve skills, tactics and performance. Similarly, in Australia it was professional sports that led the way with the appointments of and systems for the development of coaches. It could be argued that (in performance terms) we have caught up with the rest of the world – our Beijing Olympic results more than confirm this claim. However, with no more than 3 per cent of coaches in the United Kingdom being full-time and the status of coaches and coaching being still some way short of ambitions, there is much progress yet to be made.

MOVING INTO THE PRESENT

As an illustration of the prevailing attitudes in Britain, consider the scene from the Oscar-winning movie *Chariots of Fire* set in the lead-up to the Paris 1924 Olympic Games, where the Master of Trinity College, Cambridge tells the young Abrahams that his should be 'the way of the amateur'. So after almost a hundred years of effort to drive out the perceived corrupting influence of coaching from sport, the final third of the twentieth century saw British sport begin to establish formal provision for coaching. A system for producing qualified coaches is now virtually universal. There are probably four key reasons for this shift, not all of which are directly attributable to sport in its traditional sense. First, sports organizations in Britain recognized not only that sport had become more complex but also that the increase in skill levels meant that specialist knowledge was needed beyond that which could be provided by captains and senior players. For example, the game of football may have been invented in England, but, until the 1966 World Cup, its home country had never produced a team capable of progressing beyond the quarter finals of the global tournament. Second, changes in the commercial structure of professional sports since the 1960s meant that individual sports organizations were carrying greater financial risks, so greater skill development was required to minimize that risk. Third (and perhaps most significantly), the structure of British education and training changed markedly during this period, with the extensive development of more specialist awards, more staged qualifications and a growing demand for recognized credentials. Whereas this was not necessarily directly related to formalized systems of coach training and qualifications, it was a sign of a broader cultural shift and one that continues to have an impact today. Finally, since the early 1990s there has been a growing concern about generic issues such as child protection and the criminal abuse of athletes by coaches at all levels. Formal systems of coach education and accreditation became widely seen as one mechanism by which sports organizations could exercise their duty of care to sports participants. Although some have argued that in creating the 'space' for this content in coach education courses, sports have had to reduce the amount of technical input to their programmes. The contemporary coach, then, operates in a world of centrally-regulated, highly organized and rationalized sport. In Britain, the status of coaches and coaching still has much catching up to do when compared with those of North America and Australia, but policies such as the United Kingdom Coaching Framework have set out to change that in the next decade.

3

Research into Sports Coaching

'Coach', he whispered. His voice shook just a trifle. 'I found it, coach, the thing you wanted me to learn for myself.'

Jackson Scholtz, *Tales of the Cinder Track* (1926)

A number of recent commentators in the academic world (myself included) have suggested that the study of coaching has been at best neglected, or at worst ignored. We have suggested that the place of coaching studies in the academic world has been 'compromised', while calling the existing research limited and peripheral to the conceptualization of coaching and coach effectiveness. Researchers in the domain of sport and exercise psychology may disagree to some extent, and the excellent review paper by Gilbert and Trudel (2004) gives credence to counter claims of increased research activity in recent years, but the central question of whether coaching research is an established academic pursuit remains.

Until now, research into coaching practice and the coaching process has been fragmented. There are precious few coaching journals for scholarly work and, although there have been some notable recent additions to the literature in the form of books, the topic still appears to be marginalized in the research community.

COACHING RESEARCH

There are three sets of arguments to support coaching research. First, there is no ready store of conceptual frameworks or mature theories within which to locate coaching research. The lack of attention to the coaching process would seem to fly in the face of an agreed recognition, perhaps tacit at times, of its importance. Although some individual, often mature, athletes are self-coached, experience tells us that the coaching role is considered to be essential. This probably somewhat understates the weight given, rather belatedly in the United Kingdom, to the role of the expert coach in producing competitive excellence on the world stage (but do you know who the current Coach of the Year is in your sport – or in any sport for that matter?).

Second, there is what might be termed a common-sense argument. The coach, rather than the performer, is most often the end-user of knowledge. Despite the variability in coaching roles, some elements of the coaching process are normally the prerogative of the coach, for instance, programme planning, the control of training sessions, interpersonal relationships and competition management (including strategy and tactics – much of what this book is about, in fact). These elements suggest that the coach will always have the strongest influence on performance preparation and should be the focus of applied research.

Third, there is an argument based on a classification of research forms. This suggests, not that sport-performance research be replaced by coaching research, but that research into coaching is complementary (perhaps essential) if the full picture is to be achieved. It may be more accurate to say that sport-performance research is incomplete without much greater attention to sports-coaching research. It is certainly incomplete if implementation in an applied coaching setting has not been taken into account. We must also acknowledge that the complexity of the coaching process, its multivariable nature, the contested activity (there is usually at least one other coach trying his best to outdo you), the reliance on cognitive skills and the prominence of interpersonal relationships have each and together contributed to a difficult research environment.

In summary, there can be little doubt that the research policy community has focused on athlete performance, although perhaps less so on athletes performing. This community in most countries has treated sports coaching with benign neglect. It is indefensible that with the goal of improving sports performance, the coach, the coach's behaviour and the coach's intervention programme and impact can have been purposefully treated as unproblematic variables. It might be helpful now to set out what is meant by 'coaching' and to establish the concept of a 'coaching process'.

Figure 9 Coach in direct intervention mode.

THE COACHING PROCESS

Coaching is a generic term and there is an extensive literature to support the use of coaching in its counselling/mentoring, training, preparation and more general management function. There is ample evidence of the transfer of sport coaching 'principles and experience' to the corporate training industry. The term 'coaching' has a recognizable meaning in acting, dance, drama, examination preparation and even pregnancy and other areas. In addition, the term has come to be used for almost any guidance role which is intended to lead to 'improvement'; for example, all the competitors in television talent shows such as *Fame Academy* and *The X-Factor* have a voice coach in singing.

The term 'sports coaching' is used to refer to a variety of sport leadership roles and contexts. These range across all forms of sport, from participation sport in which it is often used interchangeably with leader, teacher or instructor, to intensive performance sport, in which the coach may lead a team of contributing experts. The coaching role will vary enormously in the degree of direct (hands-on) intervention, long-term planning, control of the training environment, intervention styles, depth and form of interpersonal relationships and technical knowledge. The athletes working with the coach will vary in their motives, intensity of commitment, skill levels and the perceived rewards.

Central to this enterprise is the coaching process. This can be defined as the purposeful and coordinated series of activities and interventions designed to improve competition performance (Cross and Lyle, 1999). It is most evident in the planned, coordinated and integrated programme of preparation and competition. And the process can be applied in a range of partial/complete and less/more sophisticated ways.

However, it is perhaps more useful to distinguish between different forms of coaching. Fig. 10 shows the suggested 'sub-divisions' of participation, development and performance coaching (Lyle, 2002). Each of these different forms of coaching has its own assumptions about the role of the coach, the completeness of the preparation for competition, the mix of participant and coach goals, and the extent and sophistication of the process. Although it may seem likely that the majority of questions about coaching and the coaching process can only be addressed satisfactorily in a performance-coaching context, this can be overstated, and there will be appropriate attention needed on participation coaching.

However, conceptual clarity should not deny the human, social and emotional character of the coaching process. Recognizing the essential elements of the coaching process is important for the development of a conceptual framework, but it should be remembered that the actual relationships between coach(es) and athlete(s) include extended periods of social activity, commitment, success and failure, emotional highs and lows, personal cost and achievement, and a mix of short-, medium- and long-term satisfaction and enjoyment. Insofar as the intentions and circumstances of the athlete(s) and coach(es) satisfy the criteria of the

Participation Coaching

This is largely to do with initiation into sport and with basic skills teaching. Some individuals, usually young people with greater levels of potential, will move quite quickly through this stage. Others will become more recreational or casual participants, often as they move into adulthood; this characterized by:

- Lack of emphasis on competition goals.
- Less intensive engagement.
- Short-term horizons and immediate satisfactions.
- Absence of attention to components of performance.
- Episodic rather than continuous and regular.
- Key skills are delivery/intervention-based.
- Less concrete 'contract' between the coach and the participant.

Developmental Coaching

This is characterized by rapid skills learning and a developing engagement with a sport-specific competition programme. This is a key stage for talent identification, this stage is almost exclusively for young people in age-group sport who are accelerating their way though the performance standards. It can be argued that 'instructors' of adult participants who wish to improve but who do not satisfy the boundary criteria (for example, in golf lessons) should be included in this category. It is characterized by:

- Engagement in competition.
- Identifiable performance goals.
- Degree of coordination and planning, although still perhaps some episodic engagement.
- Longer-term goals.
- Individuals having made a commitment to the sport.
- Attention to basic components, such as physical conditioning and mental preparation.
- Likely to be evidence of a meaningful interpersonal relationship between coach and athlete.

Performance Coaching

Performers and circumstances come together to fulfil the majority of the coaching process parameters. It is reflected in relatively intensive preparation and involvement in competition sport and can apply to all ages and levels of developed ability. There may be some special cases, such as representative team/group coaches. It is characterized by:

- Intensive commitment to the preparation programme.
- Intention to control performance variables in integrated and progressive fashion.
- Clear competition goals, within recognized organizational structures.
- Key skills in decision making, planning and data management.
- More extensive interpersonal relationship between coach and athletes.
- Performance components individualized.

Figure 10 Forms of coaching.

purpose and rationale of coaching, they become engaged in a coordinated, integrated and serial process, which is focused on the achievement of sport-performance goals (an early section in Part II deals with coach–athlete relationships). This recognition of coaching as a process is important because it highlights two key issues: the boundaries of the process and the skills that are particular to that process. This book is primarily concerned with the latter.

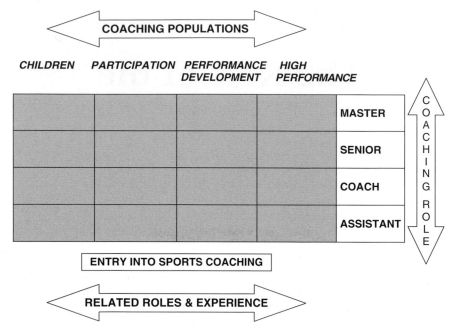

Figure 11 UK coach development model?

As a further development of the 'forms of coaching' concept, sports coach UK have proposed a 4 × 4 coach-development model integrating coaching roles and coaching domains, shown in Fig. 11. This is very much a work in progress within the United Kingdom Coaching Framework, but it does give a clear indication as to the scale and complexity of understanding what it is that coaching is about and what it is that coaches actually do.

Where are you on the 4 × 4 model? Do you 'exist' in more than one box?

4

The Role of the Coach

A coach is someone who can give correction without causing resentment.

John Wooden

Children often receive their first exposure to sport through community-based, organized sport. They typically spend considerably more time per week in these non-school-based programmes than they do in their school physical education classes. For this reason youth sport coaches are often considered to have significantly more impact on youth development than teachers. In addition, children typically begin their involvement in organized sport when they are in the formative years of their development. For example, in most countries, 50 per cent of youth sport participants start their involvement by age eight or younger and continue well into their teenage years. Some of the learning outcomes that can result from participation in organized sport include an appreciation of a healthy lifestyle, a positive self-image, teamwork, social skills and respect for others. In a review of the literature on peer relations among children it was concluded that those who developed physical competence in sport experienced higher levels of social success than their less physically competent peers. Furthermore, youth sport involvement has long been considered an important character builder for adolescents and young children (Coakley, 1993).

COACHES AS ROLE MODELS

Youth sport coaches serve as significant role models and can exert a strong influence on athletes' values and attitudes. An athlete's degree of enjoyment and the desire to continue an involvement in youth sport are largely determined by the youth sport coach. Research has shown that the coaches' verbal behaviour can influence the athletes' feelings of self-worth and desire for future participation. For example, an examination of male youth competitive wrestlers found a significant relationship between positive adult involvement and the level of enjoyment in the sport experience. Furthermore, the early sport experience goes a long

31

Figure 12 Children's coach.

way to determining future participation in it. When a child experiences a positive early involvement it serves as a hook and fosters the continued pursuit of physical activities. The potential impact of organized sport participation on the physical development of young people has also been noted. Although it is sometimes difficult to illustrate causation because of the normal growth and maturation of children, research has repeatedly shown that young athletes are more physically fit than nonathletes. It may be counter-intuitive to think otherwise, but clearly some people are not getting this message.

While participation in youth sport can be a positive experience for children, it can also be an extremely negative one that leaves an individual emotionally or physically scarred for life. There are far too many examples of incompetent or ill-intentioned coaches who contribute to high drop-out rates in youth sport. One study in Australia, for example, found that one-third of all youth sport participants quit organized sport because of poor coaching. Also, under inappropriate guidance the potential physical benefits of sport can easily turn into serious negative consequences. There is always the risk of physical injury in youth sport, ranging from minor sprains and contusions to serious injuries leading to stunted growth, paralysis or, in extreme cases, even death.

To summarize, participation in organized sport can have a tremendously positive influence on youth development or seriously negative consequences. The key to a successful and safe experience in youth sport is the coach: coaches are enormously influential in determining whether children's sport experiences are positive or negative.

The role played by the youth sport coach, therefore, is critical. However, this role is also complex and multidimensional. Research in this field commonly identifies at least twelve possible roles for coaches: instructor, teacher, trainer, motivator, disciplinarian, social worker, friend, scientist, student, manager, administrator and publicity fund-raiser. Nevertheless, it is generally regarded that the primary responsibility of the youth sport coach is to promote athletes' personal growth and development and physical competence in a fun and positive environment. Unfortunately, many coaches tend to place more emphasis on winning than on personal development or fun.

To accomplish their several roles, youth sport coaches are expected to understand and use an increasingly complex and specialized body of knowledge. The knowledge base in coaching may be divided into two large domains of knowledge: sport-specific knowledge and general coaching knowledge. The former relates to the techniques, tactics and strategies of a particular sport. It is also considered declarative knowledge that is easily verbalized and has been explicitly defined. The second area, general coaching knowledge, refers to the knowledge required to set up optimal learning environments (and we shall look at this specifically as one of the 'nine expert coaching actions' in Pa[rt ...] [...]hing knowledge is considered implicit, a[nd ...] [...]om-prising habits and routines based o[n ...] [...]s of knowledge for coaching comprise in[...] [...]isci-plines, such as anatomy, biomechan[ics ...] [...]tion and sport psychology.

[handwritten note: Below section will help with effective coach paragraph]

WHAT COACHES NEED

The extensive knowledge base required for competent coaching is obvious. The reality of the youth sport environment is that many coaches are volunteers (over 800,000 people in the United Kingdom alone) and have sparse or no formal training (more than 400,000 of these). Although comprehensive coach education programmes are now available, certification is not mandatory in most countries (and coach licensing certainly is not). Individuals usually assume the role of the coach because their son or daughter is in a team and there is a need for a coach. Because most coaches' involvement is linked to their children's participation, there is also a high turnover rate, with the average coach lasting five years or fewer. As a result, virtually anyone can assume the role of a youth sport coach, entry into coaching at the community level is not difficult – if you are willing to put on a track suit and turn up regularly, you are a coach in most people's eyes. The gap between expected competencies and the profile of the typical youth sport coach has long been considered one of the major challenges in sport. Throughout this book we are looking at how coaches can become more knowledgeable, more competent and more effective at improving the athletes and players in their charge. Part II deals specifically with the key 'how to coach' skills and focuses on coaching the individual first and the sport or activity second.

5

Developing a Coaching Philosophy

Philosophy may be likened to trying to open a safe with a combination lock: each little adjustment of the dials seems to achieve nothing, only when everything is in place does the door open.

Ludwig Wittgenstein

It is generally accepted that what coaches do in their practice, and how they do it, tends to be shaped by their personal principles and values: attributes that are thought to comprise their coaching 'philosophy'. It is also believed that to clearly articulate one's own philosophy is a prerequisite to good practice, as it provides direction and focus in relation to how one goes about doing the job of coaching. Indeed, exercises aimed at developing a coaching philosophy can be found in almost every coach education publication or course. Despite this official recognition that a philosophy has a direct impact on behaviour, many coaches consistently fail to engage adequately with the concept, not really grasping its relevance and accompanying influence over practical problems. It appears that they just cannot see how investing in the process of developing and defining a clear philosophy can really have an impact on their daily coaching practice.

Coaches on coach education courses will often ask, 'What's the point of spending time on my coaching philosophy, when what I really need are practical coaching tips?' The answer lies in accepting the role of philosophy and its underpinning value system as the precursor to action, because every element of coaching (that is, the what, why and how of it) is affected by personal beliefs. A common analogy is to view the coaching philosophy as a pair of glasses, created by personal opinions, experiences and values, through which a particular perception of reality is filtered. It has, therefore, a direct bearing on how we understand the world, what actions we take and why we take them.

I was fortunate enough a few years ago to hear the legendary American swimming coach Mark Shubert give a talk on his coaching philosophy. I'd heard bits of this speech before, because most of it had been reported over the years across several forms of the media, but hearing it at first-hand was very informative and inspiring. One of the first things that Coach Shubert did was to ask the audience (comprising almost exclusively of other swimming coaches) how many of them had a coaching philosophy? Almost everyone raised their hands. He then asked, how many of them could say what their philosophy was in fifty words or fewer? Hands dropped rapidly – only a dozen or so remained. He then said, 'Great, because I'm going to pick one of you to come up here and tell us all what your philosophy is.' Instantly that dozen became around three, and none of those three hands was raised very high. Shubert did not, in fact, ask any of them to come up and relate their personal coaching philosophy, but he did use it to highlight his main point, which is that if you don't have a distinct philosophy that you believe in and can defend, then you haven't decided what is important to you. And, if you don't know what is important, then you won't be able to tell your coaches or athletes what is important. If they don't know what your philosophy is, then they can't be held accountable when they don't perform. Shubert's philosophy in two words (no more) was 'Win forever!' Keep doing things better than you've ever done them before in order to replicate winning records and a winning culture for years and years. But just like the quotation that opened this section, you won't find your coaching philosophy overnight; however, when you do, you need to be consistent in applying it.

THE NATURE OF A PHILOSOPHY

A coaching philosophy can be considered to be a set of principles that guide a coach's practice. Consequently, an examination of it asks questions of the coach's actions, investigating why he coaches as he does. The value of developing a philosophy is to allow both coach and athletes a foundation from which to build and learn according to a consistent, coherent way of thinking. More specifically, it can help coaches to clarify motives and provide direction to their coaching, while addressing what uniquely valuable contributions they might make.

Without a definitive philosophy, behaviour can become too situation-specific, too reactive. A philosophy provides boundaries within which the coach–athlete relationship can be located. Writing one also has the potential to develop fresh ideas by encouraging us to think creatively and imaginatively about what we do as coaches and why we make these choices. For the individual, thinking through actions to determine their root causes can become an enlightening process, as the value systems that guide a person's coaching need to be understood if we are to comprehend his or her actions. Additionally, clarifying and adhering to a coaching philosophy can assist in reminding us of why we coach, thus guarding against the excesses that circumstances may drive us to.

Let us now examine in more depth some of the difficulties inherent in applying a definitive coaching philosophy in practice. Such a philosophy is usually given in the form of a declaration about an aspect of practice. For example, a statement regarding sincerity could be presented as 'I will be open and honest with my athletes'. The values proclaimed are clear, but the circumstances in which they will be evident are not specified, giving the assumption that a sincere coach will always be honest and open with athletes. The problem with such a declaration comes not with its worthy intent, but with its practicality and appropriateness in all circumstances. It does not address the thorny issue of whether a coach should always be honest with athletes, for instance, in terms of selection and opinions on performance. This, in turn, begs the question of whether there are certain situations where being less than honest is in the best interests of athletes or for the greater good? A principal problem here is that the statement of intent is too far removed from the ambiguous and complex reality to have much effect.

In order to generate more realistic and functional coaching philosophies, the first step is to acknowledge that they are complex. Hence, they cannot be realistically created in a 30min workshop or through a 'quickie' self-reflective exercise, since, to make them credible, they need careful and realistic consideration. Similarly, there is a need to move away from bland, generic statements written as if they were meant as ideals to aspire towards, or reflections that are too abstract for addressing actual coaching needs in practice. Alternatively, philosophies should be highly individualized, grounded in reality and be based on personal objectives founded on experiences. While acknowledging that there may be many means to the same end and that coaches will act according to their perception of the context, the clarification of purposes and guidelines encapsulated in a philosophy is still valuable as it leads to informed choices and better priorities. Within this process, we need to consider and link issues of philosophy and behaviour. Hence, not only do we need to differentiate between delivery style and core purpose, but also to sketch outlines of appropriate practice in relation to both.

How should one go about developing such a functional, yet sincere personal philosophy? As stated earlier, the aim here is not to provide 'correct' prescriptive thinking for all, but rather to assist coaches through a process by which they can arrive at their own individualized, personalized guides for action. A good place to start, however, is to use higher thinking skills in addressing fundamental questions about one's personal involvement in coaching, while allowing more detailed reflective questions to emerge once the conceptual issues have been clarified. An important point to remember is that this process should be carried out in a systematic, careful and rigorous way, so as to give the findings definitive meaning.

Prompts for Developing a Coaching Philosophy

What is coaching, and why do I think that?

Have my coaching motives changed? How? Why?

Is there another way?

Why are these athletes participating?

Why did a particular coach have such a meaningful impact on me?

What are my future hopes, both for the athletes I coach and for myself as a coach?

Are they 'my' athletes or am I 'their' coach?

Who holds the power in a coach–athlete relationship?

What is my role as a coach and why do I think that?

Although lists of similar questions appear in coach education courses, often the flimsy way with which they are engaged makes the exercise of little value. To create a worthwhile functional philosophy such questions need to be carefully and sincerely addressed. For example, in examining the last question cited above – what is my role as a coach? – instead of merely brainstorming potential functions, coaches should address such issues related to role as, how do I 'play' the role of the coach? Whose expectations am I fulfilling? Why? Is there a case for me to expand and explore the boundaries of the traditional coaching role? Do I want to, and what are the implications of doing so? How can I allow my own personality to emerge through the coaching role? Am I fulfilling myself within the coaching role? Through addressing these and other such carefully crafted questions to address both meaning and purpose, a deeper sense of a coaching philosophy and identity can emerge, one that is grounded in personal reality.

Once a philosophical framework has been established, or perhaps in tandem with it, more practical questions should also be addressed so that the philosophy maintains a working credibility and usefulness for coaches. Such questions here could include those shown in the accompanying box.

Such reflective questions could be applied to all aspects of the coaching process, from pedagogical and motivational issues to those of planning, monitoring and organizing, to ensure that the developed philosophy is realized through behaviour. In many ways, it is important to commit the philosophy to paper for all to see, because a written document easily reminds everyone of the ethos of the sporting experience undertaken. It also forces the coach to organize his or her ideas and to defend a position. It allows each to see whether his or her thoughts have really been clarified. Of more importance, however, is the need to regularly re-examine and re-evaluate the philosophy, as our experiences constantly shape and evolve our thoughts. The philosophy should perhaps be written in pencil not in ink!

Questions for Coaches

Do I create a learning environment?
Do the practices I use best serve the purpose for which they are intended?
Is the approach appropriate for the athletes?
Is there a better way of doing what I'm doing?
Can I explain and justify my coaching actions and decisions?
How do I ensure that I follow my coaching philosophy?
What happens if my coaching philosophy is challenged?
How will I deal with the different values of other people?
What is key about the interpersonal relationships I have with athletes?

As an illustration of this process, two examples of coaching philosophy are provided; the first is a complete philosophy from a young student coach in his first few years of coaching and the second is an excerpt from the philosophy of a coach with over twenty years' experience.

Coaching Philosophy I

As most of my coaching experience has been in participation or developmental contexts, I have often had a reasonably small amount of control over variables such as decision-making regarding the frequency of engagement, the level of planning, engagement in competition or attention paid to different training components. This said, my attitude and values regarding my intentions while implementing the coaching process at any level remain constant. This personal coaching philosophy has been shaped through my experiences both as a player and as coach.

With a passion for sport at any level, I instinctively strive for an improved execution of skill or a more successful performance when in a sports-coaching environment. To observe individual improvement and be involved in the process of this gives me much satisfaction. In addition, to have an impact on an individual's personal development – through an involvement in sport – I feel, at times, is an undervalued aspect of the coaching process. As a young coach, I continually endeavour to extend my knowledge base, broaden my experience in coaching contexts and develop my own coaching process to become a more effective coach. Knowledge, which I acquired from watching others or from being coached myself, has had the most significant impact on my coaching practice today.

One of my personal goals as a coach is to develop self-belief among athletes, in order that they may become confident in their own ability to achieve their potential. I believe that coaches should guide athletes, but also empower them – through delivery of knowledge and by creating a positive learning environment – to be independent individuals, motivated to set high standards for themselves and continue with their own performance development in the absence of a coach.

Of great importance during the coaching which I undertake are organization and planning (including flexibility in dealing with unforeseen circumstances). In this way I hope to deliver sessions which are specific to an athlete's needs, and ensure that I maintain control over sessions. Preparation is vital to me as it relates to commitment, which is a value I respect highly. Regarding my approach to coaching, I always try to consider how I would react as a player to a particular activity or situation. Athlete protection is also important, and I believe that part of the role of the coach is ensuring that athletes are safe and healthy (physically and emotionally) throughout training and competition.

An active, cooperative, two-way communication process between the athlete and coach, I believe, is essential in order for goals to be defined together. Conveying knowledge to athletes at the correct time and in a manner so that they will understand and value the information received requires excellent interpersonal skills. This is another factor which I regard as extremely important within the coaching process: athletes should know and understand what they are doing and why they are doing it.

Maintaining my position one step away from the athletes I like to convey an approachable manner, making it easier to develop good working relationships with them. Providing feedback to individuals in team sports (as you would in individual sports) helps me to facilitate productive training, with every team member having individual aims in addition to the overall team targets. The equal treatment of all athletes whom I coach, eradicating any favouritism, is an important value within my coaching. The emphasis put on winning varies with the level at which I am coaching, and is dependent on the overall goals for the individual or team. The coaching which I have been involved in up until now has never been results-driven, therefore I have had more focus on improvement in performance. When I am involved in coaching, regardless of the aims of the training or competition or of the athletes involved, I ask that all participants apply themselves fully. I aim to keep all participants engaged, enjoying the session, and demand that the high standards of quality which I or they set are maintained throughout.

Coaching Philosophy II

My personal preference would be towards a constructivist philoso-phy, encouraging the athletes to find solutions to problems. The key to performance success in my sport is having a well-formed and robust set of decision-making skills. The ability of the athlete to quick-ly recognize and analyse game situations then select and apply the appropriate response is crucial. The reality of the athlete's need to dem-onstrate a coherent set of cognitive skills in competitive pressure situa-tions underpins all of the work which is completed in practice sessions and establishes a clear direction and boundaries for the relationships I have with them.

Do you have a public declaration of your coaching philosophy? Can you or have you defended it?

6

Coaching Children

Children are like wet cement. Whatever falls on them makes an impression.

Dr Haim Ginott

The success of a sport depends primarily on the quality of its adult leadership. Teachers, coaches, officials, spectators and parents all affect the experience and determine to a large extent whether it will be positive. However, of all the adults involved, parents and coaches are perhaps the most important. It is their attitudes, beliefs and behaviour which undoubtedly affect the child the most. The relationship between the coach and the young athlete is critical. How a coach teaches new skills, manages a practice, gives feedback, recognizes effort and behaves with players and parents is essential to establishing a healthy environment. The role of parents is to decide what a child's sport needs are, investigate the programmes that are available, decide which ones are the most appropriate for the child's sex, age and ability, estimate the quality of the youngster's experience and decide whether a particular activity lends itself to a lifelong habit of exercise. Parents should also determine whether the coach's philosophy is compatible with their own personal values.

Parents' Involvement

Few children can participate in sport without the financial and emotional support of their families. Often, family arrangements are made around a child's sport commitments. Research shows that children are more likely to participate in sport if their parents do. A study commissioned by Sport Canada on participation by Canadians showed that a mother's participation had a greater effect than a father's on a child's likelihood of involvement.

Parents 'coaching' from the sidelines, criticizing the opposition or verbally abusing officials and coaches are common examples of parents misbehaving in children's sport. Fortunately, the majority of parents and adult spectators do not engage in this sort of excessive behaviour. Most parents spend their time silently watching the game or chatting with friends. However, one fanatical parent can ruin a child's experience and have a serious negative impact on the whole team (reconsider the ethical dilemmas for evidence of this). Research has found that certain factors

41

help to explain why some parents are intrusive. For example, the proximity of spectators to one another or to the players, familiarity with the game and the closeness and importance of the game, as perceived by adults, are all factors that may indicate a greater likelihood of parents offering verbal comments or criticisms. Another factor is the tendency to value winning above all else. In this case, parents constantly focus on what they perceive to be the mistakes players, officials and coaches make, especially in the crucial last moments of a game. In a recent article I wrote for the magazine *Coaching Edge* I advised coaches who were dealing with disruptive parents that prevention was the best cure. I suggested holding an orientation meeting to inform parents about the programme's philosophy and goals and what was expected of parents during a practice or a game. Coaches who find themselves with a disgruntled parent should meet him or her after-hours to discuss the problem openly and point out the negative effect such behaviour was having on the child and possibly also the team. Parents who are kept busy may have fewer opportunities to complain. For some parents, it can be useful to be responsible for a task, which might focus their efforts on the well-being of all of the children. Scoring, being team manager, keeping statistics, refereeing or being kit manager are all good possibilities. Parents are also less likely to intervene if they believe that the children are in the hands of a knowledgeable coach. Factors such as experience and coaching qualifications are important in convincing parents that their child is well supervised.

Children and Their Coaches

Most children have enormous respect for their coaches. Usually studies show that more than 90 per cent of young athletes state that their coaches were a greater source of influence on their behaviour than their teachers, parents or their peers (and most of my anecdotal experience would support this evidence). But when coaches encourage children to cheat or abuse them in any way, the impact can be serious. We should note that the people who are life-guards have to be licensed and trained, but any volunteer can walk in off the street and coach in some sports. We have already mentioned the issue of cheating. Parents who hear of coaches who encourage cheating should inform them that teaching children to cheat is unacceptable and should let other parents know what is going on. If nothing is done about it, look for a better sport environment. Unfortunately, taking a child off a team is hard because you are penalizing the child instead of the coach. Children are also vulnerable to sexual abuse by adults involved in sport, and sporting environments increase the potential for abuse. Sexual abusers find it easy to work in locker rooms and showers, on trips and during tournaments. The traits that make children good athletes – obedience, pliability and an eagerness and willingness to please – also make them targets for sexual abuse. Children are afraid that the coach will reject them if they say no to improper advances. As parents, be wary of situations that are inappropriate.

For example, never let your child train alone or go to a coach's house unattended. If possible, make sure another adult is involved in the coaching process. This means that any contact with children is always in the presence of another adult. If individual coaching is required, make sure that the room is open so that the children can be seen by other people. Be sure that all touching is limited to what is strictly needed for proper coaching, such as the spotting or correcting of errors. Verbal abuse is another problem that may occur in coaching. Coaches who value winning above all else may berate young children for missing a shot or not landing a jump. This type of behaviour is inappropriate for any coach, and at any level of sport.

What Coaches Need

As we have already noted, historically, coaches were selected for their athletic accomplishments and the all-too-common belief that, 'I played the sport for twenty years, so I can surely coach it.' Even though the attitude that 'coaching requires no special skills and anyone can do it' still exists, experts agree that today's coaches need training in order to be effective. Sport administrators now recognize that understanding sport techniques is only one component of being a good coach. In order to do the job effectively, coaches need to know a great deal about children. Thus, how do children grow and develop? What can coaches do to build self-esteem? What is the best method to teach new skills?

Coaches are the most important link in providing a healthy sport experience. Good coaches balance a sound philosophy of coaching with high ethical standards and a solid understanding of skill learning, growth and development and the needs of athletes. Parents should feel a moral responsibility to determine whether their children are in the hands of competent and ethical role models.

Figure 13 Children's rugby coach.

A competent coach may be defined as one who has the appropriate knowledge, skills and attitude to do the job effectively. Good coaches must have a sound knowledge of coaching principles. They must understand the principles that apply to learning, training within a sport environment and human development. They must understand the sport, its techniques, strategies and tactics. And they also need an understanding of athletes and their individual characteristics. This knowledge does not automatically come from participating in a sport for twenty years. Qualified coaches need to be trained to recognize and understand these important principles and to apply them on the field. Many of the skills that good coaches apply can also be learned or refined.

These include how to be a good leader, teacher and administrator. Watching the game, you should be able to tell very quickly whether the coach relates well and can manage the children effectively. Is the coach a good problem-solver? Can the coach motivate the group to work as a team? Does the coach recognize everyone's contribution and celebrate achievements? Does the coach set reasonable goals for the group in terms of age and ability? Is effort recognized as much as performance? Since many primary schools no longer provide children with a good grounding in sport skills, it is essential that the coach knows the fundamentals and is qualified to teach them to young children. A good coach helps players to learn by explanation, demonstration and practice. Does the coach communicate well with athletes? Does the coach crouch down to a child's eye level to give instructions? Is individual guidance provided even in a group setting? Are skills taught in a progressive manner and within a safe environment? A good coach does not have six children working like demons while the others do nothing. He or she moves easily from group to group, knowing what comes next. Is the coach well-organized? Are practices well-organized? Is there lots of opportunity for participation? Coaches are figures of authority and role models. They should have the proper attitude toward sport that will instil values of sportsmanship and fair play. Does the coach put winning in perspective? Does the coach encourage children to respect the rules and to respect others?

Sitting on the sidelines, parents and spectators are in a good position to determine whether the sport experience is a good one for children. Useful Checklists for parents are presented on pages 45 and 46.

There is more to refereeing children's sports than blowing whistles. A referee who takes on the role of supplementary coach can make a significant difference to the games played by young children. A good referee is more teacher than rule enforcer. He or she can give young players on-field lessons which they will carry through the game and into future games. Referees control the way a game is played. They are there to help the game flow and to ensure that it is played properly and fairly. Even at the World Championships, the highest level of international sport, the referees continually talk to, warn and advise the players to ensure as much continuity

Questions to Ask

Shopping around for a good sports club is worthwhile in the end. A child's early exposure to sport lays the groundwork for participation in the years to come. When registering a child in a sports programme, consider these questions:

- Are the coaches UKCC qualified? What coaching experience do they have?
- Is there a policy of equal playing time?
- Does the programme emphasize the development of skills?
- Are the play areas safe and well maintained?
- What is the ratio of practice to competition? For example, a ratio of three or four practices to one game is appropriate for young children.
- Are the groupings and teams suitable for safe and enjoyable activity?
- Are there many opportunities for children to play?
- Are youngsters encouraged and congratulated for good efforts?
- Are the needs of the children taken into consideration? For example, are practices at a convenient time and place? Are they limited to a reasonable length of time? Will time demands prevent the children from participating in other activities and assuming other responsibilities?
- Are safety rules adhered to during practices and games? Is the appropriate equipment available? Are children matched with others of the same size?

Questions to Ask Youngsters After a Competition or Match

The first question parents usually ask their child after a game is, 'Did you win?' Whether the answer is yes or no does not really tell you anything about what the child has just experienced. Ask the right questions and learn from the answers:

- Did you have fun?
- What was your favourite part of the game?
- What did not you like about today's game or practice?
- What did you learn?
- What do you need to work on?
- Can I help you to improve any skill?
- Were you nervous during the game today?
- What did the coach say after the game?
- Were you a good sport?

Questions for Parents

- Training or practice sessions should be well organized and purposeful. The coach should be in charge and well prepared. The equipment should be set up and the children organized quickly into groups to practise different skills.
- Every session should have a high level of activity and involvement for all children. Children do not like to stand around waiting for their turn to kick the ball. They should be active – most of the time!
- Every session should progress from known skills to new skills. After a proper warm-up, the children should begin familiar practices to improve or maintain their skills. Then the coach should build on these skills by introducing new ones to the group.
- A good coach communicates clearly. A picture is worth a thousand words: new skills should be clearly introduced with a demonstration. If the coach notices that the skill has not been absorbed, he or she should stop the practice and ask the children to watch while another demonstration is given as a reminder.
- A good coach makes encouraging comments to his group. Coaches should encourage their charges by praising their efforts. Children like to be told that they are doing a good job and working hard.
- A good coach provides specific instruction to individual children, 'Just try to open those fingers a bit more when you catch the ball', or 'Watch where you're throwing that ball when you throw it to your partner. Try to throw it right into her tummy, that's good, much better!'
- A good coach provides opportunities for feedback and questions from the children. Children should never be discouraged from asking questions.
- A good coach lets everybody play. Sign up with a coach who believes everybody should play even if it means not 'winning' all the time. Everybody gets to play whether they are good players or not.
- A good coach has happy children. Children who enjoy working with a good coach leave practices happy and satisfied, ready to come back the next time.

of play as possible without unnecessary stoppages. In children's games a referee who blows the whistle when an error is committed should not be afraid to stop the game and explain why the whistle was blown. Even for individual sports, officials and judges can take the opportunity to give pointers to young athletes. For example, an athletics or swimming official might explain to a youngster what the rules are for an event in which he made an error such as stepping over the take-off board in the long jump or touching the wall with one hand in the butterfly.

I first noticed the following story after a couple of years ago and I use it all the time now on coach education courses (I can't find the source). I'm not sure whether it is apocryphal or not, but it certainly made me think about my attitudes to officiating as a coach, and as a spectator.

Donald Jensen was struck on the head by a thrown bat while umpiring a Little League game in Terre Haute, Indiana. He continued to work the game, but later that evening was placed in the hospital by a doctor. While being kept overnight for observation, Jensen wrote the following letter:

Dear Parent of a Little Leaguer,

I'm an umpire. I don't do it for a living, but only on Saturdays and Sundays for fun. I've played the game, coached it and watched it. But somehow, nothing takes the place of umpiring. Maybe it's because I feel that, deep down, I'm providing a fair chance for all the kids to play the game without disagreements and arguments. With all the fun I've had, there is still something that bothers me about my job. Some of you folks don't understand why I'm here. Some of you feel I'm there to exert authority over your son. For that reason, you often yell at me when I make a mistake, or encourage your son to say things that hurt my feelings. How many of you really understand that I try to be perfect? I try not to make a mistake. I don't want your son to feel he got a bad deal from an umpire. Yet no matter how hard I try, I can't be perfect. I counted the number of calls I made in a six-inning game today. The total number of decisions, whether on balls and strikes or safe and outs, was 146. I tried my best to get them all right, but I'm sure I missed some. When I figured out my percentage on paper, I could have missed eight calls today and still got about 95 per cent of the calls right. In most occupations that percentage would be considered excellent. If I were in school, that grade would receive an A for sure. But your demands are higher than that. Let me tell you more about my game today. There was one real close call that ended the game. A runner for the home team was trying to steal the plate on a passed ball. The catcher chased the ball down and threw to the pitcher covering the plate. The pitcher made the tag and I called the runner out. As I was getting my equipment to leave, I overheard one of the parents comment, 'It's too bad the kids have to lose games because of rotten umpires. That was one of the lousiest calls I've ever seen.' Later, at the concession stand, a couple of kids were telling their friends, 'Boy, the umpires were lousy today. They lost the game for us.' I felt just terrible when I got home. Here was a group of kids who had made a lot of mistakes, which had cost them a number of runs.

The purpose of Little League is to teach baseball skills to young men. Obviously, a team which does not play well in a given game, yet is given the opportunity to blame that loss on an umpire for one call or two, is being given the chance to take all responsibility for the loss from their shoulders. A parent or adult leader who permits the younger player to blame his failures on an umpire, regardless of the quality of that umpire, is doing the worst kind of injustice to that youngster. Rather than learning responsibility, such an attitude is fostering an improper outlook toward the ideals of the game itself. This irresponsibility is bound to carry over to future years.

As I sit here writing this letter, I am no longer as upset as I was this afternoon. I wanted to quit umpiring, but fortunately, my wife reminded me of another situation that occurred last week. I was umpiring behind the plate for a pitcher who pantomimed his displeasure at any call on a borderline pitch that was not in his team's favor. One could sense that he wanted the crowd to realize that he was a fine, talented player who was doing his best to get along, but that I was a black-hearted villain who was working against him. The kid continued acting like this for two innings, while at the same time yelling at his own players who dared to make a mistake. For two innings the manager watched this. When the kid returned to the dugout to bat in the top of the third, the manager called him aside. In a voice loud enough that I was able to overhear, the lecture went like this: 'Listen son, it is time you make a decision. You can be an umpire, an actor or a pitcher. But you can only be one at a time when you are playing for me. Right now it is your job to pitch. And you are basically doing a lousy job. Leave the acting to actors, the umpiring to the umpires or you won't do any pitching here. Now what is it going to be?'

Needless to say, the kid chose the pitching route and went on to win the game. When the game was over the kid followed me to my car. Fighting his hardest to keep back the tears, he apologized for his actions and thanked me for umpiring his game. He said he had learned a lesson that he would never forget. I can't help but wonder how many more fine young men are missing their chance to develop into outstanding ball players because their parents encourage them to spend time umpiring.

The following morning Donald Jensen died of a brain concussion.

Most adults can remember street football and rounders from their childhood. It was a time when children developed a true love of sport because they played for sheer enjoyment. A lot of things have changed since those days. Adult involvement in children's sports is deeper and more influential than it used to be. This deeper involvement has resulted in a shift in emphasis from helping 'where they could' to a pretty clear domination of children's sport by adults and such that unsupervised sport may have become almost a thing of the past. Today's children should primarily be having fun in any sport they play, with winning and losing a by-product. Whatever the role of adults, it should always be encouraging, supportive and positive. The following legendary comment on children's sport is unattributed, but it sums up the issues perfectly; it reminds us that sport is for kids to enjoy:

> I believe the children's league idea is a great one with some minor changes: put an eight-foot board fence around the playing area and let only the kids inside; take away all strips/team kit and let the kids wear their own clothes; let them choose teams by the one-potato, two-potato system; let them play until it gets dark or until the kid with the ball goes home. (Author unknown)

To that, let me add a final note. Let us not as adults take the game away from children and mould it to adult standards. Let us encourage children to enjoy being active through enjoyable play and appropriately designed competition which meets their needs. If we do this, we shall have made an important contribution to their development through sport.

CHILD DEVELOPMENT

Certain changes occur as children grow and develop. These changes, called stages of development, affect how a child performs in sport. The stages of physical and motor development influence how well a child performs sport skills. The stages of emotional development dictate what kind of competition is most suitable. Some of these changes are dealt with in more detail in Part III. Motor development often does not proceed at the same rate as physical development. Rapidly growing children often appear awkward. The child may not be ready to execute or refine a skill until his or her motor ability has developed further. These stages of development are predictable and all children pass through them. However, the age at which the child enters each stage and the duration of it cannot be predicted. A youngster's developmental age can differ significantly from his or her chronological age by as much as two or more years in either direction.

Physical Development

When children grow, they experience a change in hormone levels, in their muscles, bones and joints, their energy systems and their cardiovascular systems (heart and lungs). Up to the onset of puberty, children grow at a steady pace, making regular gains in height and weight. Coaches and parents must remember that there can be a wide variation in size among youngsters of the same age. In a typical primary school classroom, height differences among children range from 4 to 5in (10–12.5cm). Just as height can vary from one child to another, so can the timing of a child's growth. Despite the averages, many youngsters experience clear growth spurts, followed by periods during which they grow very little.

Emotional Development

As the body grows, children also develop emotionally and intellectually. They gain a stronger understanding of themselves and the relationships they have in the adult world. They improve their ability to interpret, analyse, and think. A very small child thinks of himself or herself as the centre of the world. Once children reach school age, they pay more attention to other people. As they get older, they are more capable of understanding team play and the relationships involved in team activity. A good coach recognizes the importance of social and mental development within sport by using team games, cooperative skills and fair play as the basis of activity.

Flexibility

Not every child can bend and stretch like a rubber band. Some children, like some adults, are just not flexible. But, if they train, children will gain flexibility faster than adults. The muscle tissue in children is as flexible as muscle tissue in adults. What is quite different is the connective tissue. Children can extend their ligaments and tendons farther than adults can. What is sometimes remarkable is how stiff some young athletes are. Coaches are not spending enough time stretching with these children. It is the best time of their life to do it and you can get such good results with little effort. It is particularly important for children to work on flexibility as they head toward their growth spurt. During rapid growth, flexibility decreases. If a child is not naturally flexible, the best time to gain range is before the growth spurt. Increased flexibility may prevent injuries, and it also improves an athlete's performance. To improve flexibility, children should always perform a proper warm-up incorporating dynamic stretching exercises. It is also important that they perform static stretches during their recovery and cool down. Effective stretching can improve performance, but overstretching can be harmful to the body by reducing the stability of joints.

NATURE OR NURTURE?

Studies have shown that a person's performance level and response to training are strongly influenced by genetics. They have shown that children inherit not only physical characteristics, but also psychological qualities such as competitiveness and motivation as well. Heredity is therefore very important in determining how good an athlete a child can be. Studies of identical twins show that approximately 50 per cent of aerobic power and 70 per cent of endurance performance are fixed by heredity. Research also indicates that an individual's response to training is also genetically determined. This means that some athletes will show greater potential for improvement than others as a result of training, regardless of their initial level of fitness or how hard they work. If a child does not have the genetic makeup required to excel in a particular sport, it is unlikely that he or she can perform at the very highest level. Although genetics plays a key role in determining one's potential for performance, it is clear that the proper training is also critical. In fact, it is through training and hard work that the genetic potential in sport can be realized. Experts often refer to genetics as shaping the size of the 'talent bucket' and all other environmental factors (such as social, economic and coaching) determining how much of the bucket of potential is filled. Genetics may play a big part in our ultimate level of achievement in sport, but everyone can and should be encouraged to participate. All children can benefit from the life long lessons sport can bring them, regardless of their level of performance. Eventually, if performance is important to the child, it may be advisable to consider directing him or her to sports where the probability of success is highest, but not before.

Teaching children new sport skills is not easy. It requires knowing how children learn, how they pay attention, remember and make decisions. The human brain is like a computer. It receives information by using its senses, interprets the information and then produces a response. When children see a tennis ball travelling towards them, they must feel where their body is and recognize that to hit the ball they must swing the racket at a particular time and speed. The results of the swing are stored in memory for the next time. However, learning sport skills does not simply involve learning how to swing a bat or kick a ball. It also involves learning what to pay attention to. In a team sport many things compete for a child's attention: teammates, opponents, the ball, coaches and parents. Parents or spectators who shout from the sidelines can create distractions for players, making it difficult for them to perform. To play a team sport, children must pay attention to the cues that are relevant and block out those that are not. It is easy for children to become overloaded with information. Keeping practices simple by giving youngsters only one thing to work on at a time improves the learning process.

Everyone has a limited amount of information that can be processed at any one time; the speed with which we can deal with it is known as our information processing capacity. As we grow and mature, our capacity to handle information becomes more sophisticated. We can deal with more information at once, and more quickly. To help them to learn, coaches must try to reduce the information children have to deal with. Playing basketball, for example, requires the child to dribble the ball and look for a teammate – two tasks that are difficult until one of them requires less attention. To help children to cope, coaches should give them time to practise dribbling alone. Then they can practise dribbling past standing players or cones. When children know how to dribble, coaches can start to introduce passing techniques. When dribbling is automatic, the game is easier to learn. The NBA star Earvin 'Magic' Johnson famously used to dribble his basketball to and from school every day to hone his ball-handling skills.

Figure 14 Children's multi-sport coach.

Sporting situations usually require quick and complex decision-making. Which pass should I use? With how much force? In which direction should I kick? For children, to make decisions in a new situation is a slow process. With their limited experience, they are much slower at making decisions than adults. And when their young minds are distracted by the stress or tension that comes with playing sport, it becomes even more difficult to make good decisions. A child's capacity to learn new skills and to make decisions is limited by his or her capacity to process information. The more distractions children must cope with, the more difficult it is to learn. To enhance learning, a coach must free the child's attention from such distractions to make learning and decision-making easier.

To help children to learn coaches should adapt the sport for youngsters. Children are baffled by too many choices. A small group of players reduces the number of choices open to them and simplifies decision-making. Once children are confident, coaches can present more difficult situations, which offer a larger number of possibilities. Therefore three-a-side or four-a-side may be appropriate at the younger levels (one of my graduate students has been compiling data on the effectiveness of 4v4 football versus other forms of the game and it is clear that more touches and more time on the ball lead to more fun and better skills).

Coaches can also simplify the rules. Rules are normally written for games played at an adult level, but coaches should try to be flexible and think of rules as a framework that may need to be built upon slowly. Introduce rules as they are needed and adapt them in order to focus on what you want the children to learn. Coaches can focus on a few simple, key words that allow for a gradual progression of skill learning. They can also teach children how to make decisions by creating a comfortable environment. A three-on-one practice grid requires easier decision-making than a three-on-two or a two-on-two version. Coaches must accept that making wrong decisions is part of the learning process. Teaching youngsters decision-making skills is a vital link in encouraging their self-reliance and making their experience enjoyable.

When a baby learns to walk, it goes through a natural sequence of development – creeping, crawling, standing with support and then standing alone. Finally, it will walk, encouraged by delighted parents. The loving parent with the baby learning to walk is the best model to apply to children learning sport skills. A parent does not give walking lessons, he or she simply encourages the child and, of course, the child sees the parents walking all the time. Sport skills develop slowly from primitive to less primitive. Children rarely learn a new skill correctly at the start. Adults often make the mistake of trying to teach a child to throw, kick or catch the ball the way they do themselves. A coach who directs a child constantly is actually impeding the learning process. When children are learning, they make lots of mistakes, but they learn by thinking things through. When they detect an error, they are taking another step in skill development. There are generally three stages in teaching children new skills: understanding, practising and performing.

Understanding

In the first stage, children must understand what they are trying to achieve. Never assume that they know what you want – show them, then explain in simple terms. Good coaches demonstrate the skill themselves and then ask several team members to try it. It is better to choose someone who can demonstrate the skill correctly at the athletes' present level. Most people identify with average performers and learn best from them. Beginners sometimes find it discouraging to observe the best performers.

Practising

Once children understand what is to be achieved, practice is needed to refine the skills. Keep practices short, simple and fun. During practice, give feedback that is appropriate to the age and skill level of the players. Children simply cannot absorb feedback as well as adults. Start by asking questions and deal with one thing at a time. Children learn more if they have to recall and think it through themselves. Always find something positive to say after each skill attempt and focus on key points.

Performing

When a skill can be performed almost automatically, the child can then attempt it within a more complex or modified game situation. Coordination is the ability to control the body's actions in time within our environment, with the body parts moving in an appropriate manner. Just as an orchestra works together to make music, so the body parts must move in the correct direction with the right amount of force and at the right time to create a coordinated action. By about age six, most children are able to perform basic skills such as walking, running, hopping, jumping, throwing and catching. More complex skills such as skipping will be a challenge, and many children look awkward or uncoordinated when they try them for the first time. In order for children to learn how to skip, they must link the actions of walking and hopping, using the correct timing. For most sport skills, timing is one of the most difficult tasks to learn. Imagine how difficult it is to learn how to catch a thrown or batted ball on the run: actions must be coordinated to catch the ball and to move the body to the right place at the right time. Coordination naturally develops with age, but greatly improves with experience and practice. If you want a child to be an ace performer in any sport, you have to spend time playing that sport with him or her after school and at weekends. The average child can develop most skills with experience. Children who appear clumsy or uncoordinated when first learning a sport skill may be reluctant to continue their participation. Some sports such as volleyball, football and tennis can be modified to accommodate young children learning new skills. Short tennis, for example, is a good example of how to modify a sport. Growth spurts, which occur during puberty, may affect coordination. As the body's length and weight change, awkwardness and lack of coordination may result. But if the child continues to practice, this awkwardness will eventually disappear. The more time the child spends experiencing different kinds of sport and practising moving in different environments, the better the coordination will become. Involvement in sport can help children to become coordinated movers, but sport involvement will only continue if the experience is positive.

The renowned child psychologist Jean Piaget believed that the most important phase in the development of self-esteem occurs between the ages of about six and eleven. This is also a time when children are most likely to be introduced to sport. How children come to understand themselves and relate to others in social situations, such as sport, is essential in helping them develop mature social skills. Research conducted with more than 650 parents found that the primary reason they register their youngsters in youth sport is to build self esteem. And they are right. Success in sport will, in fact, help children to build a healthier self-esteem. Very early in life children begin to develop a picture of themselves, a self-image. They develop positive feelings about themselves and acquire a sense of importance and self-worth. The ways in which they see and evaluate themselves – either positively or negatively – are known as self-esteem. If children are given many opportunities to succeed in sport, they will more often come to see themselves as 'winners' rather than 'losers'. They will grow up to be better adjusted, more confident and better able to cope with stress and new challenges. A child's self-esteem is initially shaped by its parents. Verbal and non-verbal reactions, praise and criticism, smiles, other facial expressions and hugs help to influence a child's level of independence and sense of achievement. When children are given lots of praise and positive reinforcement, they develop high self-esteem. The behavioural psychologist B.F. Skinner believed that personalities are shaped by the positive reinforcement received throughout a lifetime. According to Skinner, we are what we have been rewarded for being.

BENEFITS OF SPORT

Sport provides children with the opportunities to try new skills and assess their capabilities. As figures of authority, parents and coaches have an enormous capacity to make children feel good about themselves. Even casual remarks can have a great impact. Parents and coaches should always find something each child does well, even if it is just following directions, and give praise for that. Understanding and support from parents and coaches are the main building blocks for feelings of self-worth. Children need a healthy sense of self-esteem in order to feel good about themselves and good about others. Self-esteem is more than just a sense of happiness. It is an attitude of 'I am capable, I can do this.' This kind of attitude develops when parents and coaches demonstrate a belief in children and encourage them to take responsibility for pursuing their own potential.

Low Self-Esteem

This may be the cause when a child:

- avoids a task or challenge without even trying, or gives up at the first sign of frustration; this often signals a fear of failure or a sense of helplessness
- cheats or lies to prevent losing a game or by doing poorly
- shows signs of regression, acting baby-like, or very silly. These types of behaviour invite teasing and name-calling from other youngsters, adding insult to injury
- becomes controlling, bossy, or inflexible to hide feelings of inadequacy, frustration or powerlessness
- makes excuses ('The coach is stupid') or downplays the importance of events ('I don't really like that game anyway'), using rationalizing to place blame on others or on external forces
- withdraws socially, losing or having less contact with friends, as school grades decline
- experiences changing moods, exhibiting sadness, crying, angry outbursts, frustration or quietness
- makes self-critical comments, such as, 'I never do anything right', 'Nobody likes me', 'I'm ugly', 'It's my fault', 'Everyone is smarter than I am'
- has difficulty accepting either praise or criticism
- becomes overly concerned or sensitive about other people's opinions
- seems strongly affected by negative peer influence, adopting attitudes and behaviours such as a disdain for school, playing truant, acting disrespectfully, shoplifting or experimenting with tobacco, alcohol or drugs
- is either overly helpful or never helpful at home.

To help to determine whether a child has low self-esteem, the American Academy of Pediatrics recommends watching for the signals listed below. These could be everyday responses as the child relates to the world around him or her, or they might occur only occasionally in specific situations. When the behaviour becomes a repeated pattern, parents and coaches may need to become sensitive to the existence of a problem.

Building self-esteem means helping children to feel good about themselves. In summarizing my advice to novice coaches on the UKCC Level 1 programmes, I recommended that they help children develop confidence and self-esteem through the following ways:

Confidence and Self-Esteem

- greet each child individually when he or she arrives for each session
- make them feel good about being there
- show confidence in their ability to learn
- offer activities that suit their level of development
- encourage effort without always focusing on results
- avoid elimination games and other activities that may add undue pressure
- create situations where there are lots of opportunities for success
- be specific when telling them what you like about their effort or performance
- use a smile, a nod or a wink to acknowledge them
- praise them for the good things they have done, a pat on the back means a lot
- give them responsibilities
- involve them in making decisions and give each of them a chance to be a leader
- ask them for their input and invite their questions.

When young people have fun and enjoy their experiences in sport they stay involved longer and their self-esteem grows. Win or lose, positive feedback is extremely valuable. As you and the athletes enjoy the victory, point out the things that went well, identify areas for improvement and help them to draw out lessons as building blocks for future success. Following a loss, acknowledge an honest effort, highlight the positives and ask the athletes to identify areas for improvement. Help them to understand that a loss is an important learning experience and that their individual value as a person does not depend on whether they win or lose.

PART 2: HOW TO COACH

The pedagogical principles used in this section focus on the 'how to' skills of the coaching process. These principles are mainly coaching techniques and social implications of coaching styles. They contribute to the enhancing of an individual's coaching effectiveness. They are encapsulated in the 'nine expert coaching actions' of successful sports coaches, which are (1) building relationships; (2) creating a learning environment; (3) effective communication; (4) organization and control; (5) coaching pedagogy; (6) goal setting; (7) planning and preparation; (8) observation and analysis; and (9) reflective practice. We shall look in detail at each of these in turn, but first some explanation of what the coaching process is all about.

7

The Coaching Process

The coaching process has been represented in many forms but for the purposes of this initial explanation, let us assume that it involves five steps, which are:

1. Observing and collecting information about your coaching.
2. Analysing the collected information based on your own knowledge and that of others.
3. Using the information to create a plan to change coaching behaviours.
4. Implementing the plan (plan of action).
5. Reassessing the plan of action.

Self-reflective analysis in coach education is often based on these five steps. Coaches need to continue the process and constantly reassess and design methods that produce changes in and/or maintain coaching effectiveness. This process is demonstrated in the following simple model:

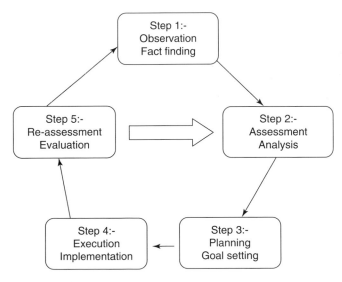

Figure 15 Simple coaching process model.

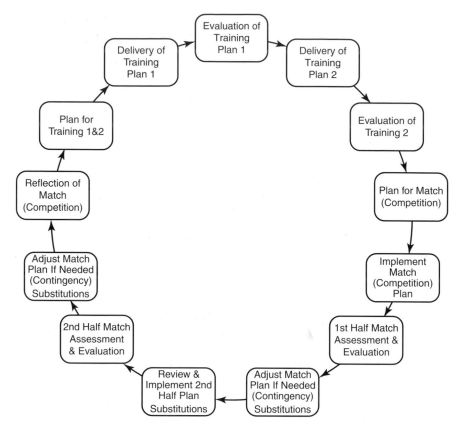

Figure 16 Amateur football coaching process model.

However, coaching is a dynamic and complex process and not easily represented in such a limited way. Fig. 16 illustrates one PG student coach's attempt to represent more adequately his coaching practice with an amateur team, training twice a week and playing a match at the weekend.

Other representations of the coaching process may stretch to many pages and there are even some attempted three-dimensional models, but suffice it to say that it is not always easy to show the complexity on paper. What is clear, however, is that we can state some assumptions about the coaching process to assist both our understanding and our efforts to improve practice. Part I of this book has already outlined three different forms of coaching (participation, development and performance), which is a good start towards delineating exactly the context we are talking about.

In considering these questions, perhaps it is helpful to think of coaches in different contexts, such as: volunteer club coach, part-time paid assistant coach, full-time school team coach and full-time national team coach. You might also want to reflect on what the key similarities and differences might be in terms of skills, attitudes, expectations and the measures of success for each of these. Where do you fit into this mix? You may play a number of different roles and adapt your behaviour accordingly.

But reflect on these other questions:

Questions for Coaches

- what is the distinction between coaching and other forms of sports leadership?
- what do coaches do that others do not or cannot?
- are there generic functions that coaches in all sports will attend to or is the coaching process sports specific?
- which factors influence how systematically a coach operates?
- what do we mean by style of coaching?
- are there some values which should be respected more than others?
- how can we decide if a coach is being effective or successful?

Figure 17 Pensive football coach during warm up.

WHY DO YOU COACH?

Have you ever asked yourself that question? There are many possible answers that won't be particularly surprising to you (as a number of them may apply), but if you haven't answered the question at all, or at least recently, perhaps completing the short survey in Fig. 18 will help to clarify your motives.

Please answer the following questions about why you coach by rating your response as:

1　Very important
2　Important
3　Some importance
4　Not important
5　Irrelevant

Reason for Coaching	Rating (1–5)
To be involved in my sport	
To earn a living	
To be in control	
To have fun	
To give something back to the sport	
To meet people	
To work with children	
To help improve performance in my athletes	
To help young people develop	
To get credit for the performances of my athletes	
To pass on my technical knowledge	
To travel	
To meet people	
To gain qualifications and get another job	

Figure 18　Why do you coach survey.

Of course, this is a very individual consideration, but there are a number of large surveys which help to give us a clearer picture of the motivations coaches have for getting involved, one of which was conducted in Scotland (over 600 coaches took part) and is summarized here.

Summary of Scottish Survey of Coaches

General Reasons

While coaches indicated a number of differing reasons for taking up coaching, these were most commonly general ones. Almost all (95 per cent) had a 'general interest' in the sport, while nine out of ten (89 per cent) indicated that 'putting something back into sport' was at least of some importance. In addition, nearly all coaches (96 per cent) indicated that 'helping young people' was at least of some importance in their decision to become a coach.

Involvement of Own Children

Although almost all (96 per cent) coaches wanted to help young people, fewer than a third made reference to their own children.

Almost three-quarters (72 per cent) indicated that their own children's involvement was of no importance or not relevant to them. Some sports are more likely to have attracted the parents of child participants than others. Over a half of athletics (58 per cent) and swimming (55 per cent) coaches indicated that the involvement of their children was at least of some importance in their original decision to take up coaching. In contrast, only 2 per cent of volleyball coaches indicated that their children's being involved was of some importance.

Financial Reward

Few coaches were first attracted by financial rewards. Only 13 per cent indicated that financial reward was of any importance in their decision to take up coaching, while almost nine out of ten (87 per cent) considered it of no importance or not relevant to them. The financial reward was of more importance to tennis coaches; over a third (38 per cent) indicated that financial reward was at least of some importance in their initial decision to become involved in coaching. This reflects the potential in tennis for remuneration for coaching activities.

Career Opportunities and Occupational Relevance

Relationships with an existing job or potential career were of limited importance in coaches' first motivations to become involved in coaching. Almost three quarters (72 per cent) indicated that starting a career in sport was not important or not relevant to their decision and over a half (57 per cent) commented that it was not relevant or not important to or in their existing occupation. Where a sport had a higher proportion of coaches with PE degrees there was a corresponding increase in the percentage of coaches, indicating that their initial decision was influenced by the relevance of their occupation. Over a half of basketball, hockey and volleyball coaches (77, 52 and 57 per cent, respectively) said that their occupation was of importance in their decision to become a coach. Swimming coaches differed slightly from others in that half (50 per cent) first became involved because the career opportunities presented by becoming a coach were of at least some importance to them.

8

Coach Profiling

INTRODUCTION

This chapter describes a self-evaluation tool for coaches to use. Originally devised and developed by the British psychologist Richard Butler (1989) for use with athletes, performance profiling is a natural application of Kelly's (1955) Personal Construct Theory to sport. The fundamental premise of Personal Construct Theory is that individuals strive to make sense of the world and themselves by constructing personal theories. These lead them to anticipate what will happen in given situations, and subsequently their theories are either validated or revised in the light of how well these theories enable and guide them to see into the immediate and the long-term future.

Helping a coach to achieve his or her potential is the premise underlying the use of this tool. Personal Construct Theory invites us to view the coach as in the business of constructing often quite an elaborate theory of his or her capacity physically, cognitively, socially and philosophically. Each coach will employ this theory to enable courses of behaviour to be charted in relation to it. However, it is often suggested that such construct systems are built up and maintained at a low level of awareness. This implies that in endeavouring to discover something about a coach's construct system, we must invite the coach to explore and communicate that which he or she is already taking for granted. Exploring the coach's perspective thus enhances his or her own awareness and enables the individual to understand better his or her needs and potential for improvement.

THE STAGES

1 Introducing the Idea

The idea of performance profiling is introduced to the coach as a means of shedding light on his current practice. Examples of completed performance profiles are shown to illustrate the basic procedure. It is emphasized that there are no right or wrong answers, but that instead the technique attempts to uncover what the coach considers important. It is pointed out that the information provided on the performance profile may improve the coach's own awareness and will help to direct the training and development in areas of perceived need.

2 Eliciting Constructs

Constructs that the coach perceives as constituting the fundamental qualities of high-performing coach effectiveness are elicited. When working on coach education courses, such constructs have been generated through brainstorming in small groups. Essentially the groups are asked to consider, 'What in your opinion are the qualities or characteristics of a high-performing coach in your sport?' Working on this for 5 to 10 min generally produces a broad range of qualities that are then shared with the whole group. The task for the coaches is then to select those qualities that are considered important for them, taking into consideration their own individual styles. When constructing performance profiles with individual coaches, the same question is addressed, often with some assistance in generating a broad range of constructs. Thus the coach might be invited to describe the qualities that mediate the different ways other coaches might cope with certain situations.

3 Assessment

The coach assesses himself against these constructs and the scores are presented on a visual profile. For each construct considered important, the coach is encouraged to rate how he currently perceives himself.

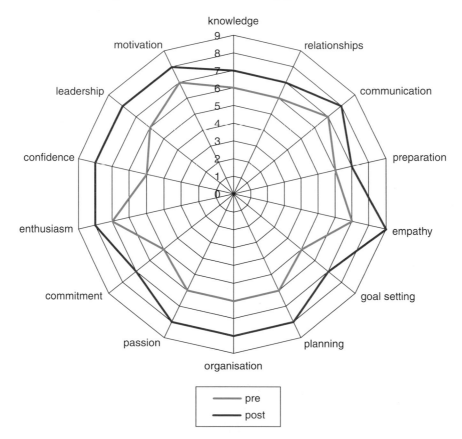

Figure 19 Swimming coach profile.

Figure 20 Blank 9-ECA profile.

Fig. 19 shows an example of one such performance profile generated by a coach at the start of a UKCC Level 3 course for swimming coaches. On this occasion, the coach generated his own categories for each segment of the profile, but it works just as well when these are already set out. Fig. 20 shows a blank copy of a profile I have compiled to be used in conjunction with this book. Once you have read the whole book and practised some of the 'nine expert coaching actions (ECAs)' you can rate yourself again and again to measure the improvement in your coaching practice. As a reminder, the nine ECAs are: (1) building relationships; (2) creating a learning environment; (3) effective communication; (4) organization and control; (5) coaching pedagogy; (6) goal setting; (7) planning and preparation; (8) observation and analysis; and (9) reflective practice.

Before getting on to the specifics of the 9-ECAs, let us briefly turn our attention to the tricky concept of effective coaching. It would be convenient to say that effective coaches are the ones who are successful, but is this enough? What about the coach who saves his team of journeymen players, exceeding expectations, from relegation? That might arguably have been a 'more effective' coaching job than the coach of the team who won the league with more talented players but which never really performed to their utmost. It is sometimes easier to recognize ineffective coaching when we see it, so what is it that makes the difference? Back to our delineations again: the judgement of effective coaching will necessarily be bound by time and place and the constraints that apply to it. We can assume that the coach acts effectively if the sum total of coaching actions produced the desired effect. So an effective Participation Coach may be one who creates a positive learning environment, improves the skills of the youngsters and has everyone turning up for sessions, eager and ready to work hard. In the Development Coach domain, effectiveness may be more closely linked to performance-improvement goals, achieving progressively challenging standards and measurable behavioural factors. Although it may seem obvious that Performance Coaches will be 'winners', this may not be the only measure and effectiveness may extend to specific aspects of play; for example, the defence coach in international rugby may be judged on how many tries are scored against his team (as well as the total score). What we can conclude is that coaching effectiveness is judged by evaluating instances of specific coaching performance.

Effective coaching = planning, managing and delivering the appropriate coaching intervention to achieve the optimum performance in relation to the achievement goals.

The coach in Fig. 21 took over a team that won just one game out of sixteen in the 2007 season (the Miami Dolphins in the NFL) and turned around their very next season to winning eleven out of sixteen and winning their division. By any measure of effectiveness, this was a tremendous achievement.

Figure 21 Effective coach in action.

9

The Nine Expert Coaching Actions of Successful Sports Coaches

In choosing these coaching actions (9-ECAs) of successful sports coaches, the intention is to illustrate what the research (and many years of experience) leads us to conclude about coaching practice. The 9-ECAs may come under different guises in other books or manuals, but they should be both recognizable and relevant to coaches in all domains and sports. There is a natural tendency towards using examples from the development coaching context (when dealing with children and young aspiring performers) and, since this is where most coaches operate, there is no apology for that. The elite performance context is dealt with in an example in Part III and there are some examples of participation coaching included where relevant.

1 BUILDING RELATIONSHIPS

> Relationships – of all kinds – are like sand held in your hand. Held loosely, with an open hand, the sand remains where it is. The minute you close your hand and squeeze tightly to hold on, the sand trickles through your fingers. You may hold on to some of it, but most will be spilled. A relationship is like that. Held loosely, with respect and freedom for the other person, it is likely to remain intact. But hold too tightly, too possessively, and the relationship slips away and is lost.
>
> *Anon*

In a sport context there are many personal relationships (for instance, coach–parent, athlete–athlete, athlete–partner) that can have an impact on performance, but the coach–athlete relationship is considered to be particularly important. This relationship is not an add-on to or by-product of the coaching process, nor is it based on the athlete's performance, age or sex – instead it is arguably the bedrock of coaching. The coach and the athlete intentionally develop a relationship that is characterized by a growing appreciation and respect for each other as individuals. Overall, the coach–athlete relationship is embedded in the dynamic and complex coaching process which provides the means by which coaches' and athletes' needs are expressed and is fulfilled at the heart of achievement and the mastery of personal qualities such as leadership, determination, confidence and self-reliance. This section offers a perspective on the coach–athlete relationship and shows how you can better understand, work at and develop your relationships with all your athletes.

Figure 22a Coach and athlete.

Figure 22b Coach and athletes.

The Significance of Coach–Athlete Relationship

The significance of this partnership has more recently been acknowledged in both the academic literature and the policies of sports organizations. It is characteristically described by using terms such as commitment, cooperation, communication, bonds, respect, friendship, power, dependence, dislike and distrust. At national policy levels, documents such as the DCMS (*A Sporting Future for All* [2000]) refer to the coach–athlete partnership and the coaches' mentoring and supportive roles as prominent issues of coach education. It is perhaps surprising then that, historically, coaching has been preoccupied with merely enhancing athletes' physical, technical and strategic skills. Now that the coach–athlete relationship is recognized as the cornerstone of coaching and a major force in promoting the development of athletes' physical and psychosocial skills, coaches' ability to create perfect working partnerships with their athletes becomes paramount. The fundamental question is 'What makes the ideal coach–athlete relationship?'

Effective vs Ineffective Relationships

Effective coach–athlete relationships are holistic in that the emphasis is placed on positive growth and development (that is, 'to be the best you can be') as an athlete/coach and as a person. Effective relationships include the basic ingredients such as empathic understanding, honesty, support, liking, acceptance, responsiveness, friendliness, cooperation, caring, respect and positive regard. In contrast, ineffective relationships are undermined by lack of interest and emotion, remoteness, even antagonism, deceit, exploitation and, sadly in extreme cases, physical or sexual abuse.

Successful vs Unsuccessful Relationships

The nature of sports coaching implies an achievement situation, where the performances of both coach and athlete are evaluated. Thus people are often inclined to evaluate a given coach–athlete relationship as either successful or unsuccessful. Successful relationships are those that have unquestionably reached a level of performance success (for instance, a Paralympic gold medal). A classification that allows us to view successful versus unsuccessful and effective versus ineffective relationships together is an interesting one. An unsuccessful yet effective coach–athlete relationship will invariably have some positive outcomes for the athlete (and the coach) in terms of psychological health and well-being – but obviously not performance-related ones. Although successful relationships are desirable, without their being effective they run a risk of breaching ethical and professional issues that are associated with codes of conduct formulated to protect coaches and athletes.

Effective and successful	Ineffective and successful
Effective and unsuccessful	Ineffective and unsuccessful

Figure 23 Simple classification of coach–athlete relationships.

Helping Relationships

A helping relationship involves an ability or desire to understand the other person's meaning and feelings, an interest without being overly emotionally involved and a strong and growing mutual liking, trust and respect between the two people. Helping relationships are optimally effective relationships, in that they facilitate self-actualization (that is, 'to be the best you can be'). According to Rogers (1967), helping relationships are not exclusive to client–counsellor but include other types of relationship such as teacher–pupil and parent–child. The task of a coach in developing optimally effective relationships that the athlete can use for growth, change and personal development is a challenging one, because it is a measure of the growth they have achieved themselves. This implies a responsibility on the part of the coach in that he must continually strive to develop his own potential. Ultimately, optimally effective coach–athlete relationships are reflected in the maturity and growth of both coaches and athletes.

Sport and exercise psychology research has largely studied the interpersonal dynamics between coaches and athletes from a leadership approach. Since the late 1970s, the multidimensional model (Chelladurai, 1993) and the mediational model (Smoll and Smith, 1989) of coach leadership have been the main frameworks for studying the behaviours, actions and styles coaches employ in their coaching. Emphasis is placed on how behaviours are perceived by the athletes and the coaches themselves, and their relative impact on outcomes such as satisfaction, self-esteem and performance. This approach may be limited, especially if we consider coach leadership as a function that can be shared, that is, 'a coach cannot do it alone'. Ultimately, a focus on what one person does to another may not accurately reflect what goes on between coaches and their athletes. To fill this gap, over the last decade a relationship approach has resulted in the development of several conceptual models, the most popular of which has been the work of Sophia Jowett and her colleagues at Loughborough University for example (Jowett and Cockerill, 2002).

Although this shift opens up an exciting direction to the study of coach–athlete interpersonal dynamics, the emphasis of most conceptual models is still on exploring coaches' and athletes' interpersonal behaviours. While there is little to argue against this investigative approach, there may be a risk of neglecting other important non-behavioural components of relationships, such as thoughts and feelings. This is where Jowett's concept of the 3-Cs (closeness, commitment and complementarity) and co-orientation come in.

This questionnaire aims to measure the quality and content of the coach–athlete relation-ship. Please read carefully the statements below and circle the answers that indicate whether you agree or disagree. There are no right or wrong answers. Please respond to the statements as honestly as possible and indicate how you personally think a specific athlete from your team or squad feels about you.

	Strongly disagree					Agree strongly	
			Agree moderately				
My athlete is close to me	1	2	3	4	5	6	7
My athlete is committed to me	1	2	3	4	5	6	7
My athlete feels that his/her sporting career is promising with me	1	2	3	4	5	6	7

These questions relate only to the commitment item in the full CART-Q. For the com-plete version, see S. Jowett and N. Ntoumanis (2004), 'The Coach–Athlete Relationship Questionnaire (CART–Q): development and initial validation', *Scandinavian Journal of Medicine and Science in Sports*, 14 (2004), pp. 245–57.

Figure 24 The Cart-Q commitment example.

The full CART-Q is an eleven-item tool and one of the dimensions (commitment) is illustrated here with the three statements in Fig. 24. A series of research studies have demonstrated that high scores along all of the three Cs dimensions are associated with higher levels of satisfaction with performance and personal treatment, higher levels of team cohesion, higher levels of harmonious passion toward the activity – as opposed to obsessive passion – and lower levels of role ambiguity in team sports. Co-orientation has recently been quantitatively examined in a study which looked at empathic understanding (or accuracy) and assumed similarity in coaches' and athletes' perceptions of their athletic relationship. The findings showed that athletes were more understand-ing or accurate in identifying the specific content of their coaches' feel-ings in terms of closeness. It has been proposed that, due to athletes' role in the relationships as the more vulnerable in terms of expert knowl-edge, power and authority, athletes' higher levels of empathic under-standing in terms of closeness cause them to feel more in control, comfortable and confident. Another finding revealed that athletes from moderately developed relationships displayed higher levels of empathic understanding in terms of commitment and complementarity. Perhaps athletes in the earlier stages of their relationship are motivated to observe their coaches closely in an attempt to build their common ground. Finally, female athletes displayed higher levels of assumed similarity in terms of commitment. Perhaps female athletes may choose to display greater levels of assumed similarity in an effort to affirm, support or indeed enhance their mental presentations of self (that is, that they are worthy of their coaches' attention).

Conflict and Communication

The measurement of the three Cs and co-orientation allows us to analyse coach–athlete relationships and to identify problem areas. Different dimensions of co-orientation can play an important diagnostic role in identifying ineffective or dysfunctional coach–athlete relationships by uncovering the points of disagreement, misunderstanding or dissimilarity across the three Cs. For instance, research has shown that athletes and coaches need to 'get on' with one another; however, getting along is difficult if coaches fail to understand the athlete's intentions or feelings accurately. Given that we are not all clairvoyant, conflict in the relationship is inevitable. Various elements can lead to conflict; for example, lack of commitment (including compromises and sacrifices), lack of a balanced approach of connectedness and autonomy and riskier and closer self-disclosure in the absence of trust. A series of qualitative case studies show that communication is an important unifying component in the coach–athlete relationship. Communication promotes the development of shared knowledge and understanding about various issues (for example, goals, beliefs, opinions and values) and forms the basis for initiating, maintaining and terminating the coach–athlete relationship. Particularly in youth sport, communication that evolves around spontaneous dialogues of daily activities related to school and training has been shown to form the basis for developing trust in the coach (Timson-Katchis and Jowett, 2004). Thus coaches that create opportunities for talk and disclosure related to the athletes' daily activities are more likely to develop trustworthy coach–athlete relationships.

2 CREATING A LEARNING ENVIRONMENT

> We learn more by looking for the answer to a question and not finding it than we do from learning the answer itself.
>
> *Lloyd Alexander*

Do you create a learning environment for your athletes? Do you know what a learning environment looks like and means? This section will look first of all at coaches as learners and then focus on the learning situations that coaches could and should create.

Coaches by definition (most coach education courses have a minimum age of 16) can be classified as adult learners. In fact, the average age of a sports coach in the United Kingdom (reported in the document *Sports Coaching in the United Kingdom* II, 2007) is 37. They are therefore likely to be rich in experience (or attitudes) relevant to the subject they are learning; goal-oriented, with their own agendas to pursue, self-aware, wanting to have their own perspective taken into account, influenced (positively or negatively) by memories of previous learning, diverse in their views about learning, balancing

Figure 25a Coach at timeout.

Figure 25b Coach at timeout.

other life interests and pressures, and expecting value for the time and effort invested. Adult learners therefore differ greatly, and it is a significant challenge to design learning experiences that will suit all learners. The coaches' study skills, experience of independent learning and familiarity with the

Figure 26 Coach education seminar.

learning process will be particularly relevant. In the context of coach education, learners will differ in their level of relevant prior knowledge, practical experience of the sport and extent of prior 'situated learning' (that is, having absorbed knowledge by being part of a community of practice).

The substantive issue is whether learning experiences (of any kind) are designed in such a way that the basic principles of successful learning are achieved. This section will demonstrate that there are explicit principles around which design can be based. A useful starting point for any learning is an early set of ideas suggesting that adults' learning is more likely to be successful in conditions of (*a*) understanding why the learning is relevant and what its immediate relevance might be, (*b*) approaching it as problem solving, (*c*) learning by doing, (*d*) having a degree of self-direction, (*e*) bringing the learner's own experience to the topic, and (*f*) having a clear goal for the learning. We can consequently summarize feedback on successful learning as (*a*) wanting to learn, (*b*) taking ownership of the process, (*c*) learning by doing (getting involved), (*d*) having an opportunity for feedback, and (*e*) 'making sense' of the material. The issue for you is the extent to which the learning materials in your coach education experience and the learning environment in your training sessions have been designed and presented in such a way as to facilitate these characteristics.

Gathering together the fundamental principles of research in learning theory, we can develop appropriate practices in creating a learning environment for our athletes. By marrying together the recommendations of Knowles (1990) – learners need to know why they are learning; they learn best experientially; they should approach learning as problem solving; learners learn best when there is immediate value from the outcomes; Kolb (1984) – experiential learning forms – concrete experiences; reflective observation; abstract conceptualization; active experimentation; and, McCarthy (1987) – recognition of different approaches to learning – dynamics learners; analytical learners; commonsense learners;

innovative learners, we can use this literature to identify and emphasize the five key factors that underpin effective learning:

* wanting to learn [intrinsic motivation]
* taking ownership of the need to learn [extrinsic motivation; recognizing need]
* learning by doing [practice; repetition; trial and error; experience]
* learning through feedback [from peers, tutors, resources, results]
* making sense of what has been learned [application, understanding].

A number of very obvious implications for coaching practice emerge from these principles. Novice coaches often present 'information' to athletes. The aim of the learning environment is to translate this into 'understanding'. Structuring the learning environment (which experienced coaches take for granted in their delivery behaviour) increases the possibility that learning will happen. Formative feedback is the most effective ingredient in any learning environment. (Does this also say something about key coaching skills?) It is important to help the learner to decide what to 'understand' and which feedback to value.

Coaching Practice Principles

* Clearly stated learning goals/outcomes for the athletes.
* Learning experiences rather than information.
* Clear tie-in to other learning experiences.
* Plenty of activity – doing.
* Manageable 'chunking' of the learning.
* Evident progression steps to reflect incremental progress.
* Self-assessment opportunities (feedback, outcome evidence).
* Clear concise instructions.
* Relevant, interesting, stimulating activity.
* Evaluative feedback given.

Coaching Practice

Let us assume that coaching is about learning (does this concur with your own experience as an athlete or your philosophy about coaching as discussed in Part I?). Do you create the appropriate conditions for that learning to take place? Much of coaching has an expectation of improved/changed skill (technique, application, tactical application). The argument presented above is that this is likely to happen better in some circumstances than in others. You may feel that these are unnecessary questions and that your coaching practice is carefully structured to enable learning to take place – but it might be valuable to reflect on that assumption.

The following table is a simple representation of learning principles with some comments added. This table was developed by Professor John Lyle for use in the CPD programme in conjunction with me.

Wanting to learn (intrinsic motivation)
- What is the incentive for learning?
- Have you established a competence motivation (rather than extrinsic reward); how did you do it?

Taking ownership of the need to learn (extrinsic motivation; recognizing need)
- Do the athletes understand why the learning is necessary?
- Is it related to their personal performance
- Have you presented 'evidence' of why the change is needed?
- Is the eventual performance outcome (contribution to competition performance) made clear?
- Do the players have a specific, individualized goal relating to this learning?
- Is each portion of learning relevant to practice?
- Is it related to your personal practice?
- Is it accompanied by reflection or evidence of existing practice?
- Is there understanding of why it is relevant?

Learning by doing (practice, repetition, trial and error, experience)
- Is there sufficient activity with repetition?
- Is it presented as a 'problem to be solved'?
- Is the decision-making element included?
- Are appropriate environmental cues identified?
- Are mistakes allowed?
- Is it put into practice?
- Is it presented with increasing complexity and accountability?
- Are there sufficient 'activities' to encourage learning?
- If so, are these presented as 'problems'?
- And is gradual learning accepted?

Learning through feedback (peers, tutors, evidence, results)
- How is the feedback provided?
- Is it individualized?
- Is the feedback evidenced or outcome based?
- Is the feedback a form of 'positive reinforcement'
- Do you provide 'markers' to recognize successful learning?
- Is there sufficient feedback?
- Does it invite the involvement of peers?

Making sense of what has been learned (application, understanding)
- Do the players/athletes know when the learning should be applied?
- Do the individuals understand how the learning relates to future learning (other skills/decisions)?
- Have you emphasized the 'learning process' rather than the outcome?
- Is it part of the new performance profile?
- Is the content applied?
- Is the process of learning explained?
- Is there an 'open' learning culture?
- Is modification invited?

Figure 27 Learning principles in coaching practice.

Taken together, these criteria reflect a 'learning culture' within your practice. Is this just good practice? Are these redundant questions? Do you put these principles into practice? And what about other coaches in your club or programme?

It might also help to think of any examples (critical incidents might be a better way of describing them) in which you felt that learning was not taking place as you expected? What is your explanation for this? And do any of these learning principles help?

You may want to argue that we do all of this as second nature because we have experience as coaches. But is this really the case? Has the exercise of examining the questions in Fig. 27 made you think about any other 'necessary conditions' that you provide or should provide for more effective learning to take place with your athletes?

3 EFFECTIVE COMMUNICATION

> The single biggest problem in communication is the illusion that it has taken place.
>
> *George Bernard Shaw*

Communication skills are often considered to be the best indicators of coaching success. Skilled orators in all walks of life are highly prized and respected, with the ability to 'communicate' (at least on the surface, verbally) seen as a great asset. The life of a coach is filled with a steady flow of communications: coaches talk, read, write, gesture, listen, teach, console, persuade, demonstrate and observe. Beyond their interaction with athletes, they spend a great deal of time communicating with parents, administrators, officials, other coaches, the media and support staff. So it is no secret that your success as a coach will depend on your ability to communicate effectively. You need a strong repertoire of communication skills to instruct your athletes clearly, motivate them and inspire confidence. Communication skills are the foundation for creating rapport with your athletes and developing team harmony. Being a good communicator can pave the way to a rewarding coaching experience, while communication breakdowns can lead to conflict, frustration, stress and job dissatisfaction.

Despite their importance, communication skills are often taken for granted. In the face of communication breakdowns, we tend to believe that our efforts are fine and that the problem lies with the people we are trying to communicate with.

> 'I know you believe what you think I said, but I'm not sure that what you heard is what I really meant.'

The reality is that we are not always effective communicators. Have you ever made a comment you later regretted? Do you sometimes unintentionally expect others to be able to read your mind? Do you find yourself talking more than you listen? Have you ever expected athletes to respond well to constructive criticism while not being open to feedback yourself? Most of us can relate to these scenarios. If you can, this section is for you.

Figure 28a Tactical coach.

Figure 28b Encouraging coach.

Figure 28c Thoughtful coach.

Becoming an effective communicator is not an easy task. Like any other skill, it takes education, hard work and practice. Part of the challenge in developing communication skills is that ineffective communication patterns are often so ingrained that it is difficult to become aware of them and let them go. The first step in improving your communication skills is to realize their importance and become aware of your communication style. This section will help you to identify your strengths and weaknesses as a communicator and provide you with essential knowledge that you can put into action to improve your skills.

What Is Communication?

Communication is the act of expressing (or transmitting) ideas, information, knowledge, thoughts and feelings, as well as understanding what is expressed by others. The communication process involves both sending and receiving messages and can take many forms. Verbal communication is the spoken word, while non-verbal communication involves actions, facial expressions, body position and gestures. Communication can occur in a one-on-one setting or group settings and in written, printed formats or visual formats (pictures, videos and observational learning). And it involves not only the content of a message but also its emotional impact, or the effect the message has on the person receiving it.

Sending and Receiving Messages

The very word 'coach' suggests that individuals in our profession send many messages. Coaches need to be able to communicate expectations, goals, standards and feelings clearly to their athletes. They instruct, encourage, discipline, organize and provide feedback. And although we tend to think of effective communicators as being able to send clear messages that are interpreted as intended, communication is a two-way street that also involves receiving messages. For a coach, this means listening attentively. As discussed elsewhere, athletes need to be able to communicate their goals, frustrations and feelings to their coaches.

Non-Verbal and Verbal Communication

As a coach, you can say a lot without uttering a word: a frown, a look of disbelief, a disgusted shake of your head, or a smile can communicate quite a bit. In fact, communication experts suggest that between 65 and 93 per cent of the meaning of a message is conveyed through tone of voice and non-verbal behaviour. Thus, in addition to becoming aware of the words you use, it is essential that you become aware of your tone and non-verbal behaviour so that you understand the messages you are sending to athletes. Have you ever seen yourself on video (with the sound off) and been surprised at the way in which you communicate non-verbally with athletes? If so, it may be time to recalibrate your communication approach.

By the same token, athletes also communicate non-verbally and coaches can learn to be more effective listeners by becoming astute observers of athlete's non-verbal communications. Understanding the non-verbal messages athletes send is a passport to greater understanding of the athletes you are coaching.

Content and Emotional Impact

When communicating, coaches tend to focus on the content or the substance of the messages they send: 'Run hard', 'Follow through strongly on your shot', 'Fake before you pass', 'Practise with intensity'. In doing so, they believe that the information is objective and that athletes will always receive the message as intended. That belief is far from the truth. When receiving messages, athletes may not share the same perception or hear the same message that the coach thought he or she was sending. For example, by saying, 'Tomorrow we are going to make sure to get this defence sorted out', a coach may mean, 'We're going to focus on the technical aspects of the defence to perfect our execution', but an athlete may interpret it as, 'Tomorrow's going to be a physically tough practice because we have been defending poorly.' Communication problems arise if a coach assumes that athletes are interpreting a message exactly as he intended. Thus effective communicators focus not only on message content but also on how a message might be interpreted by – and might affect – the receiver.

Beyond the message content then, communication also involves the emotional impact of the message on the athlete. How do your athletes perceive and react to the content of your messages? Failure to recognize the effect the message has on the athlete is all too common. For instance, a coach could intend 'Run hard!' as a positive note of encouragement, whereas the athlete could interpret it negatively, 'He never thinks I run hard enough.' Effective communicators give equal weight to message content and its emotional impact on the receiver. The challenge in effective communication is to be clear both about what you say and about how you say it by becoming more aware of the impact your messages have on your team.

Sending Effective Messages

Effective communicators are able to send messages that clearly convey the intended content and are received in the desired way. The most important judgement you need to make is whether a message needs to be sent. Some coaches talk too much, rambling on about things that bore others or distract athletes during practice. Some coaches talk too little, assuming that others know what they think or want. I have listed some guidelines for sending effective messages later in this section. Read each and then honestly rate whether this is a communication strength or weakness for you. Be sure to rate yourself objectively and take action to improve any deficiencies. Rest assured, that we all have communication strengths and weaknesses!

Effect of Your Messages

The researchers Smoll and Smith have spent hundreds of hours observing coaches and evaluating their impact on athletes (Smoll and Smith, 2006). In all, they observed dozens of coaches, coded almost 100,000 patterns of behaviour and surveyed nearly 1,000 athletes. They found that athletes responded positively to coaches who provided:

- positive feedback after a good performance effort
- corrective instruction and encouragement after a performance mistake
- technical instruction and a moderate amount of general encouragement unrelated to performance quality.

Rate yourself on each of these communication examples (1 very low, 5 is very high):

Coach Implausible

Never admitting to an error, Coach Implausible finds that he does not get the respect he demands because he does not show any for his athletes. He often does not follow through on what he says he will do, he thinks that he is far more knowledgeable about the sport than he is and he is very self-centred. When he speaks, he preaches rather than coaches so his athletes tune out because what he says never amounts to much. Coach Implausible has not yet learned that he cannot demand respect, instead it must be earned. Hence he has no credibility with his athletes. Think about how you communicate with your athletes and others. Does it add or detract from your credibility?

1   2   3   4   5

Coach Cynical

Most of the words and actions of Coach Cynical are negative, sometimes almost hostile. She frequently criticizes her athletes, which increases their self-doubts and destroys their self-confidence. Coach Cynical is slow to praise, as though she believes that it is not 'coach-like' to say a kind word, and, when she utters an infrequent kindness, she usually overshadows it with other negative comments. Think back to your own recent communications with your athletes. Are you primarily positive in the messages you deliver, or are you like Coach Cynical?

1   2   3   4   5

Coach Reviewer

Coach Reviewer continually evaluates his athletes instead of instructing them. When a player errs, he places blame rather than providing feedback or information about how to correct the error ('Who messed up here?', 'Why can't you get this right?', 'You cost us the game with that move'). When the players do well, Coach Reviewer cheers them on but does not know how to instruct them to achieve advanced skill levels. The continuous judgements, even when they are occasionally positive, cause athletes to feel uncertain and uncomfortable around this coach. Reflect a moment on the type of messages you send to your athletes. Do you give ample feedback and instructions, or are you like Coach Reviewer?

1   2   3   4   5

Coach Erratic

You are never sure what Coach Erratic will say next. Today it is one thing, tomorrow another. Last week she punished one player for fighting but not another – her star player. She tells players not to argue with the officials, but she does so regularly. It is not easy to detect our own inconsistencies, but ponder for a moment how consistent you think you are in the messages

By contrast, they found that athletes responded unfavourably to coaches who failed to notice or reinforce good performance efforts, criticized mistakes or provided instruction after a mistake in a critical fashion. How do you shape up as a communicator? Fig. 29 is a short, light-hearted survey based on mythical coaches who are poor communicators.

When you took the Communication Survey, you read about eight 'coaches' with poor communication skills. You may have identified with one of those or at least have been able to see some of the same characteristics in your own communication style. If you are like most people, you can improve in some areas of communication.

---

you send and between what you say and what you do. Is your message consistent, or are you more like Coach Erratic?

1   2   3   4   5

Coach Commentator

Coach Commentator is the most talkative person you ever met. He gives instructions constantly during practice and, when he's not yelling advice to his players during the contest, he is muttering to himself on the sidelines. He is so busy talking that he never has time to listen to his athletes. It has never occurred to him that his players might like to tell him something rather than always being told. Are you a good listener, or are you like Coach Commentator?

1   2   3   4   5

Coach Cold

Coach Cold never shows emotion. She does not smile, wink or give her athletes pats on the back. Nor does she scowl, kick at the dirt or express disgust with them. You just do not know how she feels, which leaves her players feeling insecure most of the time. Do you communicate your emotions effectively both verbally and nonverbally, or are you like Coach Cold?

1   2   3   4   5

Coach Brainy

Coach Brainy is unable to explain anything at a level understandable by his players. He talks either above their heads or in such a roundabout way that they are repeatedly left confused. In addition, Coach Brainy, who is used to dealing with abstractions, is unable to demonstrate the skills of the sport in a logical sequence so that the athletes can grasp the fundamentals. Are you able to provide clear instructions and demonstrations, or are you like Coach Brainy.

1   2   3   4   5

Coach Confused

Coach Confused just does not seem to understand how the principles of reinforcement work. Although he gives frequent rewards to his athletes, he reinforces the wrong behaviour at the wrong time. When faced with misbehaviour, he either lets the infraction pass or comes down too hard. Do you understand the principles of reinforcement, or are you like Coach Confused?

1   2   3   4   5

Rating Scale

36–40 Fantastic – you are destined for success!
31–35 Great score – but you can be a little better.
26–30 Decent – but you have plenty of room for improvement.
21–25 Poor – for those who frequently place their feet in their mouths!
8–20 Read on – you've got a lot to learn!

Figure 29 Communication survey.

Communication Tips

- Show the person speaking to you that you are interested in listening and trying to understand.
- Once someone has spoken to you, check that you understand what was said by paraphrasing the message, not only the content but also the emotion behind it.
- Express empathy, not sympathy, by showing that you care and respect what the person speaking to you has to say.
- Provide athletes with specific information that helps them to correct mistakes rather than general information that judges their performance.
- Be certain that you understand the reason for your athletes' actions before you judge their behaviour.
- Avoid making evaluative comments when athletes know they have made a mistake.
- Focus your comments on the athletes' behaviours, not on them as people to avoid damaging their sense of self-worth.
- Provide honest, direct and constructive messages.
- Embrace an attitude in which you look to catch your athletes doing something well and then tell them they have done so.
- Avoid sarcasm and put-downs, but at the same time do not sugar-coat athletes' behaviour by falsely putting a positive spin on it.
- Emphasize what can be done, not what cannot be done, and avoid language that dwells on problems; instead, use language that focuses on solutions.
- Before the season begins, define for yourself what you will reward and how you will reward your athletes; stick to this plan during the season.
- Develop team rules with your athletes so that they know what is expected and what the consequences will be if they misbehave.
- When an athlete misbehaves, follow through with the consequences.
- Reward athletes only when they have earned it.
- Use positive discipline, which uses instruction, training and correction, rather than negative discipline, which uses punishment.
- Strive hard to be consistent in your verbal messages and to ensure that your non-verbal actions are consistent with your verbal messages.
- When you promise to do something, be sure to follow through.
- Use language that your athletes will understand, keep your vocabulary simple and straightforward.
- Think through your demonstrations before you present them.
- Use analogies that your athletes can relate to.
- Recognize how much of what you communicate is in the form of non-verbal messages.
- Remember that it is not so much what you say but what you do that influences your athletes.
- How you communicate with your athletes directly affects how they perceive you and how they feel about themselves.

You can continually improve your communication skills. Doing so will help your athletes to communicate appropriately with you as well.

4 ORGANIZATION AND CONTROL

> He who controls the present, controls the past. He who controls the past, controls the future.
>
> *George Orwell*

Any time coaches meet their athletes in a training session, there is a basic need to organize and manage the session to ensure a positive learning environment. In the summary of the available research, the suggestion is for eight effective learning strategies that characterize effective coaching. They are practical tips to enhance athlete learning. These strategies do not relate to coaching approaches, they are merely strategies to ensure a smooth session that enables learning to occur (we have already looked at this specific ECA). These effective strategies are not age-specific and are relevant to every coaching context.

Teaching Strategies

1. Devote a large percentage of the time within a training session to learning key requirements for that sport (for example, sport-specific skills, psychological knowledge and understanding).
2. Devote a high percentage of the time to meaningful practice.
3. Maximize the opportunities athletes have to practice.
4. Keep athletes on task.
5. Assign tasks that are meaningful and matched to the athletes' abilities.
6. Set high but realistic expectations.
7. Give sessions flow and continuity.
8. Hold athletes accountable.

What Does This All Mean for You?

The first strategy, devote a large percentage of the time to learning key requirements for that sport, suggests that athletes will learn more if they are provided with quality learning activities and the skills, knowledge and understanding they need for a quality performance in their sport. Therefore it is important for coaches to plan and consistently provide training sessions that provide this. It is also important that athletes are engaged in appropriate learning for that sport for a high proportion of the time. For example, if an athlete is trying to practise fielding in cricket, there is no point in spending much time if he cannot throw properly. In other words, the learning activity should aim for each athlete's success in performing that activity through practising it appropriately. To encourage learning, the coach is therefore responsible for gaining an understanding of the athletes' physical, social, cognitive and emotional levels.

The second strategy – devote a high percentage of time to meaningful practice – links closely with many of the other approaches. This means that coaches should work with small groups, have plenty of equipment or have game-like situations where as many athletes are involved in a game or activity as much as possible. 'Teaching Games for Understanding' (TGfU) or 'Game Sense' is a model that ensures that coaches meet this strategy successfully (*see* Fig. 31). This provides numerous opportunities to practise because of the nature of the approach to the games. The motivation for athletes is high because they are all involved and therefore more apt to spend a larger amount of time in learning.

Figure 30 Session briefing.

Target	Net/Wall	Strike/Field		Invasion	
aim at target	consistently return the object	score runs	stop scoring runs	score	stop scoring
placement in relation to target	placement and positioning	accuracy and distance	make hitting difficult	invade	stop invading
spin and/or turn	spin and power	avoid getting out	get hitter out	maintain possession	get possession

Figure 31 The teaching games for understanding (TGFU) approach.

The TGfU approach is described by Bunker and Thorpe (1986) as game-centred games teaching where the *why* of game playing is taught before the *how* of skills to play the game. This process involves teaching children a modified or simplified game that is suitable for their physical, social and mental development. In such a game children gain an appreciation of the demands of an adult game. This appreciation invites the children to realize tactical awareness of how to play a game to gain an advantage over their opponents. With such a tactical awareness, children are capable of making appropriate decisions about 'what to do' and 'how to do it'. For children, increased decision-making encourages them to become more aware of the possibilities innate in their game playing. This awareness leads to more meaningful learning for children as they enter into practice situations to develop either a technical skill (such as trapping a ball or placing spin on a shot) or a strategic manoeuvre practised to gain a tactical advantage (such as hitting the ball short then long in tennis or using a fast break in basketball).

Thorpe and Bunker (1989) explain how games teaching strategies of sampling, modification through representation (a simplified game), modification through exaggeration (such as a long and thin area of play in net/wall games) and games focused on certain tactical complexity, allow children to become active decision-makers in their own learning. In TGfU, learners repeatedly evaluate and develop their own performance within game-playing situations that gradually, under the guidance of the coach, evolve towards the sophisticated adult games.

Primary Rules that Define the Four TGfU Games Categories

Game classification systems are based on their physical properties or their primary rules.

The primary rules for the four TGfU games categories are:

(*a*) in striking/fielding type games: i. batting players create opportunities to score by hitting balls out of an area of play and ii. batting players score by running between safe areas without the ball being caught on the fly by fielding players, or the ball reaching the safe area before the batting players;

(*b*) in target type games: players score by avoiding obstacles to get their objects closer than their opponents' to the target;

(*c*) in net/wall types games: players try to get the objects into their opponents areas of play more often than their opponents can return the objects back into their areas of play;

(*d*) in territory/invasion type games: *i.* players with the ball score by getting the object within the opponents' focused or open end target, and *ii.* players without the ball stop the opposing players from scoring without making an illegal physical contact.

The following are hints for maximizing practice time within a training session to avoid unnecessary management time that is not related to the purpose of the training session.

Routines

One of the ways to increase time to practise is to establish organizational routines for sessions. For example, do you provide a signal for the athletes to come in for an explanation or demonstration, or do you just call and wait for them to come in? It is good practice to establish a signal for gathering and dispersing. If such a signal is established, athletes will understand your expectations. For example, when you blow the whistle, athletes are to come to where you are within 5sec. Another important routine to create is how to distribute and retrieve equipment. You can delegate and distribute the responsibility for this as a reward (certainly not a punishment) or by rotating the members of the group regularly.

Such routines should be established and practised in the first few training sessions of the season so that athletes know what to do and what the group expects of each member. For example, in the first training session the team is practising a dribbling skill, in the middle of the drill, use your gathering signal to see how the athletes respond. Blow your whistle so the athletes can practise coming in quickly. Praise those athletes who do come in quickly to help to communicate your expectations.

A list of other tasks for which routines can potentially be established to minimize time away from quality training (routines) includes:

- entry to the gym/field/hall/pool
- warm-up
- attention/quiet
- moving between activities (transition)
- home base (meeting place)
- gain attention
- disperse
- collect equipment
- put equipment away
- establish boundaries
- end of training
- leaving the venue.

Prompts

Prompts are cue words to remind athletes of what should be done. If these are used when establishing the routines, they will remind them to complete the organizational task quickly. An example would be 'time-out', or 'huddle'. The cue words should encourage quick action. The comments should avoid sarcasm that creates a judging environment.

Positive Reinforcement

Positive reinforcement is essential to establish appropriate behaviours and a positive environment for the athletes. When directing or prompting athletes, coaches should use positive comments to reinforce what was done appropriately. The more you positively reinforce those who are doing constructive things, the smoother and more constructive the sessions will be (this is covered in greater detail in the section on coaching pedagogy to follow).

Organizational Games

As most sports are competitive in nature, athletes can be encouraged to compete to reduce organizational time. Tasks can also be fun and somewhat competitive. In an example of such an organizational game the coach says to children: 'Let's play a game to see how quickly you can be ready. When I call you to come in, if you come in within five seconds, you get a point. If you come in after five seconds, I get a point. If you have the most points near the end of the training session, you can choose the last activity. If I have the most points near the end of the training session, I choose what we do.'

Organizing Athletes into Groups

The organization of athletes into groups creates several issues. Remember the athlete who for one reason or another always gets left out? How can we ensure that all the athletes are included? How do we reduce the amount of time needed to get athletes into groups? There are a number of ways to organize athletes into groups. We have to be careful, however, not to hurt their feelings or lessen their self-esteem when organizing these groups.

One of the quickest ways to select groups or partners is to say 'Get a partner', or 'Get into groups of four'. This method generally works quite well with athletes, but may result in the same people always working together. Alternative methods are to have a numbering off system or have the teams pre-listed on your session plan. When athletes choose teams, there is invariably someone who gets chosen last. This is best avoided and is easily done with some preplanning.

The third strategy is maximize the opportunities that athletes have to practise. To reach a high level of skill, an athlete may need to perform a skill or game situation thousands of times. It is important to organize practices or games so that the athletes have multiple opportunities to rehearse and develop their skills. This can be done in a range of different contexts that present progressive levels of challenge and to avoid complacency or boredom.

The fourth strategy, keep athletes on task, refers to ensuring that athletes are practising and not sitting out, wasting time or waiting their turn in the queue. For learning to take place, athletes must be involved in the learning process. If athletes enjoy the activities or the subject matter, they are more likely to be involved. Also, athletes who are on task are less disruptive. To achieve this strategy, coaches need to ensure that they are monitoring athletes' activities and learning levels. If the athletes are not involved, coaches can change the activity to ensure that all are. Elimination games, 'miss and you are out', are directly contrary to the idea of ensuring that all are involved.

The fifth strategy, assign tasks that are meaningful and matched to athletes' abilities, refers to the ability of coaches to understand their athletes' ability (stage of development) levels (cognitively, physically, emotionally and socially). Coaches then must ensure that activities are at the athletes' level, not too difficult nor too easy. Again, TGfU meets this strategy if the coaches design purposeful games, where athletes need to solve relevant problems or experience relevant learning at their own level.

The sixth strategy, set high but realistic expectations, refers to the creation of expectations and then to supporting the athletes to meet these expectations within a positive, caring and motivating learning environment where athletes succeed. An example of a non-supportive environment is the 'tough' approach, where coaches feel that yelling is motivating and punishment is the way to force athletes to do what they are supposed to. There is no research that supports the belief that that approach is productive. In fact, it suggests that the more supportive the environment the more conducive the conditions to the athletes' happiness and success.

Figure 32 A coachable moment.

The seventh strategy, give sessions flow and continuity, refers to the ability of the coach to ensure that the training session flows, that interruptions are minimized and that the maximum time is devoted to athletes' learning. Sometimes coaches interrupt activities just as athletes are beginning to solve problems or at a key 'coachable moment'. It is the responsibility of the coach to be able to read when the situation needs further elaboration and when to let athletes continue with the activity.

The last strategy agreed upon in the research (Siedentop, Mand and Taggart, 1986) is to hold athletes accountable for their learning. This strategy refers to the enabling of athletes to try their best, to practise intensely, concentrate on the task and demonstrate an interest in and take ownership for their learning. To hold athletes accountable, coaches should encourage athlete and team goal setting, show an interest overtly in what athletes are learning and doing and be involved in the training session, facilitate a clear direction for each task and encourage athletes' performance. This does not mean explicitly providing information, but more of a 'setting things up and keeping an eye on things' approach, encouraging the athletes to continue asking questions to help solve problems and providing activities to extend the athletes' abilities. Setting goals, monitoring and reinforcing the team culture, listening to athletes and valuing their opinions all encourage athlete accountability.

Figure 33 Team activity away from sport.

Teams and Groups

A common problem for many coaches is how to get a group of athletes, often with varying fitness or skill levels, to perform as a team. Many great coaches have emphasized that having a group of extremely talented athletes does not guarantee a successful team, but rather that success is more often the result from a group of less talented athletes who choose to work together to achieve a shared team outcome.

The difference between a group and a team: getting a group of athletes to perform as a team is not always easy. Just because they train and compete together under the direction of one coach, does not automatically define that collection of individuals as a team. Rather, a group of athletes become a team when they all possess a common identity, have shared goals and objectives, exhibit structured patterns of interaction and communication and, most importantly, consider themselves to be a 'team'. When self-categorization is present (that is, when the collection of athletes start referring to themselves as 'we' versus 'they') coaches can feel confident that a team is beginning to emerge.

Team cohesion is crucial for team success: the factors that draw athletes to a team and help them to remain united in order to achieve a common goal is referred to as 'team cohesion'. In order to develop this coaches need to identify the contributing factors for their specific team. This can be done through survey questions or general group discussions. Questions such as, 'Why did you decide to try out for this team?', 'What attracted you to this team?' or 'What do you think makes us a team?' can help coaches to get an idea of such factors. It is also important for coaches to understand that there are often numerous factors that result in a team's cohesion, that these factors change over time and will be different for each team (for example, friendships or a chance to win a championship). Coaches must not assume that the factors reported by the team last season will be the same for the next season or even remain the same throughout one season. Having established the factors contributing to a team's cohesiveness, coaches can use this information to further build cohesion. For example, a coach has a young team of athletes who report friendship and social interaction as important factors. Using this information, the coach organizes several team get-togethers throughout the pre-season. Another example would be a team bonded by the leadership style of the coach and senior players. Among other things, this coach decides to develop a mentoring system for younger athletes to work closely with more experienced players.

Team goals: given that a key differentiation of a group from a team is having shared objectives, it is important for the goals to be established and communicated to all team members as early as possible. Often coaches make the mistake of assuming that athletes share the same goals as themselves and that everyone knows these. Rather than assume, coaches should work with the team to identify clear team outcome goals (the 'big picture' goals) and then discuss what process goals (that is, stepping-stone goals) need to be set in order to achieve them.

Basic Rules When Setting Team Goals

- Goals should be specific and measurable; coaches often make the mistake of allowing team goals to be vague and imprecise
- goals should be challenging, yet realistic, do not set the team up for failure and disappointment with impossible goals
- process goals should be linked to performance objectives; establish how the team is going to achieve these goals through smaller, short-term goals
- continually review these goals.

Coaches often fall into the trap of setting team goals at the start of the season and then never getting the team to look at them again. Having established team goals, it is important for coaches to sit down with each athlete and set individual goals. Sometimes individual goal-setting is ignored within team sports as it is viewed as unnecessary. By establishing individual goals with team members, coaches are emphasizing the importance of each athlete's contribution to the overall team success. Additionally, individual goal-setting allows goals to be set according to the ability level of each team member.

Team Roles

Regardless of the ability of the athlete within the team, all team members should have a clearly defined role. Whether the athlete's role is as team captain, key defender or as a substitute player, it is important that each individual clearly understands his importance to the team's overall performance. Typically, coaches openly define leadership roles within their team, but fail to explain the importance of the support role that substitute players perform. By sitting down with each athlete once every couple of months, coaches can clarify each individual's role within the team, review his progress and set new individual objectives.

Establishing Clear Expectations for the Team

Often in sporting groups when there are athletes of varying ability, coaches fall into the trap of having different behavioural and attitudinal expectations for different athletes. For an athletic group to become a team, all members need to understand and agree on a common set of expectations specific to that team. One way of doing this is to establish team guidelines. These are best determined by the athletes themselves, not set and enforced solely by the coach. Encouraging athletes to define what they expect from one another as members of the same team allows them to experience ownership and therefore increases the likelihood of adherence. It is always

important to document the agree   official
'team contract'. Finally, consider a   n team
meetings each week and review   that all
members understand the jargon b   e lingo
can vary from team to team and   be too
embarrassed to ask what it means

5 COACHING PEDAGOGY

> It is as much a logical absurdity to say 'one teaches children not subjects' as it is to say 'one teaches subjects not children'.
>
> *Paul Hirst*

Coaching pedagogy involves the strategies, techniques and approaches that coaches can use to facilitate the learning of sports skills. This implies that coaches must skilfully arrange an environment in such a way that athletes exhibit specifically intended learning outcomes. It could crudely be called teaching or instructing, but, as we have already discovered, coaching itself is a process and a complex one at that. So, coaching pedagogy is a bit more than traditional didactic approaches and is a much more holistic attempt to explain one of the most fundamental aspects of coaching effectiveness.

For even the most basic movements to be possible they have to be appropriate for particular circumstances. The appropriateness is encoded in the neural patterns in the brain to be called upon when environmental situations deem them appropriate. Running a 100m race requires specific movement qualities, amplitudes and precisions to be successful. If a different pattern of neurons fired when running the 100m race, an inconsistent performance would result, the degree of inconsistency being dependent upon the lack of relationship between the wrong response and the race situation. For example, if an athlete ran with his arms kept by his side, the leg action would be compromised because of the dependent relationship between all the coordinating actions. The brain will not consider the activity and then insert this arm style there. Thus any altered movement pattern that is caused by a departure from a specific situation will lead to a worse performance.

It is not hard to appreciate our needing specific neural patterns in particular situations. Imagine if a person were rock-climbing and a certain move were called for. However, if a different pattern of neurons fired each time the situation arose, there would be no way of performing the activity. Unless we are able to act appropriately to an environmental demand, in a biological sense survival would be impossible. Performing wrongly would invite disaster at almost every response.

It is impossible to have some 'general responses' being appropriate for other situations that require precise movements. There are no known generalized functions within the motor domain of the human brain. They are only discriminatory. Thus, those who advocate cross- or auxiliary activities for individuals who are expected to perform with high precision just do not understand how we function. However, when low levels of performance are tolerated, for example, in a 'learn-to-swim' class, movement patterns can be variable and quite inefficient. However, if a river rescue needed to be performed, one would not want a rescuer to perform with the lack of precision and effectiveness of a learning-to-swim swimmer. Competency tests for persons of responsibility (such as national team members or lifeguards) are necessary to ensure that the correct movement patterns will be performed when the situation demands it. Thus when considering the performances of high-level athletes, factors divorced from low-level performances must be considered. Movement representations in the brain are specific. If they are confused and elicited in other circumstances, poor performances, often with obvious 'errors', result.

If only specific movement representations are patterned in the brain, how do they get there? In some circumstances some elements in the pattern occur by chance at the outset. A familiar phenomenon is for a learner to call on 'like-experiences' and use elements which seem to be common to them. The learner consciously orders those elements and performs the best attempt at the complex skill. Response elements can be modified because of naturally occurring consequences (such as successful outcomes) or contrived consequences (such as, after instruction, teachers providing performance information indicating changes that are needed in order to enhance performance). The modification of existing elements and patterns of movement establishes a new discrete pattern that is associated with the specific situation. The modified elements and pattern serve a new specific situation and are not associated with the original starting-point situation that tolerated a different pattern.

The greater the required degree of efficiency in a movement, the more superb is the appropriate neural pattern of representation. Through repetitious training, and when facilitating contingencies are present, the movement elements and its pattern are refined. The phases of change in an element leave residual representations in the brain. Movement elements that were once considered acceptable for a stage of learning are rarely emitted but remain represented in the brain. The number of repetitions of an inappropriate element without meaningful consequences determines the likelihood of a performance error being made at a specific time. The greater the number of ignored practice errors, the greater is that likelihood. Because of this phenomenon, the importance of teaching skills efficiently and effectively should be the highest priority in coaching children. It is obvious that instruction-following procedures that have been verified as effective and economical are desirable over less efficient coaching procedures. Not only do the skills of instruction have to be the best possible, but the content of instruction also has to be correct. Unfortunately, much sports instruction and coaching is far from optimal or desirable. An interest in the sport or an adequate level of enthusiasm for doing the job of instruction or coaching is an unsatisfactory criterion for employment.

Poor instruction, wrong content and high volumes of erroneous element practice in the sporting environment do not improve performance beyond a certain level. This effect is exhibited commonly in golf. Individuals play the game for forty years and never improve beyond scoring 90+ strokes for eighteen holes. Skill elements have been adopted that are far from optimal. Without instruction, those elements become so engrained (that is, they have a high degree of conditioned strength in a psychological sense) that they are difficult to change and often impossible to change even if 'lessons' were taken.

In sports that rely on high levels of skill, it is imperative that from the outset a youngster is exposed to instructional experts who teach correct content by following developmental progressions that have been tailored to the individual. If that does not occur, performances may change, but not at a remarkable rate, up to a point and then get no better. Unfortunately, some coaches do not coach focusing on technique instruction. Much of

Figure 34a Technical and tactical instruction.

modern instruction and coaching emphasize the use of drills and equipment as avenues for improving sports skills. These activities are advocated as a means of changing the specific skills of the sport by repetition with little or no follow-up instruction. Unfortunately, all they do is clutter the motor area of the cortex with irrelevant neural patterns. If young athletes come to believe they are beneficial activities and consciously evoke them in total movement patterns, performances will suffer.

Unfortunately, the value of such practices or drills is dressed up in hope as opposed to verified knowledge. The pre-eminent researcher in this field, Robert Christina (1996), reviewed the motor learning literature and developed conclusions about the limitations and effects of drills for coaches. The implications of those conclusions follow.

Drills for Coaches

The tasks of training have to be structurally similar to a competitive task and very well learned for there to be positive transfer.

For full transfer to occur, athletes have to be aware of the elements or components practised in drills that need to be transferred to the competitive setting. Practice activities would be detrimental to competition performances when items are perceived to have few shared and many distinctive or irrelevant components.

Athletes need to be aware of the elements of a practice item that need to be transferred to a competitive setting. However, that awareness will be increasingly distorted the greater the number of irrelevant elements among those that are learned. If the belief is high that similarity exists between practice and competition tasks, but the tasks really are very dissimilar, then task transfer will be depreciated because of negative transfer, that is, too many inappropriate or irrelevant elements will be transferred. Thus, despite the well-meaning intentions of a coach and athlete, irrelevant activities are likely to harm competition skills.

Transfer of appropriate processing requires the practice of the mental content and control attempts that are likely to be used in competition. It is insufficient to have only similar physical characteristics between the tasks. The mental activity accompanying those skills also has to be of like quality and content.

Skills and their competition-specific variations should be introduced in a stepwise manner so that a general concept of the situational variants for the drill can be developed. It is necessary that each variant be learned, not just 'experienced' without forming any degree of mastery.

Increased item similarity in the original learning of a task should produce better retention and transfer when the task is the same in a competition as in original learning. Golf and competitive swimming are in this class of activity. Activities of this type were once termed 'closed' skills.

Performing skills at training needs to be contextually, biomechanically and cognitively the same as in competition. The value of drill activities decreases the greater the departure of these three characteristics from what is required in the competitive arena (again, this is concrete validation of the TGfU approach discussed previously). Despite the belief that irrelevant practice activities will actually be beneficial for athletes in competition, they will be counterproductive for subsequent competition performances. The added belief that poorly developed skill elements can be executed in competitions because of mental application (that is, attempting to alter a segment in a movement chain purely by concentrating without sufficient whole-skill practices) is also counterproductive. There is no substitute for or modification of the principle of specificity in skill training, if skill is to be an important part of a competitive performance. Most drills that contain a greater proportion of irrelevant skill elements than relevant ones will lead to poorer and incorrect performance in competition because of the flawed elements that have been practised and possibly transferred into the various competition actions.

Figure 34b Technical and tactical instruction.

Controlling and Changing Athlete Behaviour

In order to change skilled and general behaviour in athletes, the coach must be a good instructor. For effective instruction, several classes of coach behaviour have been defined under the heading of the 3Ps – Prompts, Progressions and Positive Reinforcers.

Prompts are instructions given to athletes to indicate how they should perform. Normally, these are physical manipulations of the athlete, demonstrations and visual displays, and verbal directives (instructions).

Progressions are the systems of steps that the athlete needs to follow to change from a status to a definable outcome. Unlike poor instructors who expect athletes to achieve mastery in one step, the formation of stepped-progressions needs to be a task that is carefully constructed according to a number of criteria.

Positive reinforcers are the consequences of an athlete's behaviour that cause the athlete to increase the likelihood of behaving in the desired manner. Consequential events can take a number of forms. In sports coaching, it is best to concentrate on providing positive consequences ('positive reinforcement'). Contrary to popular folklore, meaningful consequences usually do not always emanate from the coach. Among athletes, the most powerful reinforcers are those generated by individuals for themselves ('self-reinforcement'), social reinforcement (particularly 'peer-reinforcement'), naturally occurring reinforcement (usually in the form of 'intrinsic reinforcement'), vicarious reinforcement (such as watching others being reinforced) and reinforcement from influential others (such as parents, friends outside the sport and coaches). It is the responsibility of the coach to engineer high frequencies of positive reinforcement for appropriate sport-specific behaviour.

Shaping: a strategy for progressively developing and modifying sports skills (the following material is adapted from the work of Rushall and Siedentop (1972). This is the first known exposition of operant shaping as a teaching strategy for coaching and movement instruction. It is as relevant today as it was almost forty years ago.

Features of behaviour modification can be drawn together to produce a strategy for instructing new and modifying established skills. The strategy is referred to as 'shaping'. Motor learning research once addressed itself to limited aspects of skill learning, with the consideration of such themes as part versus whole learning and speed versus accuracy, but seldom has a coherent strategy for producing change been outlined. John Lawther first came close to outlining a general method with his 'gross-framework' model for teaching physical activities to beginners (Lawther, 1968). It would be desirable to control all the factors that maximize the learning of physical skills but this rarely is possible in coaching. To form a pragmatic method of instruction, it is necessary to select the features of control that are accessible, relevant to the environment and feasible for use. The adaptations and efficiency adjustments of a performer occur at some covert level and quite often at a subconscious level. Conscious performance strategies of learners are particularly individualistic. Coaches are usually unable to control such strategies, although they can be influenced with methods of prompting and guidance (such as verbal instruction, demonstrations and video). The potential for changing and developing the make-up of skilled behaviour generally lies in the manipulation of the external environment, particularly the stimulus setting and consequences.

Teaching addresses itself to developing the landscape or rate of occurrence of a new action or changing an already established movement pattern. Shaping strategies are concerned with the development of specific behaviour. A shaping strategy involves: *i.* the definition of an outcome; *ii.* the sequencing of progressive steps of closer approximation to this outcome; *iii.* the use of prompts to produce performance variations; and *iv.* the use of positive reinforcement.

Shaping consists of reinforcing progressively closer approximations to an outcome behaviour, that is, the athlete incrementally improves in technique. It is unlikely that a correct response will be produced on a first attempt, so a behaviour short of the final skill form must be reinforced. With subsequent emissions of the behaviour, the requirements for reinforcement are made stricter and reinforcement is provided only as the behaviour more closely approximates to the desired act. The criterion for reinforcement progresses from being seemingly lax to being stringent for the final performance. In shaping, as in all reinforcing contingencies, it is essential to reinforce behaviours before other responses intervene and disrupt the new pattern. During shaping, reinforcing consequences not only strengthen the particular responses but also increase the probability that a closer approximation to the final behaviour will occur. This is the main reason why shaping works. As new approximations are reached and reinforced, aspects of earlier behaviours are extinguished. This is the difference between being an effective coach and a personable one. Skilful shaping consists of selecting the right responses to reinforce and in knowing how long to reinforce each approximation before moving to the next sequenced step. It also requires a clear definition of the outcome and the planning of the sequential steps so that transitions are made easily. The administration of reinforcers is the main difficulty with shaping. It is for this reason that it is suggested that instruction be undertaken in small groups where individual reinforcers can be provided continuously and contingent upon behaviour. The first instance of the attempted skilled behaviour is far removed from the final desired product but is positively reinforced. With instruction and reinforcement, the behaviour should improve progressively by more closely approximating to the final product. Performance improvement can be observed if the shaping progression is implemented correctly.

Skilled motor behaviours usually fall into one of four instructional classes: some are highly segmented and best taught as discrete units. For example, learning to type in the beginner stage consists of a large repertoire of small skills. Each letter typed is an individual response which needs to be developed through meaningful practice. With practice and reinforcement, the nature and the size of the performance unit change from letters to words and then to phrases. In the final stages, the typing skill is smooth and flowing and is of a markedly different appearance from the requirements of the beginning skill. These skills can be influenced by drilled behaviour but do not occur in sport to any significant degree. Some motor behaviours must be performed only as whole units. It was established long ago that the basic behavioural unit for meaningful practice is the two-phase motor unit (a preparatory act and then the act itself; for example, a crouch and then a jump). These skills are best taught as an attempt at the skill itself. Such skills are usually of short duration and the resulting performance information is used to adjust subsequent trials of the skill.

Some motor behaviours are practised as whole units but are progressively changed through instruction by focusing on one movement element at a time. These behaviours are usually highly repetitive tasks (such as running, rowing and swimming). Instruction serves to alter the execution of the skill while it is in progress in its entirety (for example, changing an underwater breaststroke propulsive position of the forearms). This is what should happen in these sports once a reasonable level of proficiency is attained in executing a total movement. The use of disruptive equipment and drills is inappropriate for this classification of movement.

Some motor behaviours are briefly introduced in small units and then practised as a whole unit. For example, a beginner footballer is shown how to run and control the ball (dribbling). These units are practised before entering a game-like situation. In a short while, these segments are combined and practised as a unified activity from then on.

Figure 35 Specific technical instruction.

The implication of this brief discussion is simply that the coach needs to know the skilled behaviour that is to be shaped. It is possible to shape a behavioural element or a total activity. The procedural steps for shaping are the same regardless of the magnitude of the behaviour. In the final stages of any sports behaviour development, the behaviour must be practised in its entirety. When a technique element or segment is practised and reinforced, it should be qualitatively the same as that required in the total behaviour. That is best achieved by focusing on the element while performing the entire skill. This is the inescapable requirement for the effective coaching of sports skills.

Positive Reinforcers

The events that immediately follow a behaviour could serve a reinforcing function. If the events affect behaviour and are positive, they are termed 'positive reinforcers'. The process of applying a reinforcer after a target behaviour occurs is called 'reinforcement'. If the consequences are negative and affect behaviour they are 'aversive consequences'; if they have no effect on behaviour they are 'neutral events'. Another class of affective consequences that will not be discussed here is 'negative reinforcers'. They are the absence of aversive events; for example, achieving a level of performance that is not perceived as a failure. In order to change skilled behaviours effectively, it is important to know what events will likely serve as meaningful reinforcers for athletes and apply them frequently and consistently at every practice. For general motivation and for effective instruction, only positive consequences, that is, positive reinforcers, will be discussed here. The coach needs to engineer the occurrence of reinforcers after attempts to change any behaviour and for motivation.

There are two alternative forms of developing the atmosphere of the sport experience. The first is positive motivation. This occurs when individuals behave because of the positive, rewarding or reinforcing events that have historically followed each 'motivated' behaviour. The second form is negative motivation. In this form of control, individuals behave to avoid or escape negative, punishing, or aversive consequences. Positive motivation is the best form of coaching control and is discussed below.

If a coach wishes to change the frequency of occurrence of a behaviour, the events that follow the behaviour must be engineered and controlled. If an athlete is behaving with a certain level of adequacy then to increase that level the coach must ensure the occurrence of positive consequences following each instance of the behaviour. This constant supply of rewarding or reinforcing circumstances is called continuous positive reinforcement. The most expedient way to change behaviour rates is to use continuous positive reinforcement. This differs from a common approach to behaviour control where behaviours are reinforced 'when possible'. With such a loose definition and regimen, behaviours are reinforced intermittently, with the consequent effect that permanent changes are rarely, if ever, achieved. The usual effect is a transient one. After a significant single reinforcement, the rate of occurrence of a behaviour might change for a short period. If no other reinforcer occurs over the next few instances of the behaviour, the rate returns to its pre-reinforcement level. This is the 'transient effect' of intermittent reinforcement. Small changes in performance rate are observed immediately after reinforcement but the effect is short-lived. Thus, to alter the occurrence of a behaviour immediately, the coach has to provide the athlete with a series of continuous reinforcements.

The provision of continuous positive reinforcement requires some organizational changes in the normally accepted coaching setting. Some possibilities are as follows: *i.* teach athletes how to evaluate and reinforce their own behaviours and the behaviours of others; this is described in more detail below; *ii.* coordinate the training session to have every member evaluate each other and themselves on the same behavioural content; *iii.* develop devices that supply performance information, possibly on a continual basis.

If the coach is to be the source of the positive reinforcement, then he or she must devote blocks of time to individuals or small homogeneous groups to the exclusion of others in the squad. This is not as difficult as it might appear, particularly if positive reinforcement emanates from sources other than the coach.

The decision about which reinforcers to provide needs to consider two features, what type of reinforcer will be used? And what will be the source of the reinforcement? In the discussions that follow, the examples of types and sources of reinforcement are presented in a hierarchy from major to minor effectiveness. When changes must be made in the shortest time possible, a situation that provides the strongest type of reinforcer from the strongest source of reinforcement has to be constructed.

Type	Positive	Aversive
Performance information	*Intrinsic* fewer strokes per lap, turns notably faster, ease of stroke execution, feeling of increased power *Artificial* coach saying 'arm position correct', video shows improvement, picture of good technique	*Intrinsic* no change in number of strokes, pace time slow, no improvement in repeat times *Artificial* peer commenting 'short stroke', film shows poor timing, poor fitness results
Internal	*Self-Control* 'That felt good', 'You did it', 'Well done', 'You did what you wanted to do' *Vicarious* watching a great swimming performance, seeing consistent swimmers use a type of arm pull	*Self-Control* 'Miserable', 'I feel rotten', 'I do not have it today' *Vicarious* watching a slow swim, seeing a wrong strategy result in a slow time, watching a swimmer lose his/her temper
Social	approval, esteem, recognition, congratulations, attention, adoration, courtesy, consideration	disapproval, hate, reproof, scolding, degradation, sarcasm, rebuke, chiding
Material	badges, patches, sweets, progress charts, grades, trophies, medals, records	poor progress, demotion in grades, bad record

Figure 36 Types and examples of positive reinforcers and aversive consequences.

Types of Positive Reinforcer

Positive reinforcers are available in a variety of forms in the sports environment. They do not reside solely within the coach. A sports setting can be greatly enriched as a motivational environment if positive reinforcers represent the several types. Fig. 36 summarizes one classification of reinforcer types and lists some examples of positive reinforcers and aversive consequences (the examples are from swimming, but you can apply the concept to your own sport).

Performance Information

A significant reinforcer is information or feedback about behaviour and performance. Some information occurs naturally, it is intrinsic to the activity. Examples of intrinsic performance information are the time for a repetition (when taken by the athlete), the number of baskets per practice (when counted by the player), a good feeling when a technique change is attempted and a skill being experienced with faster (more game-like) execution. The provision of significant intrinsic performance information usually keeps athletes interested for long periods without outside prompting. However, to produce important changes in general behaviour and technique, it is necessary to provide artificial or augmented forms of performance information.

Comments about and assessment of technique by the coach, the evaluation of video-tape replays or slow-motion movies and the measurement of performance capacities, are examples of the provision of information above and beyond that which naturally occurs in the performance of sports activities. The coach needs to make athletes aware of intrinsic performance information and its significance as well as increase the sources and frequency of artificial performance information. Such information should not be limited to objective measures but can include effort level, skill level, task execution, performer interaction and activity volume. The coach has to increase the amount of performance information provided as well as expand its scope to cover the other areas of the sport.

Performance information is also known as 'feedback'. Athletes need to be supplied with feedback to improve skilled performance. Negative feedback indicates what should be avoided and positive feedback indicates what should be retained. Feedback at the end of a task is called 'terminal feedback' (if done immediately upon task completion it is 'contingent terminal feedback') and feedback during a task is called 'concurrent feedback'. When cyclic, long-duration activities (such as swimming or rowing) are performed, to wait until the total task is completed is not the best use of time or opportunity to provide feedback. For example, when running fastbreak routines in basketball and many repetitions are executed consecutively, there are opportunities for coaches to provide feedback during the task (such as at the end of each attempt) rather than to wait for full task completion.

The provision of concurrent performance information offers the opportunity to indicate to athletes how they are performing. It can be used to indicate a need to change the way a task is being executed or to sustain the way the action is being performed because it is being done correctly. It can be used to prevent a total task being performed in error and to reinforce the correct execution of task features. To provide meaningful, concurrent feedback during multi-repetitions, it is suggested that the coach do the following: develop a system of signals that indicate successful performance (such as a thumb-up sign, circled fingers to indicate the 'O' in OK), unsuccessful performance (such as thumb-down, flat hand to indicate to stop) and satisfactory performance that could be improved (such as moving the hand back and forth horizontally). It is also useful to demonstrate the correct execution of a technique (for instance, the control of the ball on the chest in football) to indicate the element in the skill (controlling a high ball) that needs to be altered and performed better. Interactions of this type contain extra information for the appraisal of performance correctness. It is therefore more meaningful (powerful) than pure right or wrong appraisals.

The frequency with which concurrent performance information is provided will contribute substantially to its effects and success. Providing concurrent feedback is perhaps one of the most effective uses of a coach's time in sessions. It has the potential to contribute to rapid and sustained skilled-behaviour changes.

Figure 37 Coach feedback to players.

Internal Reinforcers

These refer to reinforcing activities that occur within the athlete. There are two major forms of these 'covert reinforcers'. The first is 'self-control'. It entails the athlete's forming a desired criterion for performance adequacy and then giving him/herself a 'mental pat-on-the-back' or 'kick-in-the-pants', depending upon whether the criterion was or was not achieved. This extremely important source of reinforcement will be discussed in more detail shortly. The second form of internal reinforcer is 'vicarious reinforcement'. This entails the witnessing of other athletes experience reinforcement. Thus 'observing others' successes in using a particular technique, will increase the probability of the observer's behaving similarly. This is seen often when someone is successful in using a new technique or activity. After the success, observers clamour to do the same. Within the coaching situation, when demonstrations are given and important performances are achieved, if the recognition of those acts is significantly displayed in front of other athletes, there is a high probability that the observers will alter their behaviour in a similar direction. Witnessing reinforcement is the important behaviour to be controlled. One of the most important coaching behaviours is the structuring and provision of vicarious learning experiences.

Social Reinforcers

The reactions of individuals to an athlete's behaviour are potentially very effective reinforcers. Fellow athletes, the coach, parents and other influential people such as esteemed coaches, other champion athletes and the press, all have the capacity to react to an athlete's behaviour and promote a change in it. Positive social reactions to behaviour by way of approval and congratulations can serve as reinforcers. The coach's responsibility with regard to this is to expand the use of different types of social reaction to an athlete's behaviour. This can be done by allowing parents or other athletes to react to the behaviour and the performance of an individual if they are sufficiently versed in the criteria for providing positive reinforcement. The coach may have to educate these individuals so that reinforcement will be provided consistently and without contradiction of the behaviour displayed. This should be one topic of a 'parent education' programme.

Material Reinforcers

These are tangible items that are presented as a consequence of behaviour. Trite examples are badges, pennants and medals as well as sweets or treats. All of these have gimmick qualities but are not seen as being important by serious athletes. Of more importance are reinforcers such as performance progress charts, competition results, behaviour logs and rankings. The tangible recognition of behaviours also includes some social and performance information, their permanence and overt display producing a strong reinforcing function. You as the coach should try to develop technologies to produce records and evaluations of behaviour and performance for each athlete.

The purpose behind this discussion of types of reinforcer is to emphasize that coach reactions to behaviour are not the only types of significant reinforcement in sports coaching settings. If the coach sets about engineering the environment to provide reinforcers of the types described, as well as facilitating their occurrence, then athletes will be subjected to a greater frequency of positive reinforcement, which directly affects motivation as well as changing behaviour. These increases will serve to remove the transient effects of isolated reinforcements as well as affect the rates of occurrence of specific behaviour. Environments that provide frequent occurrences of positive reinforcement for varieties of behaviour are motivational environments. Thus the coach needs to create circumstances that produce high rates of positive reinforcing experiences for athletes. An aim should be to establish so much positive reinforcement that they will want to practise and compete more than take part in any other activity.

However, at the technological level and within the context of this discussion, the above descriptions suggest to the coach how to provide a greater frequency and variety of reinforcers for specific behaviours of individual athletes. When a coaching decision has been made to attempt to increase the frequency of occurrence of a particular behaviour, the continuous reinforcement of that behaviour is required until the desired new rate is achieved. The continuous reinforcement can use any or all of the reinforcing sources indicated above. Finally, a number of other important features concerning the use of positive reinforcers should be heeded.

Do not use the same reinforcer continually. This results in the 'satiation' of the reinforcer (it loses its effectiveness through overuse). Reinforcers should be varied and continually changed so that each occurrence is novel. If reinforcers can be mixed, that is, have elements of several types of reinforcement in them, then they are more potent and effective. If a reinforcer contains both social and performance information characteristics, such as recording on a progress chart in public, a very marked effect can be achieved. It is recommended that coaches, when reinforcing, at least indicate social approval followed by performance information as the basic reaction to performance.

Particular reinforcing events are not necessarily effective for all athletes. What may be a reinforcer for one may not be for another. Although coaches develop a 'fair idea' of which events are reinforcers for athletes, individual differences do occur and the possibility exists that the consequences of behaviour can be arranged for an athlete with no observable effect. Usually, this is because the consequence was not a reinforcer for that individual. Group reinforcers are largely ineffective. When the total group is told that it did well or 'played superbly' there is likely to be little effect on the behaviour of the individuals who comprise the group. Coaches should concentrate on reinforcing individuals despite its being easier to tell a group how good they were.

The previous discussion described four classes of reinforcer and aversive consequences. This final section of coaching pedagogy considers four sources of reinforcers that are arranged in a hierarchy of importance according to their effective influence.

Figure 38 Player support group.

The Athlete

Self-reinforcement is the most powerful source of reinforcement. Thus when an athlete wants something desperately, motivation is strong and consistent. When this occurs, external sources of reinforcement have little controlling effect. The major features of self-reinforcement have already been discussed above under 'internal reinforcers'.

Self-reinforcement in sport is more potent than has previously been thought. Internal control (the application of one's own reinforcement) is stronger than external control. Researchers have shown that internally controlled individuals exhibit characteristics that are more desirable and functionally effective when compared with externally controlled persons. The ability to administer self-reinforcement is associated with better performance when direction is unavailable and the continuation of functioning in the absence of external reinforcement. The quality of responses is higher in internally-controlled persons than in those without self-control.

Several studies have shown that self-controlled individuals perform better than when they are controlled by one or more coaches. The ability of an athlete to exercise self-control can be measured with higher measurements being related to higher levels of sporting excellence. Another desirable attribute of self-reinforcement is that its reinforcing potential is always present. It offers the best logistical situation for providing continuous reinforcement for behaviour-change projects. This feature is important, because the feasibility of behaviour change through self-reinforcement is manageable in sporting situations, whereas it might not be nearly so manageable if reliance on some external reinforcer source, such as the coach, were required.

An easily available method for stimulating self-appraisals in a young athlete is to have the individual rate himself (say marks out of 10 or a letter grade A–F), or relate what was done well in the performance completed. Not only do these activities provoke self-reinforcement, they also provide the coach with an insight into the athlete's thinking. It reveals the assessment of response quality and the factors appraised during the previous performance. Other valuable benefits are also derived from this activity. These two coach-instigated stimuli should be engaged in frequently because of their effects and what can be revealed to the coach. They are very valuable coaching techniques.

An internally controlled athlete who employs self-reinforcement is the best sort of motivated athlete. It then becomes a coaching challenge to teach athletes how to reinforce themselves. Some features of self-reinforcement that need to be taught are:

- set performance standards for each task attempted
- do not alter those standards once the task is under way
- only self-reinforce when the standards are equalled or surpassed
- practise self-talk that is reinforcing

By mixing the features in each section, a coach can develop a repertoire of distinctive behaviours that have strong positive reinforcing potential.

Reinforcer					
Key Words		Voice Modulation	Gesticulation	Proximity	Subject
top notch	brilliant	pitch up	wave arms	touch	individual
capital	A1	pitch down	punch air	close	sub-group
first class	grand	volume up	OK sign	medium	group
first rate	beautiful	volume down	clap	distant	
magnifique	incredible	pitch high	smile		
stupendous	unbelievable	pitch low	nod		
superlative	fantastic	volume high	pat-on-the-back		
good	proud	volume low	squeeze		
super	superb	pronunciation	thumbs up		
fabulous	splendid	slow	point		
amazing	magnificent	emphasis	hug		
dynamite	great				
phenomenal	marvellous				
tremendous	wonderful				

Figure 39 Suggested characteristics of good reinforcing behaviours for coaches.

- vary the content of self-reinforcement over time
- over time, learn to stretch the schedule of reinforcement, that is, produce behaviour permanence.

It is possible to teach the techniques below so that the athletes can reinforce their own behaviours:

- observe a successful behaviour
- ask the athlete to tell the coach something good about the behaviour
- reinforce the athlete for saying the good things
- if possible, suggest further positive features of the behaviour in order to model a greater variety of possible reactions
- once again, congratulate the athlete for doing such a good job of self-analysis
- prompt the athlete to continue with the self-analysis and self-reinforcement behaviours
- very frequently at first and then less so, enquire whether the self-reinforcement behaviour is continuing, ask for the types of reaction that are being self-enacted and provide further reinforcement.

The Peer Group

An athlete's peers are a powerful source of reinforcement. Friends, particularly those within the sport, are the most relevant others in the social domain of developing athletes. They are a good source of information, instruction, communication and the providers of standards. Peer groups are in tune with the transitory, yet significant reinforcers that are part of their subculture. Peer relationships are one of the most important motivational sources in sport. Peer approvals of behaviour are much more frequent and can be more influential than those of the coach. It is important for procedures to be developed where athletes have the opportunities to reinforce and recognize each other for good behaviours and achievements. One successful method for developing peer reinforcement is to divide teams/squads into pairs. Then define a task and have one partner evaluate the other's attempt at the task. The roles are then reversed and the procedure completed again. Many coaches doubt whether this type of peer interaction will work. If it does not, then the coach has not created the appropriate practice climate for good responding. One could assert that any failure in peer reinforcement is a failure in coaching. Cooperative peer behaviours are both motivating and necessary to increase the logistics for increased reinforcement in a practice environment with a large number of athletes in the squad.

When children and teenagers are given the responsibility of providing reinforcement for each other's behaviours they produce faster and more permanent behavioural changes than that attempted by a dominant individual such as a coach. Not only is there a change in the recipient of the reinforcement, but the individuals giving the reinforcement also improve in the same behaviour. This added spin-off from peer-reinforcement was reported by Morgan and Loy (1970) when they showed that children need the opportunity to teach in order to learn effectively. Having subgroups of athletes instructing each other in facets of skill and performance would seem to be an opportunity to enhance the motivational level of a sporting situation as well as enhancing learning opportunities.

The Coach

A coach is a logistically weak behaviour controller because the frequency with which reinforcers can be administered is inversely related to the number of athletes in a squad. Empirically, coaches have not been shown to be good motivators or sources of reinforcement. In fact, coaches are often not viewed as being great sources of positive reinforcement. In response to the question, 'What things motivate you to practice hard and compete to your maximum ability in competition?', the following sources for motivation were revealed: *i.* self-satisfaction and achievement – females 23 and males 61 per cent; *ii.* personal gains – females 55 and males 36 per cent; and *iii.* the coach – females 22 and males 3 per cent.

In response to the question, 'What things demotivate you or turn you off during practice or competition?', the following were revealed: *i.* personal displeasure – females 8 and males 12 per cent; *ii.* displeasure with others – females 41 and males 39.5 per cent; *iii.* displeasure with the coach – females 24.6 and males 12 per cent; and *iv.* practice and other factors – females 26.4 and males 34.5 per cent.

These figures indicate that the coach is not the focal motivational source that is popularly believed. It seems that females are more influenced by coaches than are males, but the major influence of coaches is negative rather than positive. If coaches are not as influential as was once thought, then they should turn to engineering occurrences in the sporting environment that have a greater potential for effect rather than pushing their own 'weak' effect. Self-orientated experiences and reasons for training and competing are overwhelmingly more motivational than is the coach.

However, coaches are very much part of the sporting scene and most likely can increase their effect, although they should not expect to become dominant. Coaches need to be more effective reactors to athletes' behaviour. They may not be good at administering social reinforcers because they do not 'emote' enough in their responses. A prompting device produced for coaches (*see* Fig. 39) indicates a large variety of words, voice inflections, bodily reactions and interpersonal distances to be used to increase the effectiveness of responses to athlete behaviour. You should use this tool as a means of expanding the scope and intensity of reactions to athlete behaviour. Coaches need to have a rich vocabulary of positive words, a variety of voice alterations to increase verbal expressiveness, a number of non-verbal, body language actions to augment verbal reactions and to consider reinforcing in sub-groups or, most preferably, on an individual basis. An increase in the intensity of any reaction will increase the reinforcing power of a coach.

Outside Sources

The remaining source of notable influence on athlete behaviour includes parents, club officials, the media and friends outside sport. These sources of reinforcement occur sporadically and are uncontrolled from a coach's perspective, but are often powerful because of their novelty. The best that a coach can do to direct reinforcing qualities from these sources is to attempt to educate them about what has been, is being and will be done in the programme for the athletes. An education/communication programme could lead these sources to react in a manner that will be beneficial to the athletes to whom they are relevant. The sources of reinforcement need to be used to promote the highest level of behavioural change and motivation in athletes. Coaches will need to concentrate on increasing the proportion and frequency of self- and peer-reinforcement. That concentration will not detract from a coach's influence, it will add handsomely to the positive control in a sports environment that, in turn, will increase the motivational qualities of the programme.

6 GOAL SETTING

The world makes way for the man who knows where he is going.

Ralph Waldo Emerson

Goal setting has become a mainstream activity in business and sport, yet, while 'good' goals improve focus, persistence, confidence and performance, poorly set goals can create anxiety or poorer performance. This section will tell you how to make the right choices or to go about the process with your athletes in the best possible way.

Why Set Goals?

A common view of goals is as a tool to be used in the quest for higher levels of motivation. Goal-setting theory and subsequent refinements based on research and practice provide a process to create goals that will motivate us to higher levels of performance. Goals, in this sense, provide a motivational focus, a purpose if you like. If you set goals appropriately you will find that you gain access to feelings of satisfaction, confidence and calm. The flip side is that inappropriate goals can be a source of anxiety or stress.

Your goals (and those of your athletes) also represent a means of evaluating your performance and represent core values and beliefs about sport and success. In short, criteria that focus on self-improvement or effort are considered to be more positive than a focus on performance against others. Of course, this is a simplified view and the context needs to always be taken into account – are you coaching a developing athlete or someone about to compete in his or her biggest competition ever at the Olympic Games?

Remember too, that goals are not the be-all and end-all of motivation. In fact, setting goals only as a source of motivation can shut off many potentially important sources of inspiration and creativity. In other words, balance is required.

How to Set Goals

There is a great deal of relevant literature and a popular way of expressing the principles of goal setting is SMART (Specific, Measurable, Appropriate, Realistic and Time-phased). There are several versions of SMART (plus SMARTER and SMARTEST), so here are some key principles to help you:

- Make goals as specific as possible – 'to be on the coaching staff for the 2016 Olympic Games'?
- Divide long-term goals into short-term goals with deadlines and priorities, thus 'to make the national team staff in 2011'. This gives more direction. However, what do you need to do in two years' time to be on track to achieve your Olympic dream? What about this season? What about this week? What about today?!
- By creating stepping stones, the path to your ultimate goal will become much more clear. It may become apparent that to achieve one goal you may have to trade it off against another – so know your priorities.
- Set measurable goals: 'work hard' indicates the right sentiment but will not provide guidance towards your goal; 'spend time every week with experienced coaches' is more appropriate.
- Make goals challenging but achievable: you have to be able to decide, with all available help, whether your goals are achievable. Even if you have been identified as a talented coach, the chances of reaching the Olympics may be slim. Slim is fine – remember your goals must be challenging – but goals set too high can demotivate rather than motivate.

Guidelines for Goal Setting

- goals should be meaningful
- goals need to be process- not outcome-oriented
- goals should be individualized
- goals must be objective and measurable
- goals must be specific
- goals must include a criterion for success
- goals must be realistic but challenging
- goals should be stated in a positive manner
- progressive short-term goals should lead to a long-term goal
- goals should have a target date for completion
- goals should be few and should be prioritized
- goals should be accompanied by strategies for achievement
- goals must be recorded and monitored
- goals must hold the coach accountable
- goals must be reinforced or supported.

- Evaluate your progress regularly and be flexible. With your measurable goals that provide stepping stones to your ultimate goal, you will be able to see how well you are progressing.
- Write down your goals and share them: we tend to commit to goals that are written down and shared goals (either as part of the process or after they have been set) are more effective still.

What activities will you undertake over the next twelve months to develop yourself as a coach? Tick the boxes in the following table to indicate the activities that you will be involved in and make notes as required.

	Competition Coaching	Qualifications	Self-analysis	Coaching Seminars	Other
January					
February					
March					
April					
May					
June					
July					
August					
September					
October					
November					
December					

Figure 40 Goal setting chart.

What are your goals as a coach? Completing Fig. 40 may help you to set appropriate targets for your development.

7 PLANNING AND PREPARATION

> It is better to take many small steps in the right direction than to make a great leap forward only to stumble backward.
>
> *Chinese proverb*

Do you want to improve the effectiveness of your coaching? This part of the book provides information, activities and exercises for you to plan and organize progressive and enjoyable sessions. You will be asked to consider: why planning is important; the extent to which you plan systematically; how and when you plan; and how you might improve your planning.

Planning is not necessarily a difficult task – we all do it everyday in organizing our time, our families – our lives basically! Planning in coaching follows the same simple process: decide where you are, where you want to be and how you are going to get there. This applies to each and every session, which is part of a week, part of a season and part of the athlete's career. The crucial aspects of long-term planning are dealt with more extensively in Part III, so we shall focus mainly on the shorter term planning process here, that is, a series of sessions.

Figure 41 Coach taking a break from session planning.

Before getting to some of that detail, consider these three scenarios:

1. You are coaching an athlete you have known for several years. The athlete is technically proficient and a good performer in training, but lacks confidence in the competitive environment. There is a big competition in four weeks.
2. You are coaching an athlete coming back from a serious injury. The athlete is desperate to get back into action, but you are being cautious about his return. The season starts in one week.
3. You are coaching a new player to your squad/team. He is lacking certain skills, but is very committed to improve. The season is under way.

In the first example, you might plan to include some simulated competitions in training before the big event. You might also include a smaller event in the build up to allow the athlete to perform under less pressure and to gain confidence. In both cases you are planning to convert the athlete's potential into competitive success by considering more than just his technical prowess.

In the second case, you will need to speak closely with the athlete (and any support staff such as physios) and to agree an appropriate schedule of reintroduction to competition. Obviously, the sport itself will play a major part in these plans, but you must be sure that there is no risk of further and more permanent damage. Perhaps your plan will include an agreed amount of competitive action to be gradually increased as the player progresses.

In the final example, your planning may focus more on technical instruction, depending on the sport, the performer and the goals you have both agreed. You will definitely make a set of decisions about when his level of skill is appropriate for exposure to the pressure of competition.

The purpose of this section is to help you to apply the principles of the previous six ECAs in developing, implementing and evaluating a developmental series of coaching sessions in your own sport. You will need to draw on the planning knowledge and awareness introduced above and your own coaching experience.

Planning a Coaching Programme for a Developmental Series of Sessions

There are many situations in which you may plan a developmental series of coaching sessions for an individual athlete or a team. Some of these are:

- at the beginning of a season
- in preparation for a major competition or key game
- to sequentially learn new skills, or
- to learn new offensive or defensive strategies or set plays.

Athlete Profiles

Before you begin to plan for a series of sessions, it is important that you understand your athletes and their development and experience levels. Preparing athlete profiles helps coaches to develop this understanding. These profiles should include the cognitive, psychosocial and physical domains of learning (similar to the process outlined for coaches in Figs. 19 and 20).

Physical Domain

- Includes the growth and changes that occur in a person's body
- the development and performance of motor skills
- cognitive domain
- includes all the mental processes that are used to obtain knowledge and/or to become aware of the environment
- involves the athletes' understanding of the tactics and strategies of the sport and their decision-making abilities.

Psychosocial Domain

- Includes emotional, personality and social development.

The athlete profiles should provide (where relevant) details of the athletes' experience, positions played, competition grade and physical, psychological, tactical, technical and leadership skills. Such profiles can be constructed in discussion with the athlete or by the coach, but this should be done with the athlete as a way of improving his/her self-knowledge and maintaining involvement in the training process.

Setting Objectives

Understanding your athletes' characteristics, abilities, needs, goals and motivation will help you to set objectives for your series of coaching sessions. These objectives include:

- keeping the fun in sport
- making training stimulating and rewarding
- designing training programmes that are appropriate for your athletes' stages of growth and development, but extend their development
- ensuring that your athletes have a solid foundation of good techniques
- setting appropriate goals and motivators
- developing a suitable competitive attitude and, with young athletes, guarding against overspecialization.

A first step in the process of planning a series of coaching sessions is to determine instructional objectives for each coaching session and for the series. An instructional objective is a statement describing a task, the situations under which it will be performed and the criteria or standards by which it will be judged. By establishing instructional objectives you can select, design and evaluate the learning activities for each session. Objectives must be achievable with effort from the athlete and coach. Meeting the discussed objectives acts as a motivator for both athletes and coaches. Objectives should be described as outcomes that can be measured and evaluated and should be discussed with the athlete at the beginning of the session (or series of sessions) and evaluated with the athlete at the completion of the session (or series of sessions).

While coaches are generally most concerned with the physical objectives, the three domains of learning, cognitive, psychosocial and physical, should be used when designing instructional objectives. You should attempt to incorporate all three learning domains in every coaching session to enhance the holistic learning of the athlete. This variety will also increase the enjoyment the athletes get out of each session.

Write down one objective in each domain of learning for the next coaching session that you will coach. You need to remember that you may have more than one objective in each domain. When you are setting your objectives, consider the following factors:

- athlete enjoyment
- athlete involvement
- physical/skill development
- cognitive development
- psychosocial development and competition.

When you have completed this task, discuss your objectives with another coach to determine their effectiveness. Remember that your session objectives should lead progressively to the achievement of your longer-term objectives.

Planning the Coaching Sessions

Once you have established the objectives for each coaching session you need to ask yourself, what will the athletes need to do to achieve each instructional objective?. The answer will consist of a list of skills, knowledge and behaviours (tasks) that athletes will need to have or complete to achieve the objectives. Developing these skills, knowledge and behaviours will provide the structure and content of the coaching sessions, for instance, the players will be able to perform all aspects of the lay-up (task), starting from the half court line (situation) and be able to make nine out of ten lay-ups with the dominant hand (criteria).

Some players may need to break the task into a number of components and to practise these separately. They may need to develop word or visual cues to focus on the task. They may need to adjust their mental thinking to believe they can achieve successful lay-ups to the specified criteria. You need to plan a coaching session that suits all the participating athletes and considers the various components of the task. You need to consider how to keep the skills practice interesting for your athletes. When planning these objectives you will also need to consider such things as the time set for each activity, the equipment needed and the safety of your athletes.

Developing the session(s) plan needed to achieve the objectives you listed in the previous activity: the requirements will include:

- session structure
- specific activities
- range of activities
- time allocated to each activity
- feedback to athletes
- equipment
- athlete safety.

It is important that you provide variety in your sessions, as well as creating opportunities for your athletes to achieve success. Within a team situation the ability of athletes varies. One way of meeting the needs of all of your athletes is to use the grid system. This is a teaching approach which increases the number of opportunities for athletes to practise at their own level. It involves forming grids or marked off playing areas and organizing your athletes to practise within the grids. Large groups can be organized efficiently using this approach. For example, a football pitch could be divided up into several playing spaces by using the existing markings. In other playing spaces, the lines and corners of the grid may be marked with cones or some other markers. The areas can then be used for practising a number of different drills, with each athlete performing at his own level. (Figs 42a and 42b give examples of this.)

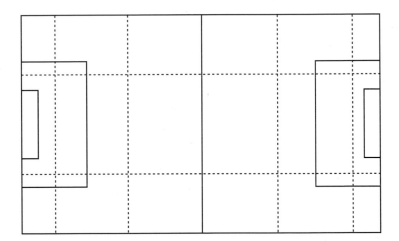

Figure 42a Grids in coaching.

Activity 1

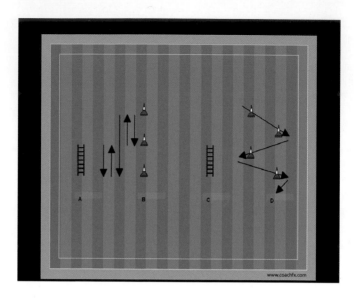

Set up:
After FIFA 11+ warm up 4 SAQ exercises are set up to work on Speed (Time 20mins):
A – Fast feet work both feet in the ladder
B – Forward and back running always facing forward
C – Lateral ladder work, Icky Shuffle
D – Cutting and planting through cones.

Instructions:
Normally 18 players = 3 groups of 6 players with a 1 to 5 work rest ratio.
Each exercise lasts for 5mins and is repeated for 5 reps each, when complete, active recovery in the form of light jog and passing within group until coach signals change over.

Coaching points:
Maintain good form throughout the exercises, maximum effort during each repetition and light jog back to start.

Activity 2

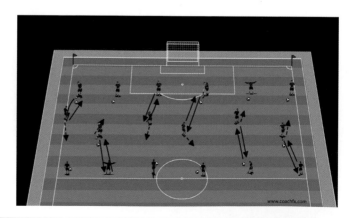

Set up:
Speed Endurance Technical Work (20mins) Work to rest 2 to 1, Load 5 reps
Groups of 3 Players Set out as shown, with 2 end players who are stationary with a ball each, the middle player is active.

Instructions:
Active player works for 1minute, he must move towards end player and perform technical skill as directed by coach, then quickly spin and sprint to opposite end player and repeat; exercise play continues for 1min.
Exercises – Left foot pass, Right foot pass, Left foot volley, Right foot volley, Header.

Coaching points:
Technical and tactical ability is paramount players are reminded to receive ball at an angle and to maintain quality technical work. Effort is almost maximal and continuous for 1min. Side players are encouraged to motivate and keep on their toes. If intensity drops, players are given a target amount of repetitions to reach within the time frame.

Activity 3

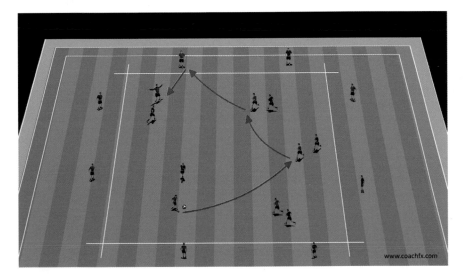

Set up:
Small Sided Game (Time 20mins) work to rest 1 to 1
5v5 in the middle the other 8 players are positioned on the outside as wall players which creates an 8v4 overload when in possession. Wall players have limited touches.

Instructions:
Normal possession to start work for 5mins then swap over, added conditions to manipulate work rate/intensity:
1 touch
2 touch
All in
Must jog around outside player after pass
Can't pass to player who passed.

Coaching points:
Emphasis on good passing under pressure, give coaching point during to keep intensity up, supply of footballs around square to maintain tempo of game.

Figure 42b Football session planner.

In football, for example, the grids may be used as follows:

- all players practise the same skill with the same equipment, for instance, passing and control on the volley from a throw-in
- all players practise the same skill at different levels, for instance, some practise passing without opponents and some with opponents
- players practise different skills in different grids, for instance, in two of the grids, players practise one-on-one defence, in another two grids, players practise receiving the ball and turning, and in the other grids, players practise creating and moving into a space to receive the ball.

The grid system allows you to observe performances effectively, correct individual faults and provide effective feedback on skill acquisition. Athletes may be observed from outside the grids, or you may observe as you move through the grids.

When conducting your sessions, there are a number of things that you need to be aware of and monitor: the following general reflective questions will help you to focus on effectively monitoring a coaching session or series of coaching sessions. They will also help you to identify aspects of your coaching that you may wish to improve.

The Safety of Your Athletes

[this is also dealt with in Part III]
Have you completed a risk assessment?
How have you planned your session to ensure the safety of your athletes?
What steps have you taken to ensure that your athletes are supervised adequately at all times?
What steps have you taken to prevent injury to your athletes?
How do you ensure that the equipment your athletes are using is safe and appropriate for their abilities and stage of growth and development?

Session Objectives

How do you observe your athletes in order to assess whether your session objectives are being achieved?
If your session objectives are not being achieved, how will you modify your session in an appropriate way?

Athlete Profiles

How do you involve your athletes in reassessing their performance profiles as you progress through the series of sessions?

How are you analysing your athletes during your coaching sessions and competitive situations?

How will you modify your coaching programme as a result of these assessments?

Series Objectives

How do your session objectives lead progressively towards your objectives for the series of sessions?

How do you observe your athletes in order to assess whether your series objectives are being achieved?

If your series objectives are not being achieved, how will you modify your sessions in an appropriate way?

Your Own Coaching

What did you learn about your coaching during your last session?

What effect did your coaching during the session have on your athletes?

What will help you to improve your coaching sessions?

How do you plan to act on the improvement needed in your next coaching session?

Evaluating Programmes

There are a number of techniques you can use to evaluate your series of sessions. One is to establish an objective measuring system. To do this, you will need to identify suitable criteria by which to measure improvement in the physical condition or performance of your athletes. Then you need to establish a test using these criteria and assess your athletes at the beginning of the series of sessions and again at the end. You will then have objectively evaluated whether there has been an improvement in the athletes' physical condition or performance. Other factors that must also be evaluated include: athlete safety, athlete injuries, adherence to the programme, and whether the series and session objectives have been achieved or not.

Your evaluation could use one or all of these evaluation techniques:

- observations and feedback from a suitable observer
- feedback from the athletes themselves
- analysis of a video recording of your sessions and/or
- a coach self-analysis.

Date . . . . Venue.	
Characteristic	*yes/no*
Individual interactions occurred more often than group instruction	
More time was spent coaching than in watching/managing	
Positive reinforcement occurred much more frequently than correction/ direction	
Few sets of instructions or directions lasted more than 30sec	
Coaching was performed in a variety of locations	
Demonstrations/models were used appropriately	
Comments were made to every athlete about the quality of perform- ances in the practice	
Interactions were made with every athlete during the session	
Athletes established goals for each important training item	
Athletes were asked or given an opportunity to evaluate whether they achieved or did not achieve their self-set goals for each important training item	
Each athlete was asked for his/her perception of his/her performance quality.	
Training session content was made known to the athletes before the start of practice.	
Athletes were kept busy all the time.	
Each athlete left the practice with a positive feeling.	
Indicate the type of primes used in the session: • manipulation • verbal guidance • visual guidance • demonstrations by the coach • demonstrations by athletes.	
Provision of prepared pictures and illustrations.	
Indicate the types of reinforcer provided in the session: • social reinforcers (usually swimmer interactions) • material reinforcers • performance information • internal reinforcers • vicarious reinforcement.	

Figure 43 The coaching-practice assessment form (C-PAF).

The purpose of this self-analysis is to provide a form of coaching behaviour evaluation that will sensitize you to develop effective coaching behaviours. The Coaching-Practice Assessment Form (C-PAF) is a self-appraisal technique designed for use by development and performance coaches in preparation for competitive settings. The form is to be completed periodically to evaluate whether the basic principles and behaviours of good coaching are being considered and performed. You should attempt to produce as many of the included features as possible.

The items evaluated are those that are important for effective instruction and provide the central features of an adequate programme and motivational environment. It is contended that if these behaviours are the central focus of coaching at training and practice, then athletes will enjoy a very positive experience and will look forward to each session. The scope of the C-PAF serves as a model for effective, ethical and professionally-acceptable coaching. That scope is derived from valid items from the motivational factors preferred by champion athletes (*see* pp. 139–40 in *High Performance Swimming* [Crowood, 2008]).

The intent of the C-PAF is to assist coaches to become better and more refined practitioners. This tool cannot and should not be used punitively. Coaching competence should be evaluated by a variety of other methods, perhaps including this. You should attempt to use this tool at least once a week with at least two days between each self-appraisal. Each evaluation result should be recorded on the progress log shown. This analysis form is an example of a self-observation schedule. It requires the coach to become familiar with the definitions that are listed in the following explanation. The total training session should be evaluated. A decision has to be made as to whether each behaviour category was ('yes') or not ('no') in evidence during the session. The number of 'yes' decisions should be recorded on the C-PAF Coaching Progress Log; recording the 'no' responses is optional.

Become familiar with the definitions of each entry on the C-PAF. Determine when evaluations will occur so that you will be able to get a consistent and representative 'picture' of your coaching performance. Immediately following the practice session, conduct the evaluation. For each entry, you have to decide whether your coaching performance did or did not conform to the item definition. If it did, then record a check mark in the 'yes' column on the recording sheet. If there is any doubt then place a check mark in the 'no' column. Once every item is evaluated, count the number of 'yes' check marks and record that on the bottom of the sheet and on the C-PAF Coaching Progress Log. Determine where coaching improvements can be made and set those behaviours as goals for behaviour changes in future coaching sessions. Retain the completed recording sheet in a personal file. Every two weeks, review the items that have been checked during the previous period. Consider whether your coaching is consistent or improving; there will come a time when further improvement is extremely difficult. At that stage, attempt to maintain the exhibition of a high number of desirable coaching behaviours. The higher the number that is set, the more satisfied you should be with your performance.

Definitions of Desirable Behaviors Evaluated on the Coaching Practice Assessment Form (C-PAF)

The greater part of the coaching time was spent on technique/tactics instruction. The most important factor in sports from an athlete's viewpoint is improvement in technical features. It is necessary for coaches to concentrate on providing this type of information. This contrasts with the more usual coaching emphasis on effort. To accomplish this behaviour, the coaching focus should be on skill (technical) features of performance and/or tactical factors for competitive situations. This must be the most frequently exhibited category of behaviour in the coaching session.

At the end of most repetitions, comments were made to individual athletes about the technique emphasis of the session or a technique characteristic covered in an earlier session. This behaviour is required to break with the traditional ineffective behaviour of being a commentator-coach. Individual interactions occurred more often than group instruction. The coach interacted with athletes on an individual basis more frequently than performing group instructional behaviours.

More time was spent coaching than in watching or managing. The most important activity of the coach was instructing. Long periods of observation or engagement in organizational or management tasks did not occur (they should be done at some other time or by some other person). Positive reinforcement occurred much more frequently than correction or direction. The coach reacted to athlete behaviours in a positive and encouraging manner. Where possible, the reactions should have occurred immediately after activity-related behaviours rather than being delayed. Few instances of negative feedback (for example, an emphasis on erroneous technical features) should have been evident.

Few sets of instructions or directions lasted more than 30sec. The coach provided directions that were simple, planned and relevant to the moment. Longer presentations should have been provided before entering the practice environment.

Coaching was performed in a variety of locations. The coach should have coached from more locations than one end of the gym/pitch/pool. The sides, the other end and even elevated positions offer different perspectives of an athlete's form and therefore increase the reliability of a coach's evaluations and suggestions.

Demonstrations/models were used appropriately. Verbal instruction was supplemented with demonstrations by the coach or team participants and/or the use of teaching aids.

Comments were made to every athlete about the quality of performances in the practice. The coach communicated to each athlete a general assessment of his or her performance quality for the total session.

Interactions were made with every athlete during the session. The coach interacted in a meaningful way with every athlete on an individual basis.

Athletes established goals for each important practice item. When important practices were performed, athletes had a performance goal, a technique feature and, in more advanced groups, mental content for competition as the purpose of each repetition.

Athletes were asked or given an opportunity to evaluate whether they achieved or did not achieve their self-set goals for each important practice item. After such items, the athletes were given an opportunity to self-evaluate whether they achieved their self-set goals.

Each athlete was asked for his or her perception of his or her performance quality. The coach asked each athlete for a general indication of the quality of his/her performances in the practice session. This behaviour normally should occur after the last important training segment. Session content was made known to the athletes before the start of practice. Before the practice started, athletes were told what would occur in the session. This information allowed the athletes to allocate their resources and efforts appropriately.

Athletes were kept busy all the time. Athletes did not waste time by being idle or doing activities that were unrelated to competitive preparation.

Each athlete left the practice with a positive feeling. As the athletes left, they gave the impression of positive feelings indicating that they willingly wanted to return for the next session.

The following types of prompt should be used to direct athlete behaviours:

- manipulation
- verbal guidance
- visual guidance
- demonstrations by the coach
- demonstrations by athletes
- provision of prepared pictures and illustrations.

The following types of positive reinforcer should be engineered by the coach:

- social reinforcers (usually athlete interactions)
- material reinforcers
- performance information
- internal reinforcers (usually asking the athlete to grade themselves or indicate what they did well)
- vicarious reinforcement (watching others receive positive reinforcement).

Plan for Competitive Situations within the Series of Coaching Sessions

To simulate competition conditions during training is an excellent way to physically and mentally prepare athletes for competition. For mental preparation you can:

- simulate real-life situations by playing loud or crowd music
- train at the time of day or night when the competition will occur
- require your athletes to use their competition mental plans
- provide situations where athletes can practise in competitive situations in which they are leading the competition, performing relatively well, or are far behind the opposition.

For physical preparation you can:

- have athletes perform in training the way they would perform in the competition
- have athletes practise their competitive tactics, and
- maintain competition-level intensity throughout the practice.

Athletes usually feel competent in training. If you can insist on competition-like situations at training, your athletes may relax and perform better during competitions. Developing competition preparation routines is a key to ensuring that athletes regularly perform well in competition. Competition preparation routines help athletes to gain consistency in performance as they feel more confident and maintain better control of time, concentration, thought processes, mental rehearsal and reactions to pressure and emotional states. If something does happen, having a mental plan will enable your athletes to recover more quickly and to refocus on the task.

Developing a Pre-Competition Routine

Your role is to help your athletes to create their own pre competition routines. You may provide a basic structure that the athletes then fill in to best suit their individual requirements, or work with athletes to develop their own routines. A pre-competition routine will include elements of both a physical and a psychological warm-up. Most people are familiar with aspects of physical warm-up but are unaware of what a psychological warm-up entails. This usually includes a combination of structured self-talk and imagery and sometimes uses music. Self-talk should take the form of realistic, positive self-suggestions such as reminders of preparation, readiness, ability, adaptability, commitment, intensity and positiveness. Imagery can be calming or activating (depending on the required level of arousal) and typically includes reminders of the competition plan, past personal bests or good training sessions and the feeling of executing the first few moves perfectly. Music is sometimes included as part of a psychological warm-up as certain songs may help to create the preferred pre-competition state of mind. The final element of a pre-competition routine is a pre-start focus, the focus of attention just before the start of competition. The pre-start focus usually includes a brief reminder of the competition plan, final adjustment of arousal level and the focus on the first few movements required in the competition. When athletes create a pre-competition routine they can draw upon the feelings and thoughts that served them best in the past.

An example of a generic pre-competition routine:

- arrive at venue *xx* minutes before the start
- check equipment
- begin stretching and warm-up.
- think happy, relaxed thoughts
- positively image upcoming performance
- listen to coach's comments
- apply these comments to imagery
- engage in heavier physical preparation
- use more imagery if needed
- engage in more intense physical activity
- ready self for the start and think of opening skills
- use cue word for the first skill.

Developing a Competition Strategy

Athletes need to be able to maintain their focus during competition. Having a structured pre-competition routine is only part of the mental planning required to produce consistent performances. Being properly prepared for competition just gets athletes started, they need to reinforce this with a competition strategy. Basically, competition strategies are compilations of cue words. A competition strategy should help athletes to focus on the most appropriate cues during the competition. The strategy should also help athletes to get back on track if they are distracted, make an error or just have their attention drift. The make-up of the strategy will, in part, be determined by the type of sport. For team sports such as rugby, soccer or hockey, the strategy should break the sport down into specific skills or critical situations. For example, there can be a team strategy about what to focus on just after the opposition has scored. Short races or routines such as those involved in sprinting, throwing, diving or gymnastics can involve sequential checkpoints that remind the athletes of specific technical cues. Long events such as marathons can have general cues or reminders that can be used throughout the event whenever the athletes need to maintain focus. For example, cues relating to technique, arousal or self-encouragement could be used when experiencing signs of fatigue, when approaching a big hill or after being passed. The specific cues used in a competition strategy will depend on the athletes' personalities, their level of performance, their past experience and the sport itself. When creating a strategy it is important to involve your athletes as they need to decide how they want to feel, focus and function during the phases of competition.

In some sports it may be appropriate to identify the strengths and weaknesses of the opposition when this information has an influence on the performance of your athletes. These strengths and weaknesses may include physical, psychological, tactical, technical and leadership skills. You can then use this information in developing athlete and/or team tactics as part of your competition strategy.

Two examples of competition strategy follow. Note how they can be sequential or situational. In addition, cue phrases that initially are lengthy can be shortened over time and continue to retain their full meaning. You will need to develop cues for your own athletes that have meaning for them.

100m Sprint (Track)

Segment	Cue	Purpose
0–30m	'push'	acceleration phase
30–60m	'heel'	maximum velocity stage
60–100m	'claw'	speed endurance phase

Volleyball

Situation or Skill	Cue	Shortened Cue
serving	'take your time'	'slow it down'
receiving serve	'want it'	'mine'
setting	'make position'	'position'
hitting	'high elbow'	'elbow'
blocking	'thumbs up'	'thumbs'
back court	'on toes, weight forward'	'toes'
other team scored	'ready for next serve'	'ready'

The Role of the Coach During Competition

Once competition strategies are developed verbally, to remind your athletes of cues during competition is usually much more useful than to provide a long-winded explanation of what the athletes should be doing. Before and during competition, athletes and coaches should avoid any self-defeating thoughts as these lead to worry, low poor confidence and interfere with competition concentration.

You must continually be aware of potential barriers to communication with the participants during competition and have developed strategies to overcome these, within the rules and regulations of the competition. These strategies must be practised in training to be effective in competition. Some athletes will get so involved in their own game that they may be totally unaware of possibly negative reactions of other people to their intensity.

Coaches also benefit from having pre-competition routines and competition strategies. These strategies will vary depending on whether the coach also has a significant role in organizing athletes before the competition. For example, a tennis coach might have as his pre-competition routine, the following:

- choose a team space (claim an area for a team base)
- verify opponents, courts and times
- check on practice courts (if available) and organize practise times
- check that the players are happy and starting their own pre-competition routines
- timetable pre-match talks at times that suit the players
- plan playing strategies for competition against each individual competitor and
- hold pre-match talks and/or warm-ups.

Planning for the Competitive Season

In planning for a competitive season, it is important for you to be aware of the needs that you and your team will have in terms of training facilities, equipment, finance, transport and management or specialist support. At the beginning of the season it is necessary to ensure that each support participant fully understands both the extent and the limits of his or her role. Establishing brief job descriptions may be one way of achieving this. These could provide guidelines relating to the total time commitment involved, skills and tasks required of the position and lines of communication with other personnel, including the coach and athletes.

You then need to match your support needs with the resources you have available. This may involve requesting additional help and support from your club or organization or making compromises if the resources cannot be made available to meet all of your needs.

Manage and Evaluate Competitive Situations

Competition is not the time to overload athletes with information, the place to introduce new strategies or techniques, nor the time to criticize your athletes' performances. Although opportunities for coaching input vary by sport, the coaching that can actually be done during competitions is minimal. Even though athletes can learn from competition, the competitive situation is not the appropriate place for vast amounts of instruction. The anxiety of athletes increases when importance is placed on the outcome and/or when they feel uncertain about their ability, training, place on the team or any other aspect of performance.

One of the most common competitive coaching errors is to place great importance on the outcome of specific competitions. It is not unusual to hear comments such as, 'this event is what you have been training all year for', 'the upcoming game is the most important game of your life', or 'remember, the selectors will be watching this weekend, be sure to perform your absolute best'. Even young children recognize the importance of elimination matches, grand finals and selection trials. Reminding them of this only serves to place greater pressure on them, usually resulting in increased anxiety, self-doubt and poorer performance.

Some coaches feel compelled to pull out all the stops when it comes to a grand final or an unusually important competition. Instead of sticking with routines and behaviours that worked to get the athletes to where they are, they decide that fancier methods are required. No major changes should be made before or during major competitions. Things should remain as familiar as possible. Even if a particular behaviour is less than optimal, to suddenly change that before a competition usually has worse consequences than to persist with the original course of action. Coaching during competitions can be frustrating since you have limited control at this stage over how your athletes perform. In reality, coaches can often do more harm than good during a competition.

It needs to be noted that you are likely to become anxious during competition, just as your athletes do. The main difference is that your anxiety can be compounded by a sense of having little or no control. Studies have shown that the heart rate and the blood pressure of coaches on the side-lines can exceed those of the athletes out running around.

Just as athletes need to focus on controlling the controllable, you need to do the same. Maintaining self-control and remembering to implement positive coaching behaviours will be beneficial for your athletes. If you are nervous or anxious, your athletes will pick up on those feelings and become more like you. On the other hand, if you are calm, focused and positive, your athletes will tend to be the same.

Ensure that your athletes go through their pre-competition routines and that you and they work through your competition strategies and tactics during the competition. Utilize all of your available supporting resources and people as you need them.

Evaluating the Competitive Situation

You need to monitor your athletes throughout the competitive situation and assess the effectiveness of your competition strategy and tactics. Factors that should be evaluated include the physical, psychological, tactical and leadership skills of your athletes, and, in some cases, of your opponents when this may affect the performance of your athletes. During the competition it may also be important to assess the state of the competition in terms of winning or losing.

Complete this form as soon as possible after your next competition. The purpose of it is to provide you with feedback about your own coaching skills.

Name: Date:

Strategy/Characteristic	Rating 1 (never) – 5 (all the time)				
I listened to my athletes	1	2	3	4	5
I was confident with my athletes	1	2	3	4	5
I was well prepared for the competition	1	2	3	4	5
I was positive	1	2	3	4	5
I gave effective feedback	1	2	3	4	5
I was enthusiastic	1	2	3	4	5
I kept my cool	1	2	3	4	5
I treated my athletes equally	1	2	3	4	5
I avoided the pitfalls of information overload	1	2	3	4	5
I allowed some athlete decision-making	1	2	3	4	5
I remained positive even when athletes were not performing as well as expected	1	2	3	4	5
I provided coaching cues	1	2	3	4	5
I varied my tone of voice	1	2	3	4	5
I found the competition enjoyable	1	2	3	4	5
The competition environment was safe	1	2	3	4	5

Figure 44 Coach competition assessment form (C–CAF).

Finally, it is important that you evaluate your own coaching skills during competition and how well you managed the competitive situation. In analysing the competition, answer the following questions:

- What did you learn about your coaching during the competition?
- What effects did your coaching have on your athletes?
- How effective were your communication strategies in overcoming any barriers to communication that arose during the competitive situation?
- What worked well during this competition?
- What would you change about the competition or competition plan if you could coach it again?
- How do you plan to follow up your suggestions in the next competition?

8 OBSERVATION AND ANALYSIS

> We cannot create observers by saying 'observe,' but by giving them the power and the means for this observation and these means are procured through education of the senses.
>
> *Maria Montessori*

As we have already established, the coaching process is about enhancing performance by providing feedback about the performance to the athlete or the team. Scientific research has shown that human observation and memory are not reliable enough to provide accurate and objective information for athletes. Objective measuring tools may also be necessary to enable the feedback process. These can take the form of video analysis systems in- or post-event. The scope of such sophisticated tools is not within the remit of this book (and they are generally utilized with performance-level athletes), but it is appropriate to look at the principles involved in such approaches to observation and analysis.

The essence of the coaching process is to instigate observable changes in behaviour. The coaching and teaching of skill depend heavily on the observation and analytical skills of the coach to effect an improvement in athletic performance. Therefore, informed and accurate measures are necessary for effective feedback and the improvement of performance. In most sports, the analysis of the performance is guided by a series of qualitative assessments made by the coach. Our original representation of the coaching process (Fig. 15) defined a simple flowchart and a more detailed version (for football) was proposed in Fig. 16. These outlined the coaching process in its observational, analytical and planning phases. The performance is watched and the coach will form an impression of the positive and negative aspects of the performance. Often the results from previous games, as well as performances in practice, are considered before planning in preparation for the next competition. The next competitive outing ensues and the process repeats itself. There are, however, problems associated with a coaching process that relies heavily upon the subjective assessment of performance.

During a competition many events stand out as distinctive features, ranging from controversial decisions given by officials to exceptional technical performances by individual athletes. While these are easily remembered, they tend to distort the coach's assessment of the total event (think of the irate football manager immediately after the match, still raging about the last controversial decision by the referee and unable to give an honest, objective account of the game). Human memory is limited so that it is almost impossible to remember all the events that take place during an entire competition. Franks and Miller (1986) showed that soccer coaches are less than 45 per cent correct in their post-game assessment of what occurred during a half of a soccer game. While there is considerable individual variability, this rapid forgetting is not surprising, given the complicated process of committing data to memory and subsequently retrieving it. Events that occur only once in the game are not easily remembered and forgetting is rapid. Furthermore, emotions and personal biases are significant factors affecting memory storage and retrieval.

In most team sports an observer is unable to view and assimilate the entire action taking place on the playing area. Since the coach can only view parts of game action at any one time (usually the critical areas), most of the peripheral play action is lost. Consequently, the coach must then base his post-match feedback on only partial information about a team's, unit's or individual's performance during the game. This feedback is often inadequate, so an opportunity is missed to optimize the performances of players and teams.

Figure 45 Coach during competition.

Problems associated with subjective assessments would seem to present the coach with insurmountable difficulties, particularly if improving the performance of an athlete hinges on the observational abilities of the coach. Despite the importance of observation within the coaching process, little research has been completed into observational accuracy, the little that has clearly demonstrates that coaches cannot expect to remember even 50 per cent of a performance, and in most cases considerably less.

One of the coach's main tasks is to analyse accurately and assess performance. It would seem then that this could not be carried out subjectively. Any hopes for improvement through feedback would be reduced to chance. How can this be rectified? Objectivity can be obtained through the use of video, biomechanical systems for fine analyses or notational analysis. Hand notation systems are in general very accurate but have disadvantages: the more complex ones involve considerable learning time. In addition, the data these systems produce can involve many man-hours to process into output that is meaningful to the coach or athlete; for example, it can take as much as 40hr just to process the data from one squash match.

The introduction of computerized notation systems has made it feasible that these two problems, in particular the data processing, to be tackled positively. Used in real-time analysis or, with video recordings, in post-event analysis, they facilitate immediate, easy data access and the presentation of data in graphical or another pictorial form more easily understood by coaches and athletes. The increasing sophistication and reducing cost of video systems has greatly enhanced post-event feedback, from playback with subjective analysis by a coach, to detailed objective analysis by means of notation systems. But computers introduce extra problems, of which system-users and programmers must be aware, such as operator errors (such as accidentally pressing the wrong key), hardware and software errors. Such undetected perception errors, where the observer misunderstands an event or incorrectly fixes a position are particularly problematic in real-time analysis when the data must be entered quickly.

To minimize these problems careful validation of computerized notation systems must be carried out. Results from a computerized system and a hand system should be compared to assess the accuracy of the former. Reliability tests must also be performed on both hand and computerized systems to estimate the accuracy and consistency of the data.

Four major purposes of notational analysis are analysis of movement, tactical evaluation, technical evaluation and statistical compilation.

Many of the traditional systems are concerned with the statistical analysis of events previously recorded by hand. The advent of on-line computer facilities overcame this problem, since the game could first be digitally represented first, via data collection direct into the computer, then documented via the response to queries about the game. The major advantage of this method of data collection is that the game is represented in its entirety and stored in ROM or on disk, a database is therefore initiated.

Team sports can benefit immensely from the development of computerized notation; the information derived therefrom can be used for several purposes:

- immediate feedback
- development of a database
- indication of areas requiring improvement
- evaluation
- as a mechanism for selective searching through a video recording of the game.

All of these are of paramount importance to the coaching process, the original reason for performance analysis. Database development is crucial. If the database is large enough, it will enable predictive modelling as an aid to the analysis of different sports, subsequently enhancing future training and performance. Knowing when you have enough data to form a true performance profile is not easy, but there are some guidelines.

Using computer analysis systems accurately and reliably needs a structured training programme that deals with all aspects of the system. There are at least three problems in obtaining objective, accurate data from a system such as the Computerised Coach Analysis System (Franks *et al.*, 1988). The definition of behaviour given to the observer by the experimenter may be vague, subjective or incomplete. The behaviour may be difficult to detect because of its subtlety or complexity, because of distractions or because of other factors obstructing observation. Finally, the observer may be poorly trained, unmotivated or incompetent.

The two fundamental goals of a training programme are teaching the observer the data collecting and recording techniques required by the instrument. The second, more difficult task is teaching the observer the behaviour categories and their operational definitions, defined unambiguously. To be adequately trained, the observer must have some knowledge of these definitions, understand them and be able to apply them in varying circumstances.

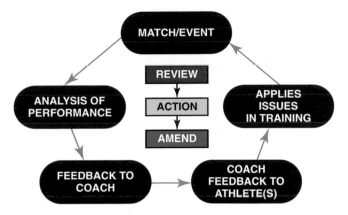

Figure 46 Coaching process incorporating performance analysis.

The training programme should train the observers to observe, that is, where and how to look and what to look for. It should also provide some method of evaluating the observer's progress toward the goals of understanding the definitions and becoming skilled. In addition, such an evaluation could be used to assess the observer's understanding of recording techniques. Because of their accumulation of these skills, these tasks have become the preserve of specialist performance analysts.

Because of the shortcomings of the human observation system and the fallibility of human memory, it is unrealistic to expect a coach to remember large parts of an athletic performance. By using objective observation systems, coaches can focus their attention on analysing what they perceive to be critical incidents in their athletes' performances. In this way they can hope to improve the performance of these athletes by planning practices based on these analyses. Hand notation and computerized notation systems and all biomechanical analysis systems have been shown to benefit these processes. Our simple model of the coaching process (*see* Fig. 15) can now be extended (*see* Fig. 46) to include some of the recent developments in computer and video technology.

Game Coaching

In the heat of the action, you cannot afford to lose your cool, coaching in the game or 'bench coaching', is arguably the most important aspect of successful coaching at elite level in team games. While thorough planning and preparation are crucial to success, months or even years of effort may be wasted because of a single error by the coach at a crucial point in the game. Clearly, some coaches do seem to have an almost uncanny ability to read a game and to make sound tactical decisions while under great pressure. In a broader sense effective bench coaching is important because it can have an impact, either positive or negative, far beyond a single game. From a positive point of view, a competitive game provides coaches with some of their best opportunities for effective teaching. In a sense, the tough game provides the perfect learning situation; the players are focused and want to do well, action is real, the learning is contextual and relevant and motivation is high. The challenge for the coach is to recognize and use every teaching opportunity that emerges. As with many highly complex human capacities, the process of bench coaching seems to be more intuitive than reflective in nature so it is not readily amenable to a simple analysis. The challenge for coach educators therefore is to tease out the critical components of this ability – make them intelligible – and find ways of helping all coaches to improve in this crucial aspect of their craft because many novice coaches often appear to be like mere spectators who simply watch the action but see little. A real game is a whirling, often chaotic, ebb and flow of action with no instant replays so the coach must note, interpret and react to continuous sequences of action, all the while remaining cool, calm and collected. The process of match analysis, that is, the ability to really see what is happening at every instant of the game underpins bench coaching. To see in this sense implies that coaches have the capacity to both direct their observation to what is really important and know what to look for.

In order to do this you need a precise model or template of the game to give purpose and focus to the observation. Effective match analysis is therefore based on a thorough understanding of the fundamental nature, strategy and tactics of a game.

For football, rugby and other invasion games these are encapsulated in the principles of effective play. These provide the verbal and conceptual template necessary for intelligent observation and thus help to simplify the process of analysis. They also provide a common tactical language for both coach and players, which makes communication easier and helps the latter more readily to understand their role in the total team effort. With such a template to provide a framework for observation, the coach is free to focus on other important factors such as one-on-one match ups, the tempo of the

Figure 47a Coaching from the bench.

Figure 47b Coaching from the sideline.

game and specific patterns of play employed by the opposition. Without the structure provided by these principles or rules a coach is like a tone deaf conductor who cannot read music, trying to improve an orchestra.

The collection of 'hard data' on performance at a basic level or advanced level can be valuable when it gives coaches a clearer picture of future opponents or when it hardens the post-match analysis of one's own team. Even though sophisticated computer programs are now beginning to give coaches in some games access to real time data, they cannot yet replace the coaches' capacity for real-time analysis, based upon intelligent eyeballing. There are also intangibles such as intensity or hustle which are not easily measured but which can change the course of a game as much by their psychological impact as by their objective value in gaining or retaining the ball. Perceptive coaches who value these elements of good play are gradually finding ways to quantify them and to factor them into any analysis of player performance. However, the fact is that most coaches will have to rely on their own powers of observation to analyse what is happening on the field and can rarely expect more data than their eyes can give them. As in our everyday lives, receiving more information is often not as important as how we interpret and respond to what we already have.

Pre-game match analysis or the scouting process involve the observation and analysis of future opponents either in the flesh or through video tape. It can give a coach invaluable insights into the strengths and weaknesses of future opponents and enables him to predict the probable reactions of opposing teams and individuals to specific tactical situations. Again, it is worth pointing out that player performance and statistics, as well as specific patterns of play, can vary from game to game, so the team you scout may not be the same team you play against statistically or tactically. Remember that they will also be preparing – to play against you! A scouting coach may learn far more that is useful about an opponent by identifying their philosophy of play rather than merely gathering statistics, for the

Figure 48 Coach making real-time adjustments.

former is unlikely to vary much from game to game. Thus a scout must try to identify the crucial elements of an opponent's style and consider a range of issues such as – how do they combine in attack?, who are their key playmakers?, how fast do they counterattack or fast break?, how well do they recover in defence?, do they play with heart?, are they tough and resilient?, do they keep coming back when they get behind? Among the most crucial issues are the philosophy and psychological make up of their coach. In order to develop the observation skills necessary for effective match analysis quickly, the serious coach must spend time watching lots of games, particularly at a level above the one he is coaching.

Post-match analysis of games combined with match statistics can ensure that an objective picture of player and team performance emerges. It gives players the chance to come face to face with their own performance and enables the coach to constructively plan future strategies for improvement. Even at the lowest level, post-match analysis is critical because it provides a coach with a specific focus for succeeding practices – it will also help players to understand the reason for that focus. It is important to use video replay of games positively, to highlight and reinforce successful aspects of play which have been emphasized in practice and which provide evidence that a team is beginning to achieve its goals even if the results are not good.

9 REFLECTIVE PRACTICE

> By three methods we may learn wisdom: first, by reflection, which is noblest; second, by imitation, which is easiest; and third, by experience, which is the most bitter.
>
> *Confucius*

Drawing on research into student learning, this section provides a rational-ale for the introduction of reflection into programmes of learning into

Developing Match Analysis Skills

The following are practical examples of learning experiences which will help novice coaches to develop match analysis skills.

Interactive simulation session: focused observation of game play. Coaches are allocated an individual player to observe as he or she is involved in a practice (that is, 3v1 continuous transition drill). They observe the player using a template of principles of play. Breaks in play are taken and the coach is able to provide feedback to the player. This exercise can be made progressively more complex by having the coach focus on an increasing number of players.

Apprenticeship: observe a game coached by a mentor. Observe and note the game with a particular focus in each half.

How would you have made your decisions and when during the game?

Describe the pattern of transition into attack used by both teams.

Describe the pattern of transition into defence.

Observe and comment on both teams' settled attacking patterns.

Observe and comment on both teams' defensive patterns.

Discuss these features of the game with your mentor.

Self-directed learning: attend another invasion-type sport and observe the game and then address the following issues:

is the template of the principles of play a valuable tool for observation?

did you find the game interesting, when comparing similar play principles?

were you able to transfer your knowledge to this game?

Talent spotting: attend a game of a younger age group. Select the five players that you would recruit for your team and outline the reasons. Detail a training session that you would plan for the team you observed as a result of what you saw in the game.

coaching and coach education. Reflection might be seen as both an approach and a method for improving the quality and depth of coach learning. Reflection is a way of thinking about learning and helping individual learners to understand what, how and why they learn. It is about developing the capacity to make judgements and evaluating where learning might take you.

Research into student learning has taught us a lot about learning styles, motivation and approaches to learning. It has also added empirical weight to what our instincts tell us, namely, that we learn by doing. We learn by experience and by trial and error. We have the potential to learn from our mistakes. In Western culture phrases such as 'that'll teach you' or 'you'll learn' are common reprimands when experience shows us the error of our ways. Yet we talk about these conditions for learning as if the experience

Figure 49 Reflective coach.

leads directly to improved ability or understanding. However, what gets us from experience to understanding is reflection. True, repetition and practice help us to learn, but they do not substitute for the process of actively thinking about how we did, what we did well and what less well. With the aid of a simple prompt question such as 'what might I do better next time?' or 'what could I do differently?' we have the potential to draw on the past and present and direct ourselves into a better future. It is this power to effect change that makes reflective practice so fundamental to coach education and to the creation of coaches as lifelong learners.

What do we mean by reflection in an educational sense? Educational researcher Phil Race describes the act of reflecting as one which causes us to make sense of what we have learned, why we learned it and how that particular increment of learning took place. Moreover, reflection is about linking one increment of learning to the wider perspective of learning – heading towards seeing the bigger picture. Reflection, therefore, helps to raise our awareness of ourselves as learners and to see that we can direct and change our learning. John Biggs takes this one step further and points out, 'A reflection in a mirror is an exact replica of what is in front of it. Reflection in professional practice, however, gives back not what it is, but what might be, an improvement on the original' (Biggs, 1999). In other words, reflection is not simply about acknowledging who we are and what went wrong but who we might become. It is a transformational process.

Reflection as a Structure for Learning

We might think of learning as a network of co-existing ideas. Learners construct their own meaning about situations drawing on both their cognitive skills (reasoning, knowledge) and metacognitive skills (intuition, self-awareness). When something new is experienced, the learner recollects prior knowledge and tries to make a connection into the existing cognitive or metacognitive network of ideas. In other words, we make the new piece of the jigsaw fit into the existing picture that we have. Whether a perfect fit is possible depends on the existing pieces of knowledge and the learner's ability to let the piece float until connections can be made. The process of reflection provides a structure for these connections and enables us to distinguish between important cornerstones of learning, prominent features and background 'sky' in a way that forms a meaningful and perhaps unique picture.

Laurillard (1993) draws a distinction between mediated learning (aided by a teacher) and non-mediated learning (experiential). Reflection can help to supplement mediated learning by helping the individual to make connections between the theory and constructs he has learnt formally. If we take driving a car as an example, the driver becomes more accomplished if she can make a connection between the learning theory and the Highway Code mediated by the driving instructor and the process of changing gear, steering and road awareness. Reflection can also enhance unmediated learning by providing a structure and framework by which the individual can 'unpack' an experience and consider the implications of what has happened. Extending the analogy, we see that car insurance claim forms require drivers to reflect by supplying prompt questions, such as 'how could the accident have been avoided?' In this and many other learning events, we might not always like what we find when we reflect, since blame often rests with our own lack of judgement (for instance, the accident could have been avoided by noting the distance between my car and the one I reversed into). The structure of reflection helps us to deconstruct an experience and find an explanation for what happened.

Structures in the form of prompt questions help students to reflect and to make sense of their understanding. Coaches on my MSc Sports Coaching programme at the University of Stirling have to complete a personal development journal throughout their studies. I use three simple questions to prompt the coaches to reflect: *i.* a description of an event or experience; *ii.* how it made them feel or how they responded to the event or the experience; and *iii.* how they might respond to a similar event in the future or what would they do differently?

As a structure, reflection provides scaffolding for the coach to make sense of experience and make connections. It clearly has a role in helping individuals to think more critically about how they learn. We shall now explore how this takes place in sports coaching.

Many coaches develop their skills and expertise through their experiences and by watching other coaches. However, simply acquiring experiences does not guarantee coaching competence. It is the integration of experience and knowledge in a meaningful way that promotes learning and in turn develops expertise. Coaches need to know how best to learn through their experiences. Reflective practice is a major learning tool in this regard.

Reflection is at the heart of the learning process. It is a necessary component in learning to regulate one's thoughts, feelings and actions. Reflection links experience and knowledge by providing an opportunity to explore areas of concern in a critical way and to make adjustments based on these reflections. This exploration enhances learning and promotes coaches' abilities to identify and respond to cues within the environment.

Coaches can use reflective practices both during an event, such as a practice or competition, and afterwards. Reflection during an activity involves the consideration of what is happening as it is happening. Coaches learn to read the environment and to respond accordingly. For example, during a practice, a coach may recognize that the skill is breaking down and then take steps to improve the execution of that particular practice element. This recognition is based on his ability to identify relevant sport-specific information and use this to guide his actions. Reflection after an event involves the consideration of what has taken place in relation to the goals of the activity. During this type of reflection, there is more time to assess the situation and consider possible alternatives or review other resources in order to improve or progress the activity. For example, after the practice and upon reflection, the coach may realize that a different drill would be better suited to help the athletes learn the concept.

Research suggests that expert coaches engage in both kinds of reflection on a regular basis and that reflective practice plays an important role in their development as experts. Learning to reflect, whether it is during or after an activity, is a skill that involves several steps. Understanding the reflective process can help coaches to make refinements and incorporate strategies at each stage. The following are the key elements of reflective practice.

Issue Identification

Reflection is usually triggered by an awareness of uncomfortable feelings or thoughts regarding an experience or issue. Some coaches may refer to this as intuition or a 'gut' feeling and use this information to examine the situation more closely. Perhaps the coach sees an athlete responding in an

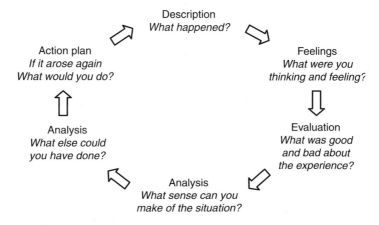

Figure 50 Reflective practice.

unusual manner or recognizes that within the practice or drill something just did not feel right. Reflection may also arise from discussions with other coaches. Another may have noticed a weakness in a drill or a lack of communication by the coach to an athlete. Reflection may also be triggered by others within the sport community, such as parents or sport governing bodies. Parents may approach coaches regarding an issue with their son or daughter and the coach may use this information to pay more attention in particular situations. Regardless of the source of the discomfort, model coaches use this discomfort as an indication of the need to acquire more knowledge to better understand the situation and themselves and to make adjustments as necessary.

Self-Awareness

It is important to note here, that whether or not coaches are triggered by certain experiences will relate to their personal approach to coaching and their level of self-awareness. For example, with respect to the personal approach, if discipline and winning define a coach's personal approach, then he is more likely to be triggered by athletes who arrive late or do not adhere to training programmes when compared with a coach whose approach is defined by fun, personal growth and development. Therefore part of reflective practice entails coaches' assessing their personal approach to coaching and taking responsibility for how their approach may be influencing their actions and reflections. Further, coaches who are self-aware or more attuned to their internal states, behaviours and intuitions are more likely to be aware of and respond to, cues within the environment that indicate that something is amiss.

Critical Assessment

The reflective process also entails a critical assessment of certain events along with a recognition of the associated thoughts, feelings and current knowledge. During an activity the assessment tends to be more preliminary and expert coaches recognize that they may not have all the information necessary to make an accurate assessment at that time. This recognition can help them to regulate their thoughts, feelings and actions until more time and information are available. Critical assessment after an activity often involves searching for more information in order to get a better picture of the situation. A clear picture needs to emerge in order for coaches to begin to generate strategies for resolving the issue. Coaches may seek advice from their peers or expert coaches, collaborate with peers to problem solve, observe other coaches, seek out additional resources (such as books and videos), review previous strategies from experience, or engage in personal creative thought to generate new solutions. Expert coaches tend to challenge their personal assumptions and envision and explore several alternatives at this stage. New knowledge may emerge from this process and this knowledge can be integrated with previous knowledge to generate problem-solving strategies.

The critical analysis stage is perhaps the most challenging, especially for developing coaches. They may not have the knowledge or support to generate creative solutions and they may be limited in their access to resources. Moreover, they may have difficulty challenging assumptions both during the activity and after, especially if they are uncertain or only beginning to develop their personal approach to coaching. Coaches designated as mentors could play an invaluable role at this stage, providing perspective as well as a forum for discussion. Research suggests that if individuals can be guided to direct their attention to their actions, thoughts and feelings in the moment, they are more likely to evaluate their personal approach critically and restructure it as necessary.

Experimentation

The next stage in reflective practice involves experimentation. Once coaches are armed with a few solutions they then need to explore the likely consequences of each and to select the most appropriate response. In some cases this experimentation may be hypothetical. They may present their ideas to their peer coaches for feedback. Hypothetical experimentation can be a practical way to reflect after a season is over and coaches are preparing for the new one. Real world experimentation occurs in the sport domain where coaches can carry out their envisioned solution and review its impact.

It is important to note that experimentation within reflective practice is different from trial-and-error practice. Trial and error simply involves doing something and, when it fails, doing something else until that something works. The approach is random and unpredictable in comparison with reflective experimentation. In reflective experimentation, the idea is to build upon existing knowledge by drawing from experiences and learning to making educated selections based on the relevant information. This approach is more predictable and thoughtful and promotes a more effective learning environment for athletes.

Evaluation

The final stage in reflective practice involves evaluation. This relates to an assessment of the meaning or value of the solution. It can be compared with some standard or criteria, or assessed based on its effectiveness within the specific situation. Model coaches often approach evaluation as a solitary endeavour. They may keep a journal related to their coaching experiences or they may simply conduct a mindful evaluation after the process. The approach is usually systematic and integrated into everyday practice. It often involves both technical evaluations and personal considerations, along with a willingness to accept responsibility for the impact of their choices. Expert coaches are willing to assume responsibility for their decisions. Sometimes strategies will work out well, while at other times they will not. Reflective coaches consider their decisions and accept the consequences of those decisions and make adjustments to their future choices.

External evaluations are also valuable contributors to reflective practice. External evaluations provide coaches with perspective and a chance to learn about themselves and view their coaching from different points of view. External evaluations may take a number of forms. They may involve informal discussions with peers or expert coaches, written feedback or more formalized questionnaires. Regardless of the form, these evaluations

---

Developing Reflective Coaches

Reflective practice can be a significant contributor to coach development. As a process, it needs to be integrated into day-to-day practice. Reflection skills in coaches can be developed and supported in a number of ways. Here a few suggestions:

Discussions: coaches can benefit from discussions with other coaches. These discussions provide a chance to reflect on current practice and be exposed to different approaches and experiences. Opportunities need to be created where coaches can engage in discussion around relevant and meaningful coaching issues. Monthly coach meetings, mentor–coach support, conferences and coaching clinics are just few avenues where discussions can occur.

Dialogue journals: in a dialogue journal coaches record their thoughts, feelings, questions and concerns related to their roles and responsibilities as a coach on a daily basis. Mentor coaches then respond to the entries providing alternatives and challenges to ways of thinking.

Season projects: at the beginning of the season coaches can designate a question about coaching or learning in regard to which they would like to explore possible solutions. Throughout the season they then attempt to address the question through various strategies and approaches. For example, a coach might wonder about the impact of a systematic team-building approach on athlete enjoyment and commitment. This coach would then develop and implement a programme throughout the season and reflect on its impact.

Practical coaching clinics: these provide the opportunity to experiment with different ideas and receive feedback from other coaches. Coaches are assigned tasks and then are required to present them to the class in a practice format.

Coaches can benefit from videotaping their performances both in practice and competitions and then review the tapes with peers or mentor coaches. The process promotes reflection on elements that are sometimes more subtle and not known to the coach, such as body language and tone of voice.

need to be meaningful to the coaches and conducted in an effective manner in order for them to contribute to reflective practice. Coaches need to be able to use the feedback and be provided with time in which to incorporate it into their regular practices. Therefore the evaluations of coaches should not occur just at the end of a season, but rather at systematic points throughout the season so that coaches can learn from the feedback and adjust as necessary.

Expert coaches learn from their experiences and, as a result, have a more extensive knowledge base than developing coaches. Reflective practice is a key factor contributing to their knowledge development. Coaches can learn to develop their reflective skills and gain the most from their experiences if they integrate reflection practices into their daily routines.

PART 3: ADDITIONAL CONSIDERATIONS

This section aims to cover some key considerations in the implementation of the 9-ECAs by looking at specific instances within coaching practice. Safety is of paramount importance with all groups, but particularly with children and when using equipment; coaching disabled athletes, although not 'special' in the integrated world of modern sport, does present some unique challenges to the coach – these will be discussed below; elite sport is presented as a specific case study and long-term planning is of paramount importance to all coaches, as are considerations in respect of child development; finally, the book ends the way it started with a discussion of the importance of all of these factors in the moral and social development of young sports participants.

10

Safety

'Don't learn safety rules simply by accident!'

Every sport contains an element of risk. One of the most important responsibilities of a sports coach is to ensure that coaching sessions are conducted in a safe and responsible manner. This section focuses on safe practice in sport, outlining the key safety issues associated with coaching. If you follow the guidelines this section offers, you may be confident that you are conducting your sessions in a safe manner and are being proactive as regards health and safety issues.

One of your most important considerations in planning for safe practice should be the physical environment in which you are coaching. It is your responsibility to identify any potential hazards in this environment and to control them, or at least to make participants aware of them, so that you can ensure safe and effective exercise.

Not all facilities are purpose-built. Nowadays many converted buildings are used in sport which are not always ideal. Ensure that objects such as radiators and glass do not pose a danger to participants and are covered and padded where necessary. The weather can also be a great danger – for example, the sun can blind the participant momentarily, causing him to lose sight of the ball or an opponent suddenly. Rain, snow and wind all pose potential hazards for outdoor sports and therefore it is your responsibility to ensure that participants are not put at risk. In indoor facilities these elements obviously do not have such a large impact. However, the sun may still present a hazard and therefore curtaining may be required, or the repositioning of the activity or any apparatus to avoid the danger. If you are coaching outdoors, make sure that appropriate lighting is available, and, if working under floodlights, make sure there is sufficient light to coach safely. Entrances and exits need to be carefully checked; for example, doors should open outwards. In a multi-use or shared facility always check everything before you use it – the previous user may not have had your high standards (*see* Fig. 51 for a suggested health and safety checklist). All facilities used for coaching should be checked by you and should meet the standards determined by the Health and Safety Executive and your sport's national governing body.

Emergency planning is an integral part of every sports programme that outlines the responsibilities all those involved in the care of the athletes, including all facility staff, coaches and players' parents. Each of these components should be included to ensure the safety of your athletes:

- have emergency contact information on each player
- have signed medical release forms on file for each athlete
- have an accessible, working telephone at practice and at games to ensure that emergency personnel can be contacted quickly in the case of an emergency
- have a first-aid kit present at all practices and games
- provide water or sports drinks for the athletes
- give numerous breaks to prevent dehydration
- examine playing fields, courts and other surfaces before practice and games for potentially dangerous obstacles such as holes, loose tiles, buckled wood, wet spots and sharp objects
- routinely check player's safety equipment before practice to make sure that it is put on correctly and that nothing is cracked or missing; if equipment is damaged the athlete should not use it
- properly store unused equipment away from the playing field so that no one trips over it while playing
- ensure that young athletes are aware of any unsafe playing conditions and report them to you
- make it your habit to check out the current health and safety regulations covering the facility where you coach
- always ensure that you and your participants are aware and have rehearsed, where possible, basic emergency procedures such as fire drills and evacuation procedures
- different sports use different types of surface, some of which are natural (such as grass, wood and water) and others synthetic
- keeping a record of the types and incidence of injuries that occur with different surfaces can assist your planning and practice (a standard injury/accident record form is shown in Fig. 52)
- the weather, as well as discarded objects such as glass and litter, will affect outdoor surfaces synthetic surfaces can be damaged by wear and tear and may be difficult to clean, thus creating the risk of injury to or the infection of participants.

Figure 51 Health and safety checklist.

As well as being aware of problems inherent in the surface itself, you should also ensure that the surface is safe to use and suitable for the activity to be undertaken. For example, dance and gymnastics sessions need a very smooth surface and a sprung floor. Certain surfaces require specific footwear and to use them without such shoes may cause injury. The space available to coach in is very important: if the numbers in the group are too large for the space, the activity could present additional hazards. You should ensure that all practices minimize the risk of participants' colliding or tripping over each other. Bags and equipment should be stored safely away from the activity area.

Practical Tips

By establishing rules and conditions for practices or drills, you can ensure that the participants are aware of the boundaries of the activity area and will not encroach into the playing area of other participants and thereby

Name of Organization:			
Particulars of Accident:			
Date:	Time:	Location:	Date Reported:
Details of Injured Person:			
Name:	Age:	Date of Accident:	Contact Number:
Type of Injury:			
Injured Part of Body:			

The Accident:

Describe What Happened:

What Were the Causes of the Accident?

How Bad Could It Have Been?

❏ Very Serious	❏ Serious	❏ Minor

What Are the Chance of It Happening Again?

❏ Frequent	❏ Occasional	❏ Rare

What Has or Will Be Done to Prevent It from Occurring Again in Future?

Treatment and Investigation of Accident:

Type of Treatment Given:	Name of First Aider:	Doctor/Hospital
Accident Investigated by:	Date:	Official Advised:	Date:

Figure 52 Injury/accident record form.

increase the risk of accidents. You should be aware of how to organize and set up skill practices and drills that promote safe working conditions for your participants; for example, by using cones to define boundaries for small-sided games. To ensure safety, make sure that the participants are aware of these boundaries by giving them some rules to play by; for example, if the ball goes outside the boundaries, stop the drill, retrieve the ball and start the drill again.

Equipment

Many sports require additional equipment, some of which will be used in participation in the sport itself, and there may be other additional safety equipment which might be worn by the athlete. The coach should check all the equipment thoroughly to ensure that it is well maintained and that there is no damage or anything untoward which could injure or harm any of the participating athletes. All equipment should be of the proper size and adhere to the regulations as set out by the sport's governing body and each athlete should use only equipment that 'fits' his needs comfortably and correctly. For beginners, in particular, it is also usually the coach's responsibility to ensure that all participants know how to use any equipment correctly and safely.

Things to Take With You

A coach should have a first-aid kit with him at all times, which should be kept fully stocked with an adequate supply of the correct medical equipment. Although some first-aid supplies will be common to all sports, the first-aid kit may have to be adapted depending on the sport in question. More importantly, the coach should know how to use all the contents of the kit properly. It is also the coach's responsibility to ensure that an adequate supply of water and/or sports drinks is available. Now that mobile telephones are an everyday part of our culture, a coach should always carry one as it could be invaluable if, for example, he needed to summon professional medical help or a hospital in an emergency.

Other Things to Consider

Beyond the basics covered above, a coach may also need to consider matters such as a medical release form for each participant and you should also have emergency contact details for each squad member. Ultimately, a participant in any kind of sport should be fully aware of the safety risks involved in his or her chosen sport and how he or she can best prevent accidents or injuries from happening, or, at least, minimize the risk and, while this would be true of most athletes, the coach also has a responsibility to ensure that the safety of the participants is continually reinforced so that all athletes under his supervision can enjoy their sport safely.

11

Coaching Athletes with a Disability

There are millions of people out there ignoring disabilities and accomplishing incredible feats. I learned you can learn to do things differently, but do them just as well. I've learned that it's not the disability that defines you, it's how you deal with the challenges the disability presents you with. And I've learned that we have an obligation to the abilities we *do* have, not the disability.

Jim Abbott
[one-handed professional baseball player for the NY Yankees]

This chapter aims to answer all the commonly asked questions about disabled participants in sport and how to set up a coaching session to suit their needs. It gives advice on how to plan a session or make minor adjustments to the way you work to make coaching more effective. You do not necessarily need special training to work with disabled people in sport. What you do need is sport-specific knowledge and skills, coupled with the confidence and understanding to make any appropriate adjustments to the ways in which you already work in your own sport.

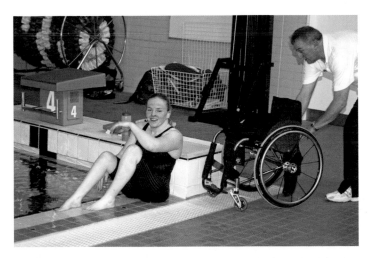

Figure 53 Disabled athlete and coach.

155

As with any athlete, the best way for people with a disability to develop sport skills is under the direction of a qualified coach. Coaching athletes or participants with a disability is fundamentally no different from coaching able-bodied people. Initially, however, it is not unusual for coaches who have never worked with such people to worry about whether they can provide the right type of support, be it at the grassroots or at more advanced competitive levels. There may be situations where coaches may not yet be totally confident with their own knowledge or abilities; there may also be questions about safety and about how to communicate properly with a person with a disability. The chapter outlines some stages that coaches may go through when working with athletes with a disability for the first time. Coaches should know that it is normal to experience some unease at first, but that they can go fairly quickly beyond these first reactions to do what they do best: coach.

When the occasion presents itself to coach an athlete with a disability for the first time, a coach's first reaction could be fear or worry about speaking to the person in terms that might be inappropriate. Some coaches may be asking themselves what they can do and have doubts about their own ability to provide adequate coaching support. Others may have a tendency to focus too much on the disability at first, to question how much a person with a disability can accomplish in the playing field or to have concerns about safety. A person new to coaching athletes with an intellectual disability may also question the level of understanding of the athlete or be concerned about behavioural issues. Finally, there may be concerns about the logistics of integrating athletes with a disability into a programme, the reactions of other participants or their parents or even the impact on team or individual performances.

Beyond these first reactions, many coaches may make assumptions about what disabled people can or cannot do. Rather than speculating about the athlete's capabilities, coaches should engage in a frank dialogue. Communication is a key component in any successful coach–athlete relationship, perhaps even more when athletes with a disability are involved. When disabled people decide to join organized sport, most have accepted their disability and are at a stage where many of the initial issues have been addressed. In general, they are also open-minded about discussing personal issues and concerns and this can help coaches better to understand their abilities and motivations.

Once the coach overcomes those initial assumptions and learns more about the person, the general conclusion is that there is not much difference in the same basic skills used for able-bodied athletes. Very quickly, most coaches become curious about the technical aspects of coaching athletes with a disability and reach a degree of comfort in the process. When this occurs, coaches seek and usually find answers to questions such as how the performance of the specific athlete can be improved? They say that reaching this stage is a major victory. The disability is no longer a factor and the focus is on coaching and on helping the person improve his or her athletic abilities.

Classification of Disability

The different types of disability are grouped into broad categories such as mobility impairment, sensory impairment and intellectual impairment. Disabilities are either congenital (present at birth) or acquired (not present at birth, but acquired through a traumatic injury or an illness). Providing extensive information about each type of disability is beyond the scope of this book, but the general classifications for disability sport are presented in Fig. 54. However, coaches should aim to develop a reasonably good understanding of the disability or disabilities of the athletes that they coach. Some basic information, including specific safety considerations and recommendations to coaches, are presented later and interested readers can also find out more about specific disabilities by contacting some of the organizations listed in the Useful Addresses section at the end of the book.

Classification is not unique to disability sport and is simply a structure for competition. In mainstream sports, such as boxing, weightlifting and judo, athletes are categorized by weight classes. In disability sport athletes are grouped into classes determined by the degree of function presented by their disability.

The International Paralympic Committee (IPC) recognizes six different disability groups. These are:

- amputees
- athletes with cerebral palsy
- blind or visually-impaired athletes
- spinal cord-injured athletes
- athletes with an intellectual/learning disability
- other athletes (*les autres*) with a physical disability who do not fit into any of the above groups.

The British Paralympic Association takes the lead from the IPC in recognizing eligible sports participants.

Each IPC sport has processes and procedures for classification which conform to guidelines laid down by the IPC. Each sport has a well trained international team of classifiers drawn largely from a medical, physiotherapy or sports technical background. Classifiers often operate in panels of three and include a representative from each professional group within each panel.

An athlete class is determined by a physical and technical assessment and observation in and out of competition. Classification is an ongoing process. On entry into international competition, new athletes will carry the status (N). Athletes whose classification is under review because their impairment is progressive or the classifiers are still undecided will carry the status (R). Athletes whose class has been confirmed will have a status (C). Some athletes are reviewed over many years, and athletes with the (C) status sometimes have their class reviewed if new information becomes available.

Classes are defined by each sport and form part of the sport rules. Individual sports have the responsibility for the education and training of classifiers. Classifiers are now largely sport-specific, whereas at one time they covered several sports.

At the Commonwealth Games there are events for elite athletes with a disability (EAD). Before each Games it is decided which sports will offer EAD events. In the major sports of swimming and athletics EAD athletes compete under their own IPC international class against the world record of that specific class. The athlete closest to the world record is judged the winner of the event.

Figure 54 Disability sport classifications.

Generally, children with a disability have limitations from congenital conditions such as spina bifida, cerebral palsy, blindness or intellectual disabilities, while people who became disabled as adults were involved in accidents or were afflicted with a major illness. For the coach, it may be important to know whether a disability was acquired or congenital. A person who acquired a disability in an accident may possess skills from previous sport experience and may know about training but now need to relearn some skills. Someone born with a disability has typically adjusted to how his or her body operates; however, sport opportunities may have been limited and as a result some motor or sport-specific skills may be delayed.

People with a disability have usually gone through rehabilitation or therapy during which they have provided their life story on numerous occasions to nurses, doctors and others. Sharing personal information about their disability is generally not an issue. You probably do not need to go into details about how someone got injured, but a good question for the coach would be how the disability affects the ability to balance or whether the athlete needs more side support – information that concerns his ability to perform in sport. Behavioural patterns may differ greatly among people with an intellectual disability. Assessment methods are available to help coaches to identify the situations that may cause changes in behaviour and information is available on specific strategies to manage these situations effectively. Some athletes with a disability may also need medication. Other than for the most severely disabled athletes (sometimes conditions such as multiple sclerosis can have associated illnesses that require regular medical attention), the general medication issues for people with a disability are the same as with able-bodied people. For example, medication may be required for diabetes, asthma, a heart condition or seizures.

Just being with the athletes and watching how they conduct themselves and react to situations on and off the playing field is a good way to know the individuals. Initially, the person with a disability (or, in the case of young children, a parent) is the best judge of what the individual can or cannot do on the playing field. The best way to get these answers is to ask. Some athletes with an intellectual disability can easily explain their needs and objectives to a coach, while others may not be as articulate or as clear. Therefore it may be essential for the coach to talk to a parent or guardian to learn more about the disability.

People with a disability will have the same goals and expectations as able-bodied athletes when they enter a sports programme for the first time. It is important for the coach to discuss with the person how those goals will be established and realized. Goals have to be realistic and achievable, but not limiting for the individual. The slogan 'see the potential, not the limitations' should apply. Everyone has the right to take risks and to fail and this applies to people with a disability as much as to any other athletes.

Assessment

An assessment of the physical, cognitive and social aspects of athletes with disabilities is essential in order to provide them with adequate support and sound programming. An athlete with a physical disability may have difficulty with movements, a low fitness level or hyperactivity. Intellectual disabilities may lead to learning delays, short attention spans, difficulty with abstract concepts and difficulty with the transferring of learning. Social aspects of athletes with disabilities are similar to those of able-bodied athletes, such as resistance to change, difficulty with transition and routines, difficulty following standard behaviours, frustration and fear of failure. One of the first challenges a coach can face with a disabled athlete is determining his or her fitness level, coordination skills and natural sport instincts. As with other matters, the process is similar to that with able-bodied athletes. However, the coach must sometimes be creative while implementing or devising tests to ensure that they are compatible for the various groups and levels of disability.

Getting to know the person first should be encouraged from the start as both the coach and the athlete with a disability get to know each other better. The coach can communicate a feeling of enthusiasm that this athlete has joined the group and how much the individual will benefit from the programme. It helps if the coach can display a knowledge of the athlete's talents, for instance, past sport or academic success. Of course, the usual questions about why a person chose a certain sport, what the short- and long-term goals are and what the commitment is to the programme are all important. Ultimately, the key is not to ignore the disability but to get past it and see the person for who she or he is.

Figure 55 Boccia timeout.

> The coach should create a welcoming environment and that includes displaying some knowledge of sport for people with disability. The coach should refer to the person as an athlete first, who just happens not to see or walk or whatever the disability is. The coach should emphasize right away that the athlete is part of the group, just like any other athlete. In the end, the most important thing is to get to know the person first, then get into specifics.

Parental Attitudes

When people dream of becoming parents, they never think that their child could have a disability. The parents of healthy children are challenged every day, but when the disability factor comes into play, both the child and the parents must face emotionally charged issues such as access and acceptance. When children with a disability join organized sport for the first time, some may not have been as active as their able-bodied counterparts and their motor skills can be delayed. Those with intellectual and learning disabilities may have been teased at school. Understandably, many parents are cautious about sport, since sometimes the basic stages of early life that able-bodied people take for granted have been more challenging for them and their children up to that point.

Experienced coaches agree that, initially, many parents tend to be nervous about registering a child with a disability in sports. Concerns include social integration, safety, access and needs. A common viewpoint from coaches is that these parents are generally overprotective. Coaches who encounter such parents may communicate that their child has the same rights as anybody else to participate in sport and enjoy its challenges and risks. Once the child is on the playing field, the goal is for the parents to discover the values of sport in social development – the increased discipline, teamwork, self-esteem, social interaction and social responsibility of the child. The overall picture with parents of disabled children is much the same as with the parents of able-bodied children. Some parents drop their children off at club sessions and return later to pick them up. Others are keen to get involved in aspects of volunteering. A parent's involvement is not necessary in most cases, but is a great benefit to the programme when offered. Many people who volunteer in sport are, or started out as, parents of participants.

How Parents and Volunteers Can Help

In sports for people with a disability, parents should be aware that, if they can spare the time, their services could be extremely valuable to a coach. A visually-impaired swimmer, for example, may need a tapper (a person on poolside with a long stick who lets them know when the wall is approaching by 'tapping' them on the head). Visually-impaired cyclists and runners may need guides. In team sports, the coach may need an assistant to keep playing time equitable. Parents can also assist in training drills and transportation issues. It is important to make sure that able-bodied help does not come only from the coach and that the mindset should start at the grassroots level.

The need for volunteers may increase when disabled athletes are involved. Tasks can include helping with transfers, loading and unloading equipment from a car and help in a change room. Such jobs are not necessarily the coach's responsibility and, by doing them, the coach might be sacrificing time that should be devoted to other athletes. These extra needs should be discussed by coach and athlete and a strategy or support to provide for these needs should be developed.

The Value of Sport

Sports can open a new world of access for the disabled: they become stronger, gain more endurance and are generally healthier and more confident outside the sporting arena. But these benefits are not limited to the

Dos and Don'ts of Coaching Disabled Participants

- Do not be scared to ask questions
- the dos and don'ts for communicating with people with a disability vary from person to person and disability to disability; ultimately, most coaches learn as they go along what is out of bounds by developing relationships with their athletes
- ensure equal treatment
- when working with a disabled athlete, the coach should aim to individualize his or her interventions as would be done with other athletes – no more, no less (a coach learns through experience how to handle these situations)
- for people with a disability, coaches must never assume that the athletes don't understand; their disability doesn't necessarily mean that they don't have the abilities to listen and learn
- have a well-structured practice plan and use a progressive approach with athletes with an intellectual disability
- activities must be adapted to the athletes' developmental age; in the same group, there may be participants of differing age and it may be necessary to implement activities and drills that suit different developmental stages, this illustrates the importance of good planning and organization.

participants themselves. Ultimately, everyone gains from the inclusion of people with a disability in sport. There are numerous illustrations of why this can be the case: parents of a child with a disability should know that sport helps the child to be more self-sufficient, which can help them to do better in school; in sport they challenge themselves and do things on their own; other children may be highly strung and sport can help them to be active; and finally, just for their health, because they are active, their whole body will be healthier. There is also a value from inclusion for able-bodied athletes. Sports such as cycling, skiing and running for the visually impaired may require guides. The Olympic gold medal sprint cyclist Craig Mclean has retired from able-bodied sport to work with Paralympic riders in preparation for the 2012 Olympic Games in London.

There is no shortage of sport opportunities for persons with disabilities. Some sports, such as goalball for the visually impaired, wheelchair rugby for quadriplegics and boccia (a popular sport for athletes with cerebral palsy at which Britain are World and Paralympic champions), are unique to them. Others, such as swimming and athletics, offer competitive opportunities at almost all levels and with all types of disability. In some instances, disabled athletes may also compete with able-bodied athletes. For instance, alpine skiing offers options to athletes with disability to compete in certain age groups with the able-bodied or with masters. Likewise, able-bodied individuals can train and compete in some sport activities for persons with disabilities, such as wheelchair basketball. But these are far from being the only disciplines in which the disabled can train and compete.

Figure 56 Paralympic champions.

Accessibility

Accessibility for the disabled remains an issue in today's society. There are many facets to it and many improvements still to be made and recognized by governments, building operators and the population in general. Improved accessibility can benefit everyone, not only people with a disability. For example, people travelling with children in prams or with heavy luggage probably prefer an elevator to an escalator. People with a temporary leg injury may benefit from a railing on an access ramp. It should be noted that the term accessibility not only means easy to reach, but also easy to use.

Transportation is an accessibility issue for persons with a disability in sport right across the board. Whether an athlete is in a wheelchair, has an intellectual disability or lives with cerebral palsy, transportation to facilities and events is an issue, particularly for adults. The cost of accessible vehicles and the availability of them are other major concerns. Hiring a bus with a lift for people in wheelchairs costs about three times more than hiring a conventional bus. Coaches should be aware of and sensitive to transportation issues and can assist in overcoming this barrier by exploring options. Perhaps another athlete in the programme lives close to the athlete with transportation needs and can help?

People in wheelchairs generally face the biggest transportation problems. Some can require adaptable vans and special buses; however, those buses don't go by the front door every 10min. They must be reserved. Most other people with a disability can generally manage with the same transportation options as anyone else, such as buses, but in smaller communities drivers could be needed for assistance.

In the United Kingdom, the Disability Discrimination Act (2005) has legislated for improved accessibility, which is good news for all disabled people in sport or not. Many facilities, whether schools or community centres, are accessible but access to playing fields can be a major barrier for anyone wanting to pursue a sport. Still, there are other facility concerns, including accessible changing rooms and toilets. However, most modern facilities house rooms that can at least be modified to be accessible.

12

Long-Term Planning

'Even the longest journey must begin where you stand.'

This quotation is a more literal translation of the popular 'a journey of a thousand miles begins with a single step' from the writings of the Chinese philosopher Lao-Tzu. It is still relevant for the planning we undertake in coaching, as no matter where we want to end up, it always starts from where we are, not where we would like to be.

PERIODIZATION

Training plans evolve from general objectives through a series of stages to the most specific objectives. Each level of planning should fit into the next, providing a framework for key programme decisions. It is best to document and review your plans from time to time to assess what progress has been made. Planning must take into account a number of variables, which may, or may not, be under the direct control of the coach. Considerations such as playing facility access, gym training facilities, squad numbers and the characteristics of squad members will differ from one sport to the next. However, the process of logically constructing both long- and short-term programmes remains the same. The operation of those plans will naturally differ from one coach to another, based upon individual circumstances. You should first have a basis for long-term programme decisions. Most sports now have a Long Term Athlete Development (LTAD) framework. Each coach's philosophy will shape decisions made at every level of planning, but it is useful to have a reference guide for several of the major developmental parameters – such as number of training sessions, type of session, age/maturation-based training objectives and number and type of competition.

LTAD is about achieving optimal training, competition and recovery throughout an athlete's career, particularly in relation to the important growth and development years of young people. If a long-term approach to training is not adopted there is likely to be a plateau in performance when growth and development slow significantly, which for some athletes may result in their performances getting worse. At this point the short-term training approach cannot be reversed. This often leads to drop out before an athlete has achieved close to his potential.

There are five clear reasons for introducing a LTAD approach:

- to establish a clear athlete development pathway
- to identify gaps in the current development pathway
- to realign and integrate the programmes for developing athletes and the sport
- to provide a planning tool, based on scientific research, for coaches, and
- administrators and to guide planning for optimal performance.

The following are some general observations on sporting systems from around the world (including Britain): young athletes under-train and over-compete; there are low training to competition ratios in the early years of development; adult competitions are superimposed on young athletes; male programmes are superimposed on females; training in the early years focuses on outcomes (winning) rather than processes (optimal training); chronological age influences coaching rather than biological age; the 'critical' periods of accelerated adaptation are not fully utilized; poor training between six and sixteen years of age cannot be fully corrected (athletes will never reach genetic potential); the best coaches are encouraged to work at elite level; coach education tends to skim the growth, development and maturation of young people; coaches, athletes and parents need to be educated in LTAD principles; and administrators and officials need to be educated in these principles.

LTAD is a sports development framework that is based on human growth and development. In short, it is about adopting an athlete-centred approach to sports development. All young people follow the same pattern of growth from infancy through adolescence, but there are significant individual differences in both the timing and the magnitude of the changes that take place (*see* the next section for more details). It is important to stress that human growth and development happen without training; however, sports-specific training can enhance all of the changes that take place. Research tells us that there are critical periods in the life of a young person in which the effects of training can be maximized. This has led to the notion that young people should be exposed to specific types of training during periods of rapid growth and that these should change with the patterns of growth. These have been used to devise a generic, five-stage LTAD framework that has been adapted by most sports to suit their specific needs (some have more than five stages):

- FUNdamentals – basic movement literacy
- Learning to Play and Practice – building skills and technique
- Training to Train – building the capacity to improve
- Training to Compete – optimizing the performance
- Training to Win – top performance.

Stage 1 – FUNdamentals: Basic Movement Literacy (girls 5 to 8 years; boys 6 to 9 years)

The FUNdamentals stage should be structured and fun. The emphasis is on developing basic movement literacy and fundamental movement skills. The skills to be developed are the ABCs (Agility, Balance, Coordination, Speed), RJT (Running, Jumping, Throwing), KGBs (Kin-esthetics, Gliding, Buoyancy, Striking with the body) and CKs (Catching, Kicking, Striking with an implement). In order to develop basic movement literacy successfully participation in as many sports as possible should be encouraged. Speed, power and endurance should be developed using fun and games. In addition, children should be introduced to the simple rules and ethics of sports. No periodization should take place, but there should be well-structured programmes with proper progressions that are monitored regularly.

Stage 2 – Learning to Play and Practice: Building Skills and Technique (girls 8 to 11 years; boys 9 to 12 years)

During this stage youngsters should learn how to train and develop the skills of a specific sport. There may be participation in complementary sports, that is, those sports which use similar energy systems and movement patterns. They should also learn the basic technical/tactical skills and ancillary capacities such as: warm up and cool down; stretching; hydration and nutrition; recovery; relaxation and focusing. This stage coincides with peak motor coordination, therefore there should be an emphasis on skill development. Training should also include the use of 'own body weight' exercises, for instance, medicine ball and Swiss ball exercises as well as developing suppleness. Although the focus is on training, competition should be used to test and refine skills. The recommended training to competition ratio is 75 to 25 per cent. If a young athlete misses this stage of development then he/she will never reach full potential. One of the main reasons athletes plateau during the later stages of their careers is because of an overemphasis on competition instead of optimizing training during this important stage.

Stage 3 – Training to Train: Building the Capacity to Improve (girls 11 to 14 years; boys 12 to 15 years)

During the Training to Train stage, there should be an emphasis on all-round conditioning. This is the stage where there is greater individualization of fitness and technical training. The focus should still be on training rather than competition and the training should be predominantly of high volume, low intensity workloads. It is important to emphasize that high volume, low intensity training cannot be achieved in a limited period and therefore the time commitment to training should increase significantly. As the volume of training increases, there is likely to be a reduction in the number of competitions undertaken. However, there should now be specific targets for each competition undertaken with a view to learning basic tactics and mental preparation.

During this stage, training should continue to develop suppleness and to include the use of 'own body weight' exercises; medicine ball and Swiss ball exercises. However, towards the end of this stage, preparations should be made for the development of strength, which for girls occurs at the end of this stage and for boys at the beginning of the next stage. This should include learning correct strength training techniques. The ancillary capacities (the knowledge base of how to warm up and warm down; how to stretch and when to stretch; how to optimize nutrition and hydration; mental preparation; regeneration; how and when to taper and peak; pre-competition, competition and post-competition routines) should already be established. As with the previous stage, if insufficient time is devoted to it or it is missed, then the young athlete will never reach his full potential.

Stage 4 – Training to Compete: Optimizing the Performance (girls 14 to 16 years; boys 15 to 18 years)

During the training to compete stage there should be a continued emphasis on physical conditioning with the focus on maintaining high-volume workloads but with increasing intensity. The number of competitions should be similar to those in the previous stage, but the emphasis should be on developing individual strengths and weaknesses through modelling and nurturing technical and tactical skills based around specific competitive goals. As a result, there should be either more patterned periodization of the training year. In addition, the ancillary capacities should be refined so they are more specific to the individual's needs. During this stage training should also focus on developing maximum strength and power gains through the use of adjunct training. This should be coupled with continued work on core body strength and maintaining flexibility.

Stage 5 – Training to Win: Top Performance! (females: 16+ years; males: 18+ years)

This is the final stage of preparation. The emphasis should be on specialization and performance enhancement. All of the athletes' physical, technical, tactical, mental and ancillary capacities should now be fully established, with the focus shifting to the optimization of performance. Athletes should be trained to peak for specific competitions and major events. Therefore all aspects of training should be individualized for specific events. There should be sport-specific periodization, depending on the events being trained for.

Start with a yearly (or perhaps a 2–3-year cycle would be more appropriate) calendar and target the important competitions that your athletes are training for. You may need to replicate this exercise for various age groupings and/or ability levels. Next, determine the long- and the medium-term preparation requirements for each training level. These requirements must satisfactorily address the background requirements needed for athletes to achieve their goals (skill, maturation, fitness, competition experience) and the intermediate performance goals that lead up to the major objective. Coaches must also ask what improvements will be required to reach the major objectives? Are these performance improvements realistic for the age/ability of athletes in the club/squad?

Now, based upon the requirements of each training group, determine the single-season objectives. A training season may be 6–7 months for some athletes or a complete year for others. This training 'season' is usually called a macrocycle. The novice coach may find it difficult to estimate the amount of improvement possible during a season, but experience and help from mentors will help in this regard. Within each season's training there may be several intermediate objectives. The length of time a coach devotes to achieving these objectives (which have a fitness or skill base) is called a mesocycle. For example, three fundamentals of every training programme are: improvement of fitness, improvement of speed and improvement of technique. The attainment of these objectives allows the athlete to train more specifically to competition objectives. Therefore specific periods during the season must focus on these fundamentals.

However, training must never focus so closely on one fundamental that the others are neglected. Training is always a mixture of several things, usually with at least a primary and a secondary focus. The length of each training cycle will depend upon the major training objective (some objectives take longer than others to achieve). There is also variation within any group of athletes that determines each athlete's ability to absorb and adapt to the training programme. Physiology texts will suggest that adaptation to specific types of training stimulus will take so many weeks to achieve. However, because coaches work with a wide range of ages, maturation levels and abilities, it would be difficult to suggest that one plan fits all. The length of any adaptation period is also influenced by each athlete's training background.

Within each mesocycle most coaches plan each week's training as a measurable training unit or microcycle. Some full-time coaches of full-time athletes use slightly smaller units (2–4 days) or somewhat longer units (for example, 14 days) to fit their plans, especially when using specialized training. Each microcycle contains smaller training units, such as individual training days or training sessions. Planning training programmes within units of time allows the coach to control the application of the stress-recovery-adaptation sequence of events. Finally, the coach must actually plan and implement each training session. Based upon the planning outline, each training session will be structured to reflect the desired outcomes within that micro-meso-macrocycle.

Every training session will contain these core components: *i.* warm-up activities that prepare the athlete for other types of training (these may also address fitness and skill-related objectives); *ii.* activities specific to one or two primary training objectives (these are designed to achieve some physiological, psychological or tactical objective); *iii.* activities that contribute to recovery (this may be the traditional cool-down or a routine that contributes to primary or secondary training objectives, if they happen to be recovery orientated). You may also wish to include a secondary training

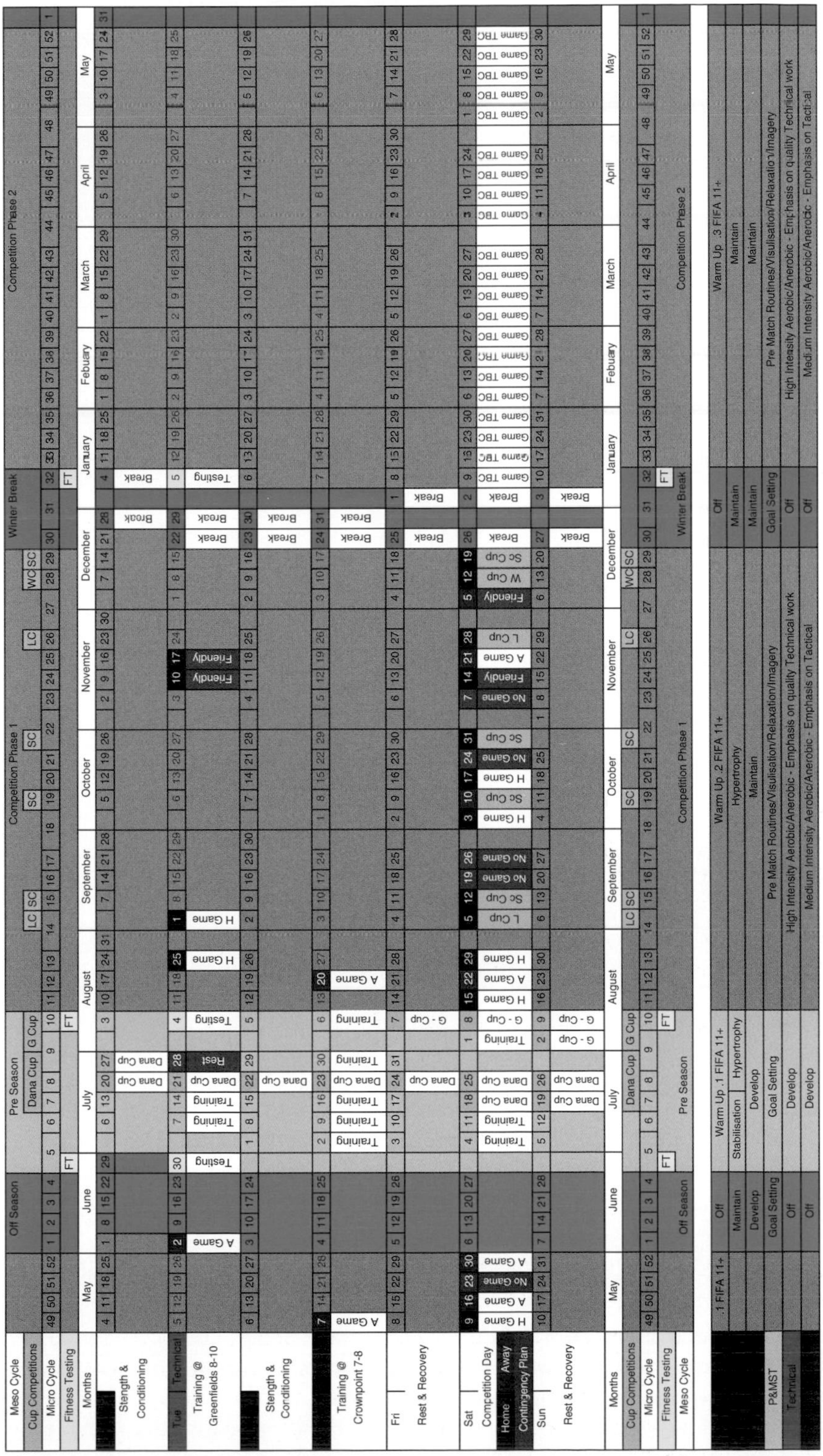

Figure 57a Annual plan for football.

Name _____

Gym based maintanance session x2 / Week		
Resistance Exercise	80% of 1RM - 1 Set x 8-10 Reps	
Load Kg's		
Leg Extension	_____	
Leg Curl	_____	
Leg Press	_____	Ab Curls	3x20
Lat Pulldown	_____	Back Extensions	3x10
Bench Press	_____	Plank	3x30s
Seated Row	_____	Side Plank	3x30s
Shoulder Press	_____	

Flexibility Programme (Focus on Development)		

Static Stretch Exercises - Hold 20s, stretch further for 10s

	Off season	Competitive Phase
Hamstrings	x4 reps	x2 reps
Quads	x4 reps	x2 reps
Glutes	x4 reps	x2 reps
Calf	x4 reps	x2 reps
Groin	x4 reps	x2 reps
Shoulders	x4 reps	x2 reps
Chest	x4 reps	x2 reps
Lower Back	x4 reps	x2 reps
Upper Back	x4 reps	x2 reps
Triceps	x4 reps	x2 reps
Biceps	x4 reps	x2 reps
Abs	x4 reps	x2 reps

Figure 57b Session plan for football during the season.

focus during some or all sessions. This type of approach addresses a secondary (minor) objective. Care must be exercised to construct secondary work that contributes to the overall session, rather than detract from it. Training content is constructed to define a specific training stress and training sets that target primary objectives must be constructed to be consistent with the overall plan.

The major questions every coach must answer (as reflected in the structure of the training programme) include:

- how long should the training season last? (macrocycle)
- how many sessions are appropriate and what am I trying to achieve with this athlete/group? (mesocycle)
- how much training volume and intensity is appropriate to each session? (microcycle)

Principles of Aerobic & Anerobic Training (Bangsbo 1996)						
Aerobic Training						
Anerobic Training	% of HR MAX		Beats/min *		%of VO2 MAX	
	Mean	Range	Mean	Range	Mean	Range
Recovery Training	65	40–80	130	80–160	55	20–70
Low Intensity	80	65 90	160	130 180	70	55 85
High Intensity	90	80–100	180	160–200	85	70–100

*Based on Max HR 200 beats/min

Anaerobic Training				
Training Type	Duration		Intensity	Reps
	Exercises	Rest		
Speed	2–10	>5 to 1	Maximal	2–10
Speed Endurance Production	20–40	>5 to 1	Almost Maximal	2–10
Speed Endurance Maintenance	30–90	Equal to or less than exercise duration	Almost Maximal	2–10

Gym based resistance session x2/Week						
Resistance Exercise	70–85% of 1RM - 3 Sets x 8–10 Reps (Bompa & Carrera 2005)					
	Sets	Reps	Rest	Tempo	Core Work	
Back Squat	3	10	60–90s	2–4	Ab Curls	3x20
Chin Ups	3	max	60–90s	2–4	Back Extensions	3x10
Dips	3	max	60–90s	2–4	Plank	3x30s
Bench Press	3	10	60–90s	2–4	Side Plank	3x30s
Seated Row	3	10	60–90s	2–4		
Shoulder Press	3	10	60–90s	2–4		
Press Ups	3	max	60–90s	2–4		

Figure 58a Training phases for football.

For example, an average twelve-year-old footballer can be expected to handle five training sessions per week of 90min duration or slightly longer. During the course of a season (that may last up to 40 weeks) this player will accumulate well over 200hr of training background. The various training outcomes, skill objectives, cognitive and competition objectives are all identified within the relevant LTAD framework. However, there may be variation based upon individual ability, maturation or past training history. Some twelve-year-old footballers will respond more like a ten-year-old and some like a fourteen-year-old. A young athlete new to the sport may have great physical capacities, but lack the skill components

Under 21's Fitness Test Results

Name:
Test location: Crownpoint
Test conditions: Dry/Sunny
Conducted by:

Body Composition				
Age		20		
Gender		M		
Height (cm)	184cm	184cm		**Target**
Weight (kg)	75	74		Maintain
Skinfolds (mm)	**1**	**Retest 2**	**Retest 3**	**Target**
Bicep	4	5		Maintain
Triceps	6	5		Maintain
Subscapular	4	5		Maintain
Suprailliac	6	5		Maintain
Sum of skinfolds	20	20		Maintain
Body Fat (%)	11%	11%		Maintain
Field tests	**1**	**Retest 2**	**Retest 3**	**Target**
Illinois agility run combined	36	34.4		**<35secs**
Left to right	18.2	17.4		**17.5secs**
Right to left	17.8	17		**17.5secs**
5 hops	11.2	11.8		**>12.00m**
Sit and reach (cms)	10	9		**>20cms**
Abdominal curls (60secs)	40	46		**>55**
Core plank (mins/secs)	50	60		**>60secs**
Standing stork balance test L	22	34		**>40secs**
Standing stork balance test R	15	30		**>40secs**
MSFT	11.2	12.4		**>12**
Press ups (60secs)	33	52		**>40**
20m Sprint	4.2	4		**<4**
Vertical Jump	45	45		**>50cms**
Pull Ups	4	5		**10**

Feedback:

1. Good results for beginning of preseason, work hard to reach your targets
2. Well done, shown great improvements on most aspects, keep up flexibility

Figure 58b Fitness testing for football.

characteristically acquired by others at eight or nine years of age. Therefore the LTAD framework is used as a guide. It should help the coach to identify which developmental areas are on track and which are advanced or behind, but not followed slavishly as a prescriptive tool for all planning.

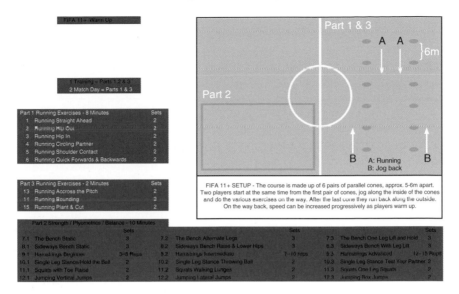

Figure 59 Match-day preparation for football.

TRAINING OBJECTIVES

The planning process outlined above makes reference to training objectives at every stage. Successful planning incorporates all the coach's conceptual models, that is, physiological, technical and psychological. The greatest mistake made by most coaches is their failure to look at the total picture and to keep that in perspective with the age and ability of their athletes. In particular, many coaches do not consider the integration of complementary training within this 'big picture'; for instance, strength and conditioning. Planning a training programme for very young athletes is therefore clear, because the primary objectives of training are narrowly defined. Skill development, aerobic capacity and having fun are the primary objectives, maintaining natural speed and developing competition skills are the secondary objectives. The complexity of the objectives (or lack of complexity in this case) determines the amount of detail that the coach needs to plan. Young athletes do not require large variation in the training plan from one cycle to the next because their training needs are simple. Good advice for coaches working with very young athletes is to devote most of the planning to fun, skills and general fitness. Also, learn how to construct training content that may look different but achieves the same objective. In terms of complementary training, the emphasis should be on general aerobic conditioning, fun games and teaching the key skills and techniques to be used in later, more demanding training cycles. Activities like Swiss ball work and core stability exercises are applicable throughout an athlete's career and should be initiated at this early stage. During the years in which children experience their most rapid physical changes the complexity of training variables changes. Consolidation of technique and continued increases in physical capacity are still important objectives, but factors such as muscle strength to body weight ratio, speed and acceleration and training volume/intensity must also be addressed in the training plan. There should also be an emphasis on improving specific functional strength to be applied in the sport and on developing a platform of sound training habits and routines.

Yet, there are still training variables that should be held in reserve for older athletes. For example, pre-pubertal children will probably increase their aerobic capacity more through maturation and appropriate amounts of training than from frequent exposure to high-intensity training. Young athletes will improve speed and efficiency of movement by perfecting technique and core body strength. Large volumes (as a percentage of the total work accomplished) of high-intensity training will wear children down and can be harmful to their development. Coaches often overestimate the progress of youngsters aged from ten to twelve and begin to train them like mini-adults; resulting in the application of an unrealistic programme and possibly their loss of many to other sports or physical activity altogether. Training objectives for girls aged twelve to thirteen and boys aged thirteen and fourteen begin to change dramatically because their needs are more complex. Provided that earlier training has given these athletes the correct background in technique and aerobic capacity, for example, there are many new training objectives, which must be included in the coaches' plan. The emphasis on training volume and intensity and how they interact, must be carefully reviewed at this stage of an athlete's career. Anaerobic capacity begins to take on greater importance and subtle changes are brought into the complexity of the training plan. There is still awareness that maturational changes are incomplete, very few twelve to thirteen-year-olds reflect the characteristics of senior athletes and the coach must be able to recognize signs of maturity and adjust the programme for both advanced as well as late maturing individuals.

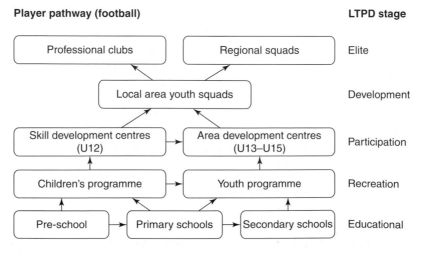

Figure 60 Football player pathway.

Planning training for most mid age-group athletes (fourteen to sixteen-year-olds) is closer to that of seniors, with the exception that recovery mechanisms are still very robust. As a general rule, these teenagers (particularly the girls) will be able to absorb large amounts of work in training. Planning the desired emphasis of training volume and intensity becomes the greatest challenge for the coach. The more talented athletes will now be getting ready to make the transition to higher levels of competition. At this time the coach must be able to assess whether there are significant weaknesses present in the athlete's training profile. In fact, at every stage of development the coach must assess the relative strengths and weaknesses and plan to fill the gaps left from earlier stages or correct potential problems before they become limitations for a senior athlete. Training complexity is again expanded because competition objectives begin to narrow. During the early years there is a relatively equal emphasis on the development of all skills and competition routines, but from the mid-teen years the athlete begins to specialize more. The coach must respond with more specific programmes every year, which require more detailed planning.

The complexity of objectives in the training programme for senior athletes is enormous. Higher levels of competition create different demands on the athlete in every aspect of performance, such as nutrition, mental skills, strength/flexibility, physiological preparation and tactical preparation. Although most coaches (particularly novices) do not train elite level athletes, the training plans designed for these performers are usually the ones every coach wants to study and emulate. Learning from the success or experience of others is important, but learning why and how those results were achieved is perhaps more so. Almost every elite performer can trace his or her training history through a similar process of successfully achieving age-related training objectives. Planning and seeing the whole picture are key to a coach's success.

TRAINING MODEL

This section is about the content of your coaching intervention. Planning is about devising or constructing the most appropriate coaching intervention to achieve the goals that have been agreed. The emphasis is often on the 'structure' of the intervention – periodization, yearly plans, levels of intensity, peaking and so on. However, we need to have attention given to the 'content'. The available literature, such as it is, is all about the appropriate manipulation of the content, without comment on what this is, how it is devised, how it develops and how decisions are made about it. It may also be the case that content-related matters are considered to be 'not for discussion' in order to preserve each coach's secrets. Nevertheless, it is assumed that coach education is devised to give coaches the 'technical' knowledge required to do the job. You may question whether this is done well and you may speculate that the packaging of 'content' is easier for the novice coach than for the more experienced one, for whom the technical package is more extensive, more sophisticated and (perhaps) more individual. You may have views on this and how your sport disseminates its technical information, advice and guidance.

Many books on planning have sections on modelling the training process. This is a useful device for introducing the 'technical model' into the planning context. To some extent, modelling performance is relatively straightforward as a concept and something that you might take for granted. Nevertheless, it raises questions about the coaches' interventions that are a valuable reflective tool.

Modelling simply refers to establishing an 'image' of the intended performance and using this to plan or devise the training or preparation context. Note that when you do this you 'image' it and not 'imagine' it. The capacity to image the required performance is something that is not often mentioned in coaching education or other literature. To some extent this is not rocket science – clearly coaches would be expected to have something to guide the decisions they make – having a clear idea of the required and intended performance model might be a minimal expectation. However, there are significant questions:

(a) Do you have this as a mental model?
(b) What is this 'image' like – is it a series of 'pictures', a set of propositions, or a list of requirements?
(c) Is this image flexible, can it be contextualized and can it be individualized?
(d) Do you find it easy to 'de-image' it into component requirements?
(e) How is this used to devise your coaching intervention?
(f) How 'sophisticated' is this? In other words, is it detailed or is it a 'big picture'?

This concept of modelling asks you to reflect on what you do. However, it is sometimes described in a narrower way, as an attempt to direct and organize training in such a way that the objectives, methods and content are similar to those of a competition. It may be that this is a useful reminder that a significant part of the team's preparation should include demands that match those of the competition. This would apply to physical conditioning, technical, psychological and tactical interventions.

Are you able to 'deconstruct' the image/model into priorities, component requirements and training loads in such a way that it retains this planning integrity, but addresses immediate needs? Perhaps if training is 'modelled', there will not be any distance between the immediate needs of the competition (that is, next week's game) and longer-term developments – which may be an answer for the team sport coach, particularly the part-time one.

TRAINING PRINCIPLES

Individuality

Every individual is different and will respond to training in a unique way. This may seem obvious, but research conducted in the United Kingdom has shown that most swimming programmes are conducted on a group or squad basis and that only the highest level performers have anything close to an individualized programme. There are many reasons for this (with lack of resources the major one cited), but, nevertheless, acknowledging the individual response to training is a fundamental tenet of designing and implementing effective training programmes. For example, in designing a land training programme for swimmers, coaches should consider the participants' chronological age, training age, sex, the event, the distance and so on.

Adaptation

Training has an effect on the human body, indeed, the very purpose of training is to have the desired effect on the body or, more specifically, its processes. This, or these, effect(s) are governed by the principle of adaptation. Placing the systems in the body under stress will produce responses associated with the type of training performed. For example, a common adaptation (inappropriate for many sports) to strength training is hypertrophy of muscle fibres. Unless the correct training is prescribed, this may result in the athletes becoming more muscle bound, heavier and slower in the water, quite the opposite from the original intention. Some training adaptations take place in a matter of days while others may take weeks or months. For effective training adaptations there must be: *i.* correct training; *ii.* nutrients for growth and repair of tissues; and *iii.* sufficient rest for growth and repair to take place.

Overload

Probably the most important principle of all, the concept of overload in training, is almost certainly the oldest of all. In order for adaptations to take place, the stress on the body's systems must be significant enough for physiological changes to occur, that is, greater than 'usual'. The same stimuli will not provoke continued improvements and therefore the principle of overloading must be applied. There is a danger in overloading and it is the careful application of this principle that brings us to the next consideration.

Progression

Often coupled with overload as a double-whammy principle, the use of a progressive or stepwise approach to training prescription is the most obvious application of periodization in action. Too much loading at once could result in overtraining or injury and too little could result in no improvements being made. Sports like swimming, running, rowing and cycling are examples of where it is easy to see the principles of progressive overload being used, For example, longer distances, less rest, more repetitions, faster effort and so on. The systematic treatment of training programmes in a structured and progressive manner is the result of careful and considered planning by effective coaches. In terms of auxiliary training, the progressive overload principle is also easily controlled with time, resistance and sets/reps being the most dominant variables.

Specificity

Although another obvious principle, the use of specificity by coaches is at times questionable. It is easy to note that regular swimming or cycling will not improve running performance, but research again shows that coaches are less than precise about their specific, individualized prescription of training. Coaches should consider the following four aspects when applying the principle of specificity: *i.* the sport; *ii.* the position/role of the player; *iii.* the training status of the athlete and *iv.* the energy system demands of these combined. By considering these aspects alongside the individual characteristics of each athlete, an appropriate and challenging training programme can be designed.

Variation

As far as skill learning is concerned, the greater the range of opportunities given to athletes, the greater the likelihood that they will improve. In all training, this should mean that coaches are innovative and challenging with the range of exercises and options they prescribe; for example, can you devise an exercise that is more position-specific for a rugby full-back? The use of the variation principle can sometimes be overdone and care should be taken to use variety as a motivational tool rather than simply an end in its own right.

Reversibility

Often simplified to 'if you don't use it, you lose it", this principle is more obvious after a period away from training, as athletes discover how hard it is to gain fitness over a period of time, but how easy it is to lose it much more quickly. In terms of auxiliary training, this is often thought of as an issue in relation to strength gains made through weight training being lost when the training is discontinued. If no other training is done to build on these gains, then obviously they will be lost, but as long as 'conversion' training is done to apply the gains in the competition context, the issue is less important.

Balance

Associated with the principle of variation, this recognizes that you cannot do everything at once. Applying training principles successfully requires as much art as science and the principle of balance is where the coach can be creative in the design and implementation of training. For example, determining how much and what types of training to do in the gym is just as important as when and how much game/competition training should be done.

Long-Term Planning

'It takes ten years of extensive practice to excel in anything' according to the Nobel Laureate H.A. Simon. This is never more true than in the field of training for sports performance. Translating the quotation into the language of elite performance, this is 3–4hr per day of deliberate practice for ten years and is supported by empirical and anecdotal evidence from successful performers across the world in sport, the arts, music and business.

13

Elite Sport

The Olympic Games were created for the exaltation of the individual athlete.

Pierre de Coubertin

Figure 61 High-performance sport.

Although not a specific focus of this book, the consideration of the elite sport environment and subsequent implications for coaches is an interesting topic to review. The Olympic environment is thought to be an important factor affecting the performance of athletes and teams. Following the Olympic Games in Atlanta, in the USA, coaches and athletes were consistent in saying that the Olympics are unique when matched with all other competitions. Some teams and coaches used these differences to enhance performance, while other teams failed to perform up to expectations in the unique setting. Examining the reasons for these performance differences was the focus of a major study conducted by Professor Dan Gould and his colleagues.

Its purpose was to identify and examine factors that were perceived to have positively or negatively affected the performance of American Olympic athletes and coaches before and during the 1996 Atlanta Games. The study used a two-phase questionnaire and interview data collection procedure. In the questionnaire phase, surveys were developed and administered to all US athletes and coaches who participated in the 1996 Games. The questions asked in the surveys were based on interviews conducted with nine US Olympic Committee (USOC) staff members who had attended a number of previous Games (such as sport psychologists, athletics trainers and games preparation administrators, NGB high-performance plan evaluations and USOC Games debriefing coaches summit notes. Notable areas included in the survey were: participant background; Olympic expectations and readiness; the importance of mental skills in Olympic performance; factors influencing performance in the year leading up to the Games and at the Games (such as athlete preparation, media, team influences, coaching, family, sponsors, staffing and environmental). In total, 296 athlete and forty-six coach surveys were completed.

In addition to the surveys, the interview phase of the project involved interviews with individual athletes, coaches and teams. Specifically, in-person coach and focus group interviews (involving two to five athletes) were conducted with four highly successful teams that equalled or exceeded performance expectations at the Games and four teams that performed below expectations. Telephone interviews with eight athletes (four who met or exceeded expectations and four who did not) were also conducted. The interviews lasted between 30 and 90min and focused on the same types of question asked in the surveys. The goal of the interviews, however, was to try to obtain a feel for each team's or athlete's individual Olympic experience and detailed explanations of the factors that affected performance.

The several methods used focused on understanding the differences between those athletes, coaches and teams that performed well in Atlanta and those that did not meet their performance expectations. They also attempted to identify factors that athletes in general perceived to have both positively and negatively influenced Olympic performance. Results from the study were encouraging, indicating that clear differences did, in fact, exist between those who met or exceeded performance expectations and those who struggled. Major factors perceived to positively or negatively influence performance and/or to discriminate between athletes performing well and those failing to meet expectations are presented below. What is interesting about these results is that, although the context is elite sport, there are many lessons to be learned by coaches in all domains.

Major Findings (Gould et al., 1998)

Based on all the sources of information collected, one thing became clear to the investigative team: successful Olympic performance is a complex, multifaceted, fragile and long-term process that requires extensive planning and painstaking implementation. It seldom happens by chance and can easily be disrupted by numerous distractions. Attention to detail counts, but it must also be accompanied by flexibility to deal with unexpected events.

The following factors were identified as being critical considerations in Olympic preparation.

Distraction Preparation

Olympians must be ready to deal with distractions generated from a variety of sources at the Games. Successful athletes and teams drew energy from the Olympic excitement, while not getting too caught up in the distractions. Specifically, successful athletes and teams had plans and systems to deal with distractions and successfully implemented those plans. Often they were characterized by a 'single-minded focus' that helped them to make appropriate decisions relative to distractions that arose at the Games. Common distractions included such things as dealing with the media; getting tickets; getting transportation; dealing with families and significant others; participating in the opening ceremonies; and coping with all the hoopla associated with the Games.

Plans and Adherence to Plans

Unsuccessful teams and athletes more often deviated from plans and preparation routines at the Games. While making adjustments when needed, more successful teams and athletes had clear physical and mental preparation plans going into the Games and adhered to those. They also anticipated potential distractions and had plans in place to deal with such events.

Optimal Physical Training

As one would expect, optimal physical conditioning and training are needed for Olympic success. These results, however, revealed that there is a fine line between training intensively to gain an edge over your opponents and going too far and overtraining. Athletes and teams that did not perform well often overtrained. This seemed to result from two factors: (1) when athletes are in optimal condition they are very 'fragile' and can easily become ill or overtrain; and (2) because of Olympic pressure to perform there is a tendency to overdo preparation in an effort to get the 'edge' and, in so doing, not take enough mental and physical breaks.

Mental Preparation

Both successful and less successful teams and athletes experienced stress at and leading up to the Games. More successful teams and athletes, however, had mentally prepared themselves to deal with unexpected events and stressors. They had worked with sport psychology specialists and integrated this mental training into a total preparation package via coach involvement and understanding. Hence, they were prepared to deal with the stress associated with the Games and either neutralized negative events or reframed them as positive influences. Interestingly, less successful teams and athletes often had some exposure to mental training, but noted that they did not do enough or spend enough time on this area.

Team Cohesion and Harmony

Regardless of whether an individual or team sport was involved, team cohesion and harmony factors were critical for Olympic success. Successful teams had a single-minded focus and a trust in their ability to succeed. Not only did this trust and focus come from experience (which was critical), but also from team-building activities that occurred in the years before the Games. Athletes on these teams were also confident in their own abilities and provided peer leadership for their teams.

Coaching

As one would expect, coach–athlete relationships and coaching issues were critical factors involved in Olympic performance. If personal, as well as appointed team coaches, were involved in a sport, successful teams made provisions to provide access to those coaches and/or to clearly define coaching roles. In addition, successful teams had coaches who were able to 'read' their athletes' physical and psychological readiness states and adjust training accordingly. More successful coaches knew what to expect at the Games, were able to stay focused and did not over-coach. They also had the ability to handle crises and stay cool under pressure. Finally, coach–athlete trust and respect was fostered.

Support Personnel

While NGB and support personnel are critical to Olympic success, having the right support personnel in place is even more critical for the athletes' best performances. These individuals must understand the performance demands of elite sport and balance the provision of services with staying out of the way and not interfering with other performance factors. Inexperienced support personnel who lacked

Continued

knowledge of high performance sport had negative effects on performances. Organizational consistency is critical in this regard, as well
as the importance of minimizing NGB politics in the process. Finally,
athletes indicated that the ideal support team personnel would include
specialists in sports medicine, massage therapists, personal coaches
and sport psychology specialists.

Team Training/Residency Programmes

Successful teams spent a good deal of time training together before the
Games. In some cases this may have involved a residency programme.
In other cases, it was characterized by having the ability to bring a team
in for numerous competitions and training and competitive camps.

Family/Friends

Family and friends were found to be either a tremendous source of
support or a major distraction for the athletes. Athletes and teams that
performed more successfully at the Games had helped family and
friends to understand how to support the athletes without interfering
with preparation and competition. Planning and structure were especially important when dealing with this issue.

Media

The two media factors that most affected performance were the
amount of media attention received and whether the athlete or team
had media training and a coordinated media plan. Media issues were
not major performance concerns for those teams and athletes that
had media training, an effective media coordinator and a media plan.
Finally, support personnel dealing with media and public relations
need to balance the need/desire for PR and promotion of the sport
with the athletes' needs for preparation and competition.

Sponsors

For the most part, sponsors were not identified as a factor that im-
pacted on performance. However, business decisions were noted as a
source of distraction that did for a substantial number of athletes.

International Competition

While being careful not to overtrain, to participate in a number of high
quality international competitions in the year before the Games was
identified as a critical factor for performance success.

Team Selection and Trials

The timing of team trials and selection was seen as a critical perform-
ance-influencing factor, especially if the selection process occurred too

close to the Games. Moreover, team selection controversies were noted as factor that could negatively influence Games performance. Athletes need time to regroup physically and mentally after the stress of the trials. They also need time to 'gel' as a unit.

Coach Actions Perceived by Athletes to Enhance Performance

When asked to list the best things their coaches did to enhance performance before and at the Games, athletes identified the following coaching strategies and actions:

- providing excellent physical/technical training
- facilitating mental preparation and training
- providing support and confidence
- organizing the environment
- preparing and protecting athletes from distractions
- scheduling of international competitions in year before the Games.

Coach Actions Perceived by Athletes to Hurt Performance

The following were coaching actions the athletes identified as hurting their Olympic performance:

- overtraining athletes and not making provisions for getting enough rest
- failing to individualize training
- implementing problematic team trial/selection procedures and policies
- failing to handle pressure well
- not providing enough training and competition scheduled in year before the Games
- failing to facilitate team cohesion
- lacking confidence in athlete.

Second Chances: What Athletes Said They Would do Differently if They Could Perform Again at the Games

- Focus more on sport psychology and mental preparation
- not overtrain and get more rest
- optimize their physical training and preparation
- plan and be better prepared to deal with distractions
- adhere to and follow their personal plan
- focus more on team cohesion
- focus more on relaxation and stress management.

OTHER LESSONS LEARNED

In addition to the above general factors, a number of specific lessons learned were reported by the coaches and athletes. Some of these are listed below:

- peak performance results from a complex interplay of many factors, including many small details; you must play close attention to these
- detailed, focused and consistent preparation is needed
- many of the factors affecting performance seem simple, but in reality they are complex
- achievement of peak performance at the Games appears to be a complex and delicate process that can easily be disturbed.

Coaching Lessons

- Focus more attention on team issues and team building by getting to know your team better and establishing a sense of purpose and collective strength
- provide some type of closure for athletes and coaches after the Games as they may have considerable psychological baggage that could stay with them for many years (including into the next Olympics) if not dealt with; going to closing ceremonies is not enough, because athletes and coaches need some time to gain perspective
- this issue is relevant for both athletes and coaches who fail and for those who succeed – set definite rules about media and interviews at the Games (such as allowing athletes to be interviewed only at certain times, for instance, right after the event on the field and not late at night on national talk shows) and coordinating media requests through only one person
- make the athletes' lives simple at the Games by setting specific rules that make things very clear – 'black or white'
- realize that Olympic athletes are not well-rounded; they are perfectionists and may need help in dealing with the pressure of the Olympics and especially when the Games have ended
- be careful not to set NGB high-performance plan Olympic medal 'markers' too high just to get more money before the Games
- allow teams with their own athletic trainers (who have relationships with the athletes) to have the same trainer at the Olympic Games
- before the Games, recognize that athletes close to retirement worry about their careers being over; this needs to be addressed in the sport psychology programme
- confront issues arising at the Games squarely in the eye – be direct and let people know where you stand
- research the decision on whether or not to go to the opening ceremonies and talk to coaches and athletes who have been there;

some suggested guidelines for deciding whether to take part in the opening ceremonies include: (a) if the ceremony is one day away do not go; (b) if it is three days away go for sure; and (c) if it is two days away obtain as much information as possible about the pros and cons of attending and make a decision

- if you go, the key is the ability to make it happen with the least amount of fatigue; doing it with the least amount of fatigue will require a great deal of work
- try to eliminate travel close in time to the Games
- details are very important, do not assume anything at any level; planning is vital
- you must plan the entire approach; consider athlete selection, a long-term performance prognosis, programme objectives, a systematic, controlled training environment, expect changes in food, housing and social factors, know the competition, travel/jet lag, daily plans (especially recovery), at-games factors (climate, weather, transportation, media, pressure)
- the number of competitions involved and how you will filter communication from home via the team leader
- at the Games, focus on what you can control
- use all the support personnel (such as sport scientists) by integrating them into a team of specialists preparing for the Olympics is not just the responsibility of the coach; he or she, however, must be responsible for integrating and evaluating the support/sport science staff
- planning and the implementation of training is part art, part science
- the coach must anticipate unexpected distractions at the Games and plan for them
- in the month before the Games every single factor is important
- the coach who can manage more factors contributing to the athlete's welfare, health and performance will be the winner
- staying positive in the last month before to the Games is critical
- athletes must be confident on both a rational and an emotional level, as well as at a deep, subconscious level
- to be successful you must have a good team leader and good lines of communication with him or her
- be careful in trying to 'get the edge' that you don't overdo it and lose the edge.

Final Thoughts

Someone once said: 'Great corporations don't do one thing right, they do a thousand little things right every day.' Professor Gould and his colleagues use this quotation when reflecting on what was learned from the athletes and coaches in this study. Successful Olympic performance does not require that an athlete, team or NGB does only one thing right.

In contrast, the key is to do many things right on a consistent basis and in an integrated fashion. Hence it is a mistake to focus on only one or two of the factors listed above. The key seems to be to develop a plan that integrates and incorporates these and other factors into a successful programme that, when implemented, does not guarantee Olympic success, but provides the greatest probability of success occurring.

Plenty of food for thought with the 2012 Olympic Games and 2014 Commonwealth Games fast approaching.

Figure 62 Championship medalist.

14

Child Development

Each person's map of the world is as unique as their thumbprint. There are no two people alike, no two people who understand the same sentence the same way, so in dealing with children try not to fit them to your concept of what they should be.

Milton Erickson

In adding detail to previous sections on coaching children and planning, let us look at the specifics of child development and the implications for coaching. Many coach education programmes pay lip-service to these important concepts and I make no apology for stating them explicitly and in detail.

Definitions of the stages of growth in childhood come from many sources. Theorists such as Piaget and Vygotsky have provided ways to understand development and recent research has provided important information regarding the nature of development. In addition, the stages of childhood are defined culturally by the social institutions, customs and laws that make up a society. For example, while researchers and professionals usually define the period of early childhood as from birth to eight years of age, others might consider age five a better end point because it coincides with entry into the cultural practice of formal schooling. There are three broad stages of development: early childhood, middle childhood and adolescence. The definitions of these stages are organized around the primary tasks of development in each stage, though the boundaries of these stages are malleable. Society's ideas about childhood shift over time and research has led to new understandings of the development that takes place in each stage.

EARLY CHILDHOOD (BIRTH TO EIGHT YEARS)

Early childhood is a time of tremendous growth across all areas of development. The dependent newborn grows into a young person who can take care of his or her own body and interact effectively with others. For these reasons the primary developmental task of this stage is skill development.

Figure 63 Children's coach.

Physically, between birth and age three a child typically doubles in height and quadruples in weight. Bodily proportions also shift, so that the infant, whose head accounts for almost one-fourth of the total body length, becomes a toddler with a more balanced, adult-like appearance. Despite these rapid physical changes, the typical three-year-old has mastered many skills, including sitting, walking, toilet training, using a spoon, scribbling and sufficient hand–eye coordination to catch and throw a ball.

Between three and five years of age, children continue to grow rapidly and begin to develop fine motor skills. By age five most children demonstrate fairly good control of pencils, crayons and scissors. Gross motor accomplishments may include the ability to skip and to balance on one foot. Physical growth slows down between five and eight years of age, while bodily proportions and motor skills become more refined.

Physical changes in early childhood are accompanied by rapid changes in the child's cognitive and language development. From the moment they are born, children use all their senses to attend to their environment and they begin to develop a sense of cause and effect from their actions and the responses of caregivers.

Over the first three years of life, children develop a spoken vocabulary of between 300 and 1,000 words and are able to use language to learn about and describe the world around them. By age five, a child's vocabulary will grow to approximately 1,500 words. Five-year-olds are also able to produce five-to seven-word sentences, learn to use the past tense and tell familiar stories using pictures as clues.

Language is a powerful tool to enhance cognitive development. Using language allows the child to communicate with others and solve problems. By age eight, children are able to demonstrate some basic understanding of less concrete concepts, including time and money. However, the eight-year-old still reasons in concrete ways and has difficulty understanding abstract ideas.

A key moment in early childhood socio-emotional development occurs around age one. This is the time when attachment formation becomes critical. Attachment theory suggests that individual differences in later life functioning and personality are shaped by a child's early experiences with their caregivers. The quality of emotional attachment, or lack of attachment, formed early in life may serve as a model for later relationships.

From age three to five, growth in socio-emotional skills includes the formation of peer relationships, gender identification and the development of a sense of right and wrong. Taking the perspective of another individual is difficult for young children and events are often interpreted in all-or-nothing terms, with the impact on the child being the foremost concern. For example, at age five a child may expect others to share its possessions freely but itself still be extremely possessive of a favourite toy. This creates no conflict of conscience, because fairness is determined relative to the child's own interests. Between ages five and eight, children enter into a broader peer context and develop enduring friendships. Social comparison is heightened at this time and taking other people's perspective begins to play a role in how children relate to people, including their peers.

Implications for Sports Coaches

The time from birth to eight years is critical in the development of many foundational skills in all areas of development. Increased awareness of and ability to detect developmental delays in very young children has led to the creation of early intervention services that can reduce the need for special education placements when children reach school age. For example, the earlier detection of hearing deficits sometimes leads to correction of problems before serious language impairments occur. Also, developmental delays caused by premature birth can be addressed through appropriate therapies to help children to function at the level of their typically developing peers before they begin school. Many local authorities (and some sports governing bodies) introduce mini versions of their games and activities at this age. Coaches need to be aware and very skilled at dealing with this clientele in order to make the experience meaningful, enjoyable and a grounding for later, more specific work to be done.

An increased emphasis on early learning has also created pressure to prepare young children to enter school with as many prerequisite skills as possible. In other words, 'all children will enter school ready to learn'. While the validity of this goal has been debated, the consequences have already been felt. One is the use of standardized readiness assessments to determine class placement or retention in nursery schools. Another is the creation of transition classes (an extra year of schooling before either nursery or the first year at primary school). Finally, the increased attention on early childhood has led to renewed interest in preschool programmes as a means to narrow the readiness gap between children whose families can provide quality early learning environments for them and those whose families cannot. It is unusual nowadays for nurseries not to have physical literacy programmes alongside more traditional numeracy and literacy ones.

Figure 64 Early years coach.

MIDDLE CHILDHOOD (EIGHT TO TWELVE YEARS)

Historically, middle childhood has not been considered an important stage in human development. Sigmund Freud's psychoanalytic theory labelled this period of life the latency stage, a time when sexual and aggressive urges are repressed. He suggested that no significant contributions to personality development were made during this period. However, more recent theorists have recognized the importance of middle childhood for the development of cognitive skills, personality, motivation and interpersonal relationships. During middle childhood children learn the values of their societies. Thus the primary developmental task of middle childhood could be called integration, both in terms of development within the individual and of the individual within the social context.

Perhaps supporting the image of middle childhood as a latency stage, physical development during middle childhood is less dramatic than in early childhood or adolescence. Growth is slow and steady until the onset of puberty, when individuals begin to develop at a much quicker pace. The age at which individuals enter puberty varies, but there is evidence of a secular trend – the age at which puberty begins has been decreasing over time. In some individuals, puberty may start as early as age eight or nine. The onset of puberty differs across the genders and begins earlier in females.

As with physical development, the cognitive development of middle childhood is slow and steady. Children in this stage are building upon skills gained in early childhood and preparing for the next phase of their cognitive development. Children's reasoning is very rule based. They are learning skills such as classification and the forming of hypotheses. While they are cognitively more mature now than a few years earlier, children in this stage still require concrete, hands-on learning activities. Middle childhood is a time when children can gain enthusiasm for learning and work, for achievement can become a motivating factor as children work toward building competence and self-esteem.

Middle childhood is also a time when children develop competence in interpersonal and social relationships. Children have a growing peer orientation, yet they are strongly influenced by their family. The social skills learned through peer and family relationships and children's increasing ability to participate in meaningful interpersonal communication provide a necessary foundation for the challenges of adolescence. Best friends are important at this age and the skills gained in these relationships may provide the building blocks for healthy adult relationships.

Implications for Sports Coaches

For many children, middle childhood is a joyful time of increased independence, broader friendships and developing interests, such as sports, art or music. However, a widely recognized shift in school performance begins for many children when aged eight or nine. The skills required for academic success become more complex. Those students who successfully meet the academic challenges during this period go on to do well, while those who fail to build the necessary skills may fall further behind in later years. Recent social trends, including the increased prevalence of school violence, eating disorders, drug use and depression, affect many upper primary school students. Thus there is more pressure on schools to recognize problems in eight- to eleven-year-olds and to teach children the social and life skills that will help them to continue to develop into healthy adolescents. Sport has been recognized as an ideal medium with which to tackle some of these wider social issues and to regain its previous role as a vehicle to teach integrity, fair play and cooperation. This need not be 'serious' adult-type sport, but, in the hands of highly competent sports coaches, it can be a powerful antidote to some of the problems mentioned above.

Figure 65 Middle years coach.

ADOLESCENCE (TWELVE TO EIGHTEEN YEARS)

Adolescence can be defined in a variety of ways: physiologically, culturally or cognitively; each way suggests a slightly different definition. For the purpose of this discussion adolescence is defined as a culturally constructed period that generally begins as individuals reach sexual maturity and ends when the individual has established an identity as an adult within his or her social context. In many cultures adolescence may not exist, or may be very short, because the attainment of sexual maturity coincides with entry into the adult world. In the current culture of developed countries, however, adolescence may last well into the early twenties. The primary developmental task of adolescence is identity formation.

The adolescent years are another period of accelerated growth. Individuals can grow up to 4in (10cm) and gain from 8 to 10lb (3.6–4.5kg) per year. This growth spurt is most often characterized by two years of fast growth, followed by three or more years of slow, steady growth. By the end of adolescence, individuals may gain a total of 7 to 9in (18–23cm) in height and as much as 40 or 50lb (18–23kg) in weight. The timing of this growth spurt is not readily predictable; it varies across both individuals and gender. As noted earlier, females begin to develop earlier than do males.

Sexual maturation is one of the most significant developments during this time. Like physical development, there is significant variability in the age at which individuals attain sexual maturity. Females tend to mature at about age thirteen and males at about fifteen. Development during this period is governed by the pituitary gland through the release of the hormones testosterone (males) and oestrogen (females). There has been increasing evidence of a trend toward earlier sexual development in developed countries – the average age at which females reach menarche dropped three to four months every ten years between 1900 and 2000.

Adolescence is an important period for cognitive development as well as it marks a transition in the way in which individuals think and reason about problems and ideas. In early adolescence individuals can classify and order objects, reverse processes, think logically about concrete objects and consider more than one perspective at a time. However, at this level of development adolescents benefit more from direct experiences than from abstract ideas and principles. As adolescents develop more complex cognitive skills they gain the ability to solve more abstract and hypothetical problems. Elements of this type of thinking may include an increased ability to think in hypothetical ways about abstract ideas, the ability to generate and test hypotheses systematically, the ability to think and plan about the future and meta-cognition (the ability to reflect on one's thoughts). As individuals enter adolescence, they are confronted by a diverse number of changes all at one time. Not only are they undergoing significant physical and cognitive growth, but they are also encountering new situations, responsibilities and people.

Entry into high school thrusts students into environments with many new people, responsibilities and expectations. While this transition can be frightening, it also represents an exciting step toward independence.

Adolescents are trying on new roles, new ways of thinking and behaving and they are exploring different ideas and values. Erikson addresses the search for identity and independence in his framework of life-span development. Adolescence is characterized by a conflict between identity and role confusion. During this period, individuals evolve their own self-concepts within the peer context. In their attempts to become more independent adolescents often rely on their peer group for direction regarding what is normal and accepted. They begin to pull away from reliance on their family as a source of identity and may encounter conflicts between their family and their growing peer-group affiliation.

With so many intense experiences, adolescence is also an important time in emotional development. Mood swings are a characteristic of adolescence. While often attributed to hormones, mood swings can also be understood as a logical reaction to the social, physical and cognitive changes facing adolescents and there is often a struggle with issues of self-esteem. As individuals search for identity, they confront the challenge of matching who they want to become with what is socially desirable. In this context, adolescents often exhibit bizarre and/or contradictory behaviours. The search for identity, the concern adolescents have about whether they are normal and variable moods and low self-esteem all work together to produce wildly fluctuating behaviour.

The impact of the media and societal expectations on adolescent development has been far-reaching. Young people are bombarded by images of violence, sex and unattainable standards of beauty. This exposure, combined with the social, emotional and physical changes facing adolescents, has contributed to an increase in school violence, teenage sexuality and eating disorders. The onset of many psychological disorders, such as depression, other mood disorders and schizophrenia, is also common at this time of life.

Figure 66 Adolescents' coach.

Implications for Sports Coaches

The implications of development during this period for sport are numerous. Coaches must be aware of the shifts in cognitive development that are occurring and provide appropriate learning opportunities to support individual students and facilitate growth. Coaches must also be aware of the

All the domains of development and learning; physical, social and emotional and cognitive are important and they are closely interrelated. Children's development and learning in one domain influence and are influenced by what takes place in other domains:

- many aspects of children's learning and development follow well documented sequences, with later abilities, skills and knowledge building on those already acquired
- development and learning proceed at varying rates from child to child, as well as at uneven rates across different areas of a child's individual functioning
- development and learning result from a dynamic and continuous interaction of biological maturation and experience
- early experiences have profound effects, both cumulative and delayed, on a child's development and learning; and optimal periods exist for certain types of development and learning to occur
- development proceeds toward greater complexity, self-regulation and symbolic or representational capacities
- children develop best when they have secure, consistent relationships with responsive adults and opportunities for positive relationships with peers
- development and learning occur in and are influenced by multiple social and cultural contexts
- always mentally active in seeking to understand the world around them, children learn in a variety of ways; a wide range of teaching strategies and interactions are effective in supporting all these kinds of learning
- play is an important vehicle for developing self-regulation as well as for promoting language, cognition and social competence
- development and learning advance when children are challenged to achieve at a level just beyond their current mastery and also when they have many opportunities to practise newly acquired skills
- children's experiences shape their motivation and approaches to learning, such as persistence, initiative and flexibility; in turn, these dispositions and behaviours affect their learning and development.

challenges facing their athletes in order to identify and help to correct problems if they arise. Sports coaches often play an important role in identifying behaviours that could become problematic and they can be mentors to athletes in need.

CONCLUSION

The definitions of the three stages of development are based on both research and cultural influences. The implications for sport and education are drawn from what is known about how children develop, but it should be emphasized that growth is influenced by context and sport for many (alongside education) can be a primary context of childhood. Just as educators and others should be aware of the ways in which a five-year-old's reasoning is different from a fifteen-year-old's, it is also important to be aware that the structure and expectations of sport influence the ways in which children grow and learn.

For the most up-to-date research and guidance we need look no further than the 2009 position statement by the National Association for the Education of Young Children (USA). I would challenge you to look at these considerations in your coaching practice.

15

Conclusion

People are always blaming their circumstances for what they are.
Never esteem anything as of advantage to you that will make you
break your word or lose your self-respect.

Marcus Aurelius

I started this book with a clear message about the importance of coaches developing ethical standards of behaviour and setting examples for their athletes to follow. Building on the previous section about child development, let me finish with a similar theme.

For most people the development of social roles and appropriate social behaviours should occur during the childhood years. Physical play between parents and children, as well as between siblings and/or peers, serves as a strong regulator in the developmental process. Physical play may take the form of chasing games, wrestling or practising sport skills such as jumping, throwing, catching and striking. These activities may be competitive or non-competitive and are important for promoting the social and moral development of both boys and girls. Unfortunately, fathers will often engage in this sort of activity more with their sons than their daughters. Regardless of the sex of the child, both boys and girls enjoy these types of activity. Physical play during infancy and early childhood is central to the development of social and emotional competence. Researchers have reported that children who engage in more physical play with their parents, particularly with parents who are sensitive and responsive to the child, exhibited greater enjoyment during the play sessions and were more popular with their peers. Likewise, these early interactions with parents, siblings and peers are important in helping children to become more aware of their emotions and to learn to monitor and regulate their own emotional responses. Children learn quickly, through watching the responses of their parents, that certain behaviours make their parents smile and laugh while other behaviours cause them to frown and disengage from the activity. If children want the fun to continue, they engage in the behaviours that please others. As children near adolescence, they learn through rough and tumble play that there are limits to how far they can go before hurting someone (physically or emotionally), which results in the termination of the activity or the later rejection of the child by peers. These early interactions with parents and siblings are important in helping children to learn appropriate behaviour in the social situation of sport and physical activity.

Children learn to assess their social competence (that is, their ability to get along with and their acceptance by peers, family members, teachers and coaches) in sport through the feedback received from parents and coaches. Initially, children are taught 'You can't do that because I said so.' As children approach school age parents begin the process of explaining why a behaviour is right or wrong because children continuously ask why? Similarly, when children engage in sports, they learn about taking turns with their teammates, sharing playing time and valuing rules. They understand that rules are important for everyone and that without these regulations the game would become unfair. The learning of social competence is continuous as we expand our social arena and learn about different cultures. A constant in the learning process is the role of feedback as we assess the responses of others to our behaviours and/or comments.

In addition to the development of social competence, sport participation can help children to develop other forms of self-competence. Paramount among these is self-esteem. Self-esteem is how we judge our worthiness and indicates the extent to which an individual believes her or himself to be capable, significant, successful and worthy. Educators have suggested that one of the biggest barriers to success in the classroom today is low self-esteem. Children are coming to our schools and sport teams with low self-esteem. This is developed through evaluating our abilities and by evaluating the responses of others to us. Children actively observe parents' and coaches' responses to their performances, looking for signs (often non-verbal) of approval or disapproval of their behaviour. No feedback and criticism are often interpreted as a negative response to the behaviour. Within the sport arena, research has shown that the role of the coach is a critical source of information which influences children's self-esteem. In their seminal study with Little League baseball players in the USA, Smith, Smoll and Curtis (1979) found that children whose coaches had been trained to use a 'positive approach' to coaching (more frequent encouragement, positive reinforcement for effort and corrective, instructional feedback) had significantly higher self-esteem ratings over the course of a season than children whose coaches used these techniques less frequently. However, the most compelling evidence supporting the importance of coaches' feedback was found for those children who started the season with the lowest self-esteem ratings. In addition to evaluating themselves more positively, these children evaluated their coaches more positively than did children with higher self-esteem who played for coaches who used the 'positive approach.' Some years later, Barnett, Smoll and Smith (1992) found that 95 per cent of the children who played for coaches trained to use the positive approach signed up to play baseball the next year, compared with 75 per cent of those who played for untrained adult coaches.

The importance of enhanced self-esteem on future participation cannot be overlooked. A major part of the development of high self-esteem is the pride and joy that children experience as their physical skills improve (as adults we experience the same feelings when our boss compliments us on a job done well). Children will feel good about themselves as long as their skills are improving. However, if children feel that their performance during a game or practice is not as good as that of others, or as good as they think their parents would want, they often experience shame and disappointment. Some children will view mistakes made during a game as failure and will look for ways to avoid participating in the task if they receive no encouragement to continue. At this juncture, it is critical that adults (parents and coaches) intervene to help children to interpret the mistake or failure. Children need to be taught that a mistake is not synonymous with failure. Rather, a mistake means a new strategy, more practice and/or that greater effort is needed to succeed at the task. Because children often use social comparisons as a way of determining their ability in sport, the highly visible arena of youth sports provides them with many opportunities to determine their ability compared with that of others on their teams.

Unfortunately, given the influence of other factors, such as maturation and previous knowledge of a sport on one's ability to perform a sport skill, children often reach incorrect conclusions about their abilities. Thus the roles of parents and coaches become significant in helping children to interpret the failure.

The development of self-esteem and perceptions of competence are not as simple as providing only positive feedback. The role of coaches' feedback, while critical, is complex. For example, among thirteen- to fifteen-year-old female softball players, skill development was the primary contributor to positive changes in self-perceptions of ability (Horn, 1985). However, certain coaching behaviours also influenced perceptions of self-esteem during practice situations. Specifically, players who received more frequent positive feedback or no feedback in response to desirable performances during practice scored lower in perceived physical competence, while players who received more criticism in response to performance errors had higher perceptions of competence. Although these results appear contradictory to interpretations of the roles of positive and negative reinforcement, Horn attributed them to the specific nature of the comments. Positive reinforcement statements given by coaches were often unrelated to the players' skill behaviours. That is, statements were not responses to desirable skill techniques and behaviours, but rather were more general (such as, 'good job, Sally' rather than 'good job, Sally, on using two hands to catch the ball'). Coaches' use of criticism was often a direct response to a skill error and usually contained skill-relevant information on how to improve (such as, 'That's not the way to hit a ball, Jill! Put both hands together and keep your elbows away from your body'). Thus, the quality of coaches' feedback is critical to children's understanding of the feedback. Specifically, instructional content, rather than the quantity of the feedback, is the key to helping athletes develop skills and perceived competence.

Another issue related to social competence, particularly during the adolescent years, is how teenagers perceive their competence in an activity, including sport. Research has shown a significant relationship between physical competence, interpersonal skills and peer acceptance (Weiss and Duncan, 1992). Boys and girls who believed that they were physically competent in sport were rated as having higher physical competence by their teachers. Those who believed that they were physically competent were also those who perceived themselves to be more popular with their peers, were competent in social relationships as rated by their teachers and expected to be successful in interpersonal situations. Finally, the development of high self-esteem is critical in helping older children buffer the negative influences experienced by youth in today's society. For example, the Women's Sports Foundation has proposed that girls who have high self-esteem are less likely to become pregnant as teenagers and are more likely to leave an abusive relationship than girls with low self-esteem. When teenagers evaluate themselves in a positive way, they are more capable of saying 'no' to drugs and gang culture. High self-esteem will not guarantee that teenagers will make the right decisions, but it does provide a stronger basis for resisting the pressures that currently exist. Coaches, of course, have a massive role to play in developing high self-esteem in these groups.

In addition to developing a positive sense of self, involvement in sport activities can assist children in learning what is right from wrong (that is, moral development). Indeed, moral concepts of fairness support the very existence of the notion of sport. For children to learn about fair play, sports activities must be designed to facilitate cooperation rather than just competition. One of the best ways that participation in sport can teach our children about fair play is through teaching the rules of the game and, more importantly, abiding by the rules during competition. If the rules mandate that every member of the team plays for a specified amount of time (such as, one period of the game or a specified number of points or minutes), parents and coaches should follow the rule without grumbling about what will happen when they 'have' to put a 'lower ability athlete', in the game. Equally important is instilling the understanding that time and positions must be shared during the early learning periods. In addition, many of children's early experiences in informal and formal sports require that children serve as their own officials. Tennis players must call their own lines during competitions while informal football games require that children call their own fouls. These games continue peacefully only to the extent that everyone cooperates to have a game and is fair in their officiating calls. If fair play is to be taught and learned, it is the responsibility of all those associated with the experience to help athletes learn and appreciate the concept of fair play.

Parents, coaches and officials will undermine the learning of the concept of fair play if they are not consistent in their teaching and personal conduct. Most coaches and parents espouse the virtue of fair play until they perceive that the opponent is gaining an advantage or winning unfairly. Parents may even chastise the coach who abides by the rules and does not win, which sends a mixed message to children about the importance of fair play. Journalists and broadcasters have fallen into the same trap of believing that the only worthy performance was that given by the winning team, regardless of whether they abided by the rules or not. For example, the media may laud the cleverness of a basketball team which is able to confuse the official and send a better free throw shooter to the line instead of the person who was fouled. Parents and coaches must help children interpret the appropriateness of these behaviours in the light of what is right or wrong.

The development of appropriate social behaviour begins before children enter sports. Parents and siblings provide important information to infants, toddlers and young children about acceptable ways to respond to being frustrated. For example, children learn that biting, hitting, pinching and kicking are not acceptable ways to retaliate because: (1) these actions hurt others and (2) the play often stops when children act inappropriately. Learning the limits to which one can go and still maintain the 'game' is one way children learn how to interact successfully with other children. Participation in sport extends the learning of social competence by teaching children to cooperate with their teammates and opponents as well as to abide by the rules. Without this cooperation the game will not continue. Parents and coaches must be persistent and consistent in teaching the value of cooperation.

Parents must provide opportunities to learn social competence to both their daughters and their sons. Fathers, in particular, are often more involved in teaching social competence through physical activity and sport to their sons. The outcomes of a high level of perceived competence (that is, enhanced self-esteem, higher perceptions of competence and greater acceptance by friends) are equally important to both girls and boys. Coaches can facilitate the development of social competence through the use of positive feedback. When teaching sport skills coaches should provide plenty of instructional and encouraging statements. Children are going to make mistakes while learning and performing sport skill. The use of a positive approach to error correction will ensure that children will want to continue to practice and will enhance self-esteem, particularly among youth who have lower self-esteem. Sport provides numerous opportunities to teach moral principles. The key to children learning what is right and wrong starts with coaches and parents being consistent in their own behaviour. Coaches should use situations that arise in sport as opportunities to teach why certain behaviours are right and others are wrong; talk about the importance of being honest; promote acceptance of responsibility for one's actions; and teach children to respect teammates, opponents and officials.

References

PART I

American Academy of Pediatrics, http://aappolicy.aappublications.org/cgi/content/full/pediatrics;107/6/1459

Coakley, J., 'Sport and socialisation', *Exercise and Sports Sciences Reviews*, 21:1 (1993), pp.169–200.

Cross, N. and Lyle, J., *The Coaching Process: Principles and Practice for Sport* (Butterworth Heinemann, 1999).

Curriculum for Excellence, http://www.ltscotland.org.uk/curriculumforexcellence/index.asp

Gould, D., Collins, K., Lauer, L. and Chung, Y., 'Coaching life skills through football: a study of award winning high school coaches', *Journal of Applied Sport Psychology*, 19:1 (2007), pp.16–37.

Lyle, J., *Sports Coaching Concepts: A Framework for Coaching Behaviour* (Routledge, 2002).

McGeechan, I., *Lion Man* (Simon & Schuster, 2009).

Piaget, J., *The Child's Conception of the World* (Littlefield Adams, 1975).

Skinner, B.F., *Science and Human Behavior* (Macmillan, 1953).

Trudel, P. and Gilbert, W., 'Coaching and coach education', in Kirk, D., O'Sullivan, M. and McDonald, D., *Handbook of Research in Physical Education* (Sage, 2004).

World Anti-Doping Agency, http://www.wada-ama.org/

PART II

Biggs, J., *Teaching for Quality Learning at University* (Society for Research into Higher Education and Open University Press, 1999).

Brackenbridge, C., *Spoilsports: Understanding and Preventing Sexual Exploitation in Sport* (Routledge, 2001).

Bunker, B. and Thorpe, R., 'The curriculum model' in Thorpe, R., Bunker, D. and Almond, L. (eds), *Rethinking Games Teaching* (University of Technology, Loughborough, 1986, pp.7–10).

Butler, R.J., 'Psychological preparation of Olympic boxers' in Kremer, J. and Crawford, W. (eds), *The Psychology of Sport: Theory and Practice* (British Psychological Society, 1989, pp.74–84).

Chelladurai, P., 'Leadership' in Singer, R.N., Murphey, M. and Tennant, L.K. (eds), *Handbook on Research on Sport Psychology* (Macmillan, 1993, pp.647–71).

Christina, R.W., 'Major determinants of the transfer of training: implications for enhancing sport performance', in Kim, K.W. (ed.), *Human Performance Determinants in Sport* (Korean Society of Sport Psychology, 1996, pp.25–52).

Franks, I.M. and Miller, G., 'Eyewitness testimony in sport', (*Journal of Sport Behavior*, 9 (1986), pp.39–45).

Gilbert, W.D. and Trudel, P., 'An evaluation strategy for coach education programs', *Journal of Sport Behavior*, 22 (1999), pp.234–50.

Gilbert, W.D. and Trudel, P., 'Learning to coach through experience: reflection in model youth sport coaches', *Journal of Teaching in Physical Education*, 21 (2001), pp.16–34.

Jowett, S. and Cockerill, I.M., 'Olympic medallists' perspective of the athlete–coach relationship', *Psychology of Sport and Exercise*, 4 (2003), pp.313–31.

Jowett, S. and Ntoumanis, N., 'The coach–athlete relationship questionnaire (CART–Q): development and initial validation', *Scandinavian Journal of*

Medicine and Science in Sports, 14 (2004) PP. 245–57.

Kelly, G.A. *The Psychology of Personal Constructs* (Norton, 1955; reprinted Routledge, 1991).

Knowles, M.S., *The Adult Learner: a Neglected Species* (Gulf Publishing, 1990).

Kolb, D.A., *Experiential Learning: Experience as the Source of Learning and Development* (Prentice-Hall, 1984).

Laurillard, D., *Rethinking University Teaching: A Framework for the Effective Use of Educational Technology* (Routledge, 2nd edn, 2002).

Lawther, J., *The Learning of Physical Skills* (Prentice-Hall, 1968).

Lyle, J., Allison, M. and Taylor, J., *Factors Influencing the Motivations of Sports Coaches* (Research report, Scottish Sports Council, 1997).

Lyle, J., 'Coaching philosophy and coaching behaviour' in Cross, N. and Lyle, J. (eds), *The Coaching Process: Principles and Practice for Sport* (Butterworth-Heineman, 1999, pp.25–46).

McCarthy, B., *The 4Mat System: Teaching to Learning Styles with Right/Left Mode Techniques* (Excel Inc., 1987).

Race, P., *The Lecturer's Toolkit* (Routledge, 2nd edn, 2002).

Rogers, C.R., *On Becoming a Person: A Therapist's View of Psychotherapy* (Constable, 1967).

Rushall, B.S. and Siedentop, D., *The Development and Control of Behaviour in Sport and Physical Education* (Lea & Febiger, 1972).

Siedentop, D., Mand, C. and Taggart, A., *Physical Education – Teaching and Curriculum Strategies for Grades 5–12* (Mayfield, 1986).

Smoll, F.L. and Smith, R.E., 'Coaching behaviour research and intervention in youth sports' in Smoll, F.L. and Smith, R.E. (eds), *Children and Youth in Sport: A Biopsychosocial Perspective* (Kendall-Hunt, 2002, pp.211–33).

Smoll, F.L. and Smith, R.E. (1989), 'Leadership behaviours in sport: a theoretical model and research paradigm', *Journal of Applied Social Psychology*, 19 (1989), 1522–51.

North, J. and Townend, R., *Sports Coaching in the United Kingdom II* (sports-coach United Kingdom, 2007).

Thorpe, R. and Bunker, D., 'A changing focus in games teaching', in Almond, L. (ed.), *The Place of Physical Education in Schools* (Kogan Page, 1989, pp.163–9).

Timson-Katchis, M. and Jowett, S., 'Social networks in the sport context: the influences of parents on the coach–athlete relationship', unpublished (2004).

PART III

Barnett, N.P., Smoll, F.L. and Smith, R.E., 'Effects of enhancing coach–athlete relationships on youth sport attrition', *Sport Psychologist*, 6 (1992), pp.111–27.

Gould, D. *et al.*, *Positive and Negative Factors Influencing US Olympic Athletes and Coaches: Atlanta Games Assessment*, US Olympic Committee Sport Science

and Technology, Final Grant Report, Colorado Springs, CO, 1998.

Horn, T.S., 'Coaches' feedback and changes in children's perceptions of their physical competence', *Journal of Educational Psychology*, 77 (1985), pp.174–86.

National Association for the Education of Young Children, http://www.naeyc.org/

Piaget, J., *The Child's Conception of the World* (Littlefield Adams, 1975).

Smith, R.E., Smoll, F.L. and Curtis, B., 'Coach effectiveness training: a cognitive-behavioural approach to enhancing relationship skills in youth sport coaches', *Journal of Sports Psychology*, 1:2 (1979), pp.59–75.

Vygotsky, Lev, *Thought and Language* (MIT Press, 1986).

Weiss, M.R. and Duncan, S.C., 'The relationship between physical competence and peer acceptance in the context of children's sports participation', *Journal of Sport & Exercise Psychology*, 14:2 (1992), pp.177–91.

Useful Addresses

UNITED KINGDOM

sports coach UK
114 Cardigan Road,
Headingley, Leeds LS6 3BJ
tel: 0113 274 4802
fax: 0113 275 5019

sports coach UK Workshop
Booking Centre
tel: 0845 6013054

Coachwise [Coachwise is
the trading subsidary of
sports coach UK]
Coachwise Ltd, Chelsea
Close, off Amberley Road,
Armley, Leeds LS12 4HP
tel: +44 (0)113-231 1310
fax: +44 (0)113-231 9606
email: enquiries@
coachwise.ltd.uk

UK Sport
40 Bernard Street, London
WC1N 1ST
tel: +44 (0) 20 7211 5100
fax: +44 (0) 20 7211 5246
email: general
enquiries info@uksport.
gov.uk
drug-free sport enquiries:
drug-free@uksport.gov.uk
job vacancy enquiries: jobs@
uksport.gov.uk

sportscotland
Doges, Templeton on the
Green, 62 Templeton Street,
Glasgow G40 1DA
tel: 0141 534 6500
fax: 0141 534 6501
email: sportscotland.enquir-
ies@sportscotland.org.uk

Sports Council for Wales
Sophia Gardens, Cardiff
CF11 9SW

tel. 0845 045 0904
fax: 0845 846 0014
e-mail: scw@scw.org.uk

Sport England
3rd Floor Victoria House,
Bloomsbury Square, London
WC1B 4SE
tel: 08458 508508
fax: 020 7383 5740
email: info@sportengland.
org

Sport England Regional
Offices
i. Crescent House, 19 The
Crescent, Bedford MK40
2QP
tel: 01234 345222
fax: 01234 359046
email: infoe@sportengland.
org

ii. Grove House
Bridgford Road, West
Bridgford, Nottingham
NG2 6AP
tel: 0115 982 1887
fax: 0115 945 5236
email: infoem@sporteng-
land.org

iii. 3rd Floor Victoria House,
Bloomsbury Square, London
WC1B 4SE
tel: 020 7242 2801
fax: 020 7383 5740
email: infol@sportengland.
org

iv. Aykley Heads, Durham
DH1 5UU
tel: 0191 384 9595
fax: 0191 374 1970
email: infone@sportengland.
org

v. Suite 1, 3rd Floor,
Building 3, Universal
Square, Devonshire Street,

Manchester M12 6JH
tel: 0161 834 0338
fax: 0161 835 3678
email: infonw@
sportengland.org

vi. 51a Church Street,
Caversham, Reading RG4
8AX
tel: 0118 948 3311
fax: 0118 947 5935
email: infose@sportengland.
org

vii. Ashlands House,
Ashlands, Crewkerne,
Somerset TA18 7LQ
tel: 01460 73491
fax: 01460 77263
email: info@sportengland.
org

viii. 5th Floor, No. 3
Broadway, Five Ways,
Birmingham B15 1BQ
tel: 0121 616 6700
fax 0121 633 7115
email: info@sportengland.
org

ix. 4th Floor, Minerva
House, 29 East Parade,
Leeds LS1 5PS
tel: 0113 243 6443
fax: 0113 242 2189
email: infoy@sportengland.
org

Disability Sport

British Paralympic
Association
40 Bernard Street,
London WC1N 1ST
tel: 020 7211 5222
fax: 020 7211 5233
email: info@paralympics.
org.uk

Scottish Disability Sport
The Administrator,
Caledonia House, South
Gyle, Edinburgh EH12 9DQ
tel: 0131 317 1130
fax: 0131 317 1075
email: admin@scottishdisa-
bilitysport.com

Disability Sport Wales
Welsh Institute of Sport,
Sophia Gardens, Cardiff
CF11 9SW
tel: 0845 846 0021
fax: 029 20 665 781
email: office@fdsw.org.uk

English Federation of
Disability Sport
Manchester Metropolitan
University, Alsager Campus,
Hassall Road, Alsager, Stoke
on Trent ST7 2HL
tel: 0161 247 5294;
fax: 0161 247 6895

INTERNATIONAL

International Council
for Coach Education
[John Bales, President,
ICCE, c/o Coaching
Association of Canada]
141 Laurier Avenue
West, Suite 300, Ottawa,

Ontario K1P 5J3, Canada
tel: 613-235-5000 ext.9-2363
fax: 613-235-9500
email: jbales@coach.ca

Positive Coaching
Alliance
1001 N. Rengstorff Ave.,
Suite 100, Mountain View,
CA 94043, USA
toll free #: 866-725-0024
fax #: 650-969-1650
email: pca@positivecoach.
org

Coaching Association of
Canada
141 Laurier Avenue West,
Suite 300, Ottawa, Ontario
K1P 5J3, Canada
tel: 613-235-5000
fax: 613-235-9500
email: coach@coach.ca

Australian Sports
Commission
Leverrier Street, Bruce ACT
2616, PO Box 176,
Belconnen ACT 2616,
Australia
tel: +61 02 6214 1111
fax: +61 02 6251 2680
email: coaching@ausport.
gov.au

Index

Happy Birthday Sam

1971.

hi hi

SCOTS PROVERBS
and Rhymes

SCOTS
PROVERBS and RHYMES

Selected and compiled
with introduction, comments
and a glossary
by

FORBES MACGREGOR

Illustrated by JOHN MACKAY

W. & R. CHAMBERS LTD
EDINBURGH AND LONDON

First Published 1948
Reprinted for W. & R. Chambers Ltd 1970

ISBN 0 550 21267 1

PRINTED BY GILMOUR & DEAN LTD. HAMILTON

INTRODUCTION

ALTHOUGH many nations of the ancient and medieval world were noted for their wealth of proverbs, the Scots had a pre-eminent reputation in this respect. It was said in England that no Scot could talk without using a proverb. The Scots thus held, until comparatively recent times, this reputation for terse and sententious language and they were exceptionally reluctant, even after the Union in 1707, to abandon their ancient modes of thought and speech.

This disinclination for change was due to several factors, the chief of which was a popular prejudice against England; it was because England was the source, or at any rate the channel, of the knowledge gained by the new scientific methods, that Scottish feeling was, by mere association, directed against those new ideas. Such a feeling, which amounted to hatred, was not lessened even by the great contributions to the new age of the many Scottish philosophers, historians, scientists and political theorists like Robertson, Hume, Watt and Adam Smith. Indeed the achievements of these men and their followers, throughout the 18th century, widened the gulf between the two Scotlands : one resisted, the other encouraged, the imposition of intellectual conformity with England.

It is considered that the friction between the ancient and modern worlds of thought helped to ignite the genius of both Burns and Scott.

Burns, although well educated along the new lines, gained national popularity by his championship of the older Scotland of the proverbs and songs : but even before his short life closed, this resurgence of national spirit was much discredited, in certain influential political quarters, on account of its association with the ideals of the French Revolution.

Scott was not of the same political colour as Burns, so his decision to devote his talents mainly to the depicting of the fast-disappearing Doric world arose more from a dislike of the bustling industrialism of the early nineteenth century than from a political bias in favour of a resurgent nationalism. However this may be, his novels, which embody hundreds of Scots proverbs, form the perfect complement to Burns's poems ; and so the two geniuses, different in outlook, left for future generations a true perspective of that vanished

5

Scottish world with its quaint manners and turns of expression.

Unfortunately, as Scott anticipated, he, as well as Burns, was to be followed by multitudes of imitators, who succeeded generally in making mere parodies of the literary achievements of their masters. These imitators include most of the Kailyard writers, who provide the whipping-boys for many modern Scottish critics. In this Kailyard period Scots proverbs were no doubt overworked and ultimately sank into disrepute along with the other contemporary modes in literature.

This was unfortunate, as many of the salty and racy proverbs gave an invaluable picture of the intransigent Scottish character. It is my purpose in this booklet to make a fresh presentation of whatever proverbial expressions seem to me to be the most colourful and at the same time most peculiarly Scottish. Apart from their interest and humour, they may help to discredit the libels on Scottish character which have passed current for a long time both at home and furth of Scotland.

Mr. John Mackay, the illustrator, and myself are aboriginal Scots and we hope that our combined efforts have succeeded in creating through the proverbial medium a just and pleasing picture of our nation. If we needed a reason for bringing forward these almost forgotten sayings, I believe we could find that reason best expressed in a Scots proverb itself: ' Auld men will die and bairns will sune forget.'

F. M.

1. A blate cat maks a prood moose.

2. A bonny bride is sune buskit
   And a short horse is sune wispit.
   > A pretty bride needs little decoration; a small
   > horse little grooming.

3. A bonny grice maks an ugly auld soo.
   > An uncomplimentary reminder to pretty girls of
   > what old age brings.

4. A broken kebbuck gangs sune dune.

5. A cauld needs the cook as muckle as the doctor.

6. ' A clean thing's kindly,' quo the wife when she turned
   her sark after a month's wear.
   > This seems almost the ancestor of a Wellerism.

7. A crook in the Forth
   Is worth an earldom in the North.

The low lands about the river Forth were so fertile compared with the Highlands. The river Forth pursues a tortuous course with many crooks through the Carse of Stirling.

8. A croonin coo, a crawin hen, and a whistlin maid are ne'er very chancy.

> These were considered three unnatural things, girls were told.

9. A dish o married love richt sune grows cauld
And dozens doon to nane as folks grow auld.

> Obviously the maker of the above was beyond sentimentality.

10. A drap and a bite's but sma requite.

> Those who are our friends are welcome to food and drink.

11. A dreich drink is better than a dry sermon.

> Dreich is dry in any sense. You could take the drink or leave it, but the sermon was forced upon you.

12. A fool winna gie his toy for the Tower o Lunnon.

> So said a disgusted Scot on observing Charles II chasing butterflies for the amusement of the Court ladies, when the Dutch fleet lay off the Thames threatening invasion.

13. A gaun fit's aye gettin, were it but a thorn or a broken tae.

> The first part promises reward for enterprise and industry ; but the second part warns troublemakers how they may fare.

14. A greedy ee ne'er got a guid pennyworth.

15. A guid dog ne'er barkit aboot a bane.

> Good servants are not always looking for rewards.

16. A guid goose may hae an ill gaislin.

17. A horn spune hauds nae poison.

> Humble people do not tempt poisoners.

18. **A hungry man's meat is lang o makin ready.**
    He thinks so, anyway.

19. **A' is no gowd that glisters, nor maidens that wear their hair.**
    In olden Scotland virgins went bareheaded, but so also, according to the cynic, did many others who had forfeited their privilege to dress thus.

20. **A kiss and a drink o water mak but a wersh breakfast.**
    Love in a cottage, on these terms, was evidently not satisfying to the practical Caledonian.

21. **A layin hen is better than a standin mill.**
    A small useful thing is better than a great useless one.

22. **A man's a man for a' that.**
    The refrain of Burns's great song of brotherhood. Among all differences of rank the chief merit is character.

23. **A mile o Don's worth twae o Dee**
    Except for salmon, stane and tree.
    Donside is fertile, Deeside wild and forested.

24. **A mouthfu o meat may be a tounfu o shame.**
    This would be so if the food were stolen.

25. **A pun o oo is as heavy as a pun o leid.**

26. **A Scot, a craw, and a Newcastle grindstane traivel a' the warld ower.**
    Scots, like crows, are great wanderers. But while

some go to thieve, like the crows, many go to do honest work, like the famed grindstones.

27. A toom pantry maks a thriftless guid-wife.
    A wise saying for the present day. The housewife must have something to be thrifty with.

28. A wee bush is better than nae bield.

29. A wee spark
    Maks muckle wark.

30. A wilfu man maun hae his way.
    But there is an undertone which suggests that no good will come of it.

31. A' complain o want o siller, but nane o want o sense.
    If they had more sense they would soon have more money.

32. A' things anger ye and the cat breks your hert.
    A rebuke to a person who is put out by the unalterable perversity of nature.

33. Ane at a time is guid fishin.

34. Ane may like the kirk weel eneuch and no ride on the riggin o't.
    A canny rebuke to the over-zealous.

35. As ae door shuts anither opens.
    We are never left entirely without hope.

36. As auld as the hills.
    In the Highlands they add ' and the MacArthurs.'

37. As caller as a kail blade.
    Even in hot weather this was cool and often used to hold butter.

38. As daft as a yett on a windy day.

39. As the auld cock craws, the young ane learns.

40. As the day lengthens
    The cauld strengthens.

The coldest weather begins after New Year, when the days perceptibly lengthen.

41. Auld saws speak truth.

42. Auld sparrows are ill to tame.
    It is difficult to tame old birds, or to teach old folk new ways ; though, as a point of natural interest, old rooks are more easily tamed than young ones.

43. Auld wives and bairns mak fools o physicians.
    The first from experience know what to do ; the second from ignorance often pass unwittingly through great dangers.

44. Auld wives were aye guid maidens.
    They all say so, at any rate.

45. Aye keep your bonnet on : sheeps' heids are best warm.
    This was said to men who impolitely kept their hats on.

46. Bannocks are better than nae breid.

> Bannocks were less appetising than bread, however, being unleavened.

47. Be aye the thing ye would be ca'd.

> Let your conduct come up to your opinion of yourself.

48. Be thou weel, or be thou wae,
Thou wilt not aye be sae.

49. Better bairns greet than bearded men.

> This was commonly used to justify stern measures. John Knox, on reducing Mary to tears over her non-conformity to Protestantism, quoted this proverb, substituting "women" for "bairns."

50. Better mak your feet your friends.

> Run for your life.

51. Better wear shune than sheets.

> It is better to be running about healthy than bed-ridden, even though shoe-repairs are dear.

52. Butter to butter's nae kitchen.

> Used when women kiss each other, to imply that there would be more relish in the business if one was of the opposite sex.

53. Ca canny, lad, ye're but a new-come cooper.
> Go easy until you learn more about your business.
> This is a different matter from the modern sense
> of ' Ca canny.'

54. ' Can do ' is easily cairried aboot wi ane.
> Knowledge and skill are easily carried.

55. Carrick for a man, Kyle for a coo,
Cunninghame for butter and milk,
And Gallowa for oo.
> These districts of South-west Scotland were famed
> for the above.   This, we would suppose, is a Carrick
> proverb.   Burns was born in Kyle, though as a youth
> he lived ' upon the Carrick border.'

56. Cast a cat ower the hoose and she'll fa on her feet.
> Some people, no matter what occurs to them, never
> seem to be upset.

57. Cast not a cloot till May be oot.
> Don't put off any winter clothing until the hawthorn,
> or may blossom, is out ; or, perhaps, until the end
> of May.

58. Changes are lichtsome, and fools like them.

59. Christiecleek will come to ye.
> This was a word of terror in Scotland for centuries,
> and was used effectively by mothers to frighten way-
> ward children.
> The famines, wars and anarchy of the 14th century
> caused an outbreak of cannibalism in the Highlands.
> One of the leaders of a cannibal gang was, inappropri-
> ately enough, named Christie, and he used to carry a

large iron cleek or hook to drag down his victims. He thus earned the above name. Christie is said to have escaped the law and to have ended his life as a prosperous merchant.

60. Curse of Scotland.

The nine of diamonds. There are five good reasons given by casuists why this should be so. We may be certain of this, that the Duke of Cumberland, the Butcher of Culloden, or Stinking Billy, purposely chose that card, knowing its significance, to write on the back of it the infamous order for the massacre of wounded Jacobites.

D

61. Ding doon the nests and the rooks will flee awa.

The repetition of this at the Reformation led to the destruction of the abbeys by the populace.

62. Dinna dry up the burn because it may wet your feet.

Don't destroy a useful thing because of a small annoyance it causes.

63. Dinna speak o a raip to a chiel whase faither was hanged.

E

64. Eat-weel's drink-weel's brither.

Gluttony goes hand-in-hand with drunkenness.

65. Even a haggis will run doonhill.

A soldier is not necessarily very brave who charges downhill, though this was the favourite manner of the Highlanders.

66. Every man has his ain bubbly-jock.

It was formerly the practice to board out daft fellows to farmers, so that they might do work and be out of mischief. A gentleman visiting one of these poor souls asked him if he were happy. He began to cry. He confessed that he had a soft bed, a full belly, and pennies for sweeties. Still he was troubled. 'O, mister, my life is made a burden to me,' he wept. At last he managed to tell his worry. ' O, sir, I'm sair hauden doon by the bubbly-jock.' It seems that the turkey-cock had taken an aversion to him and chased him at sight.

67. Facts are chiels that winna ding.
    Facts cannot be denied.

68. Fair maidens wear nae purses.
    Despite the reputation of the Scots for meanness, this proverb was in common usage among them when a girl offered to pay her expenses in mixed company.

69. Fair words winna mak the pot boil.

70. Fleas and girning wives are waukrife bedfellows.

There is little sleep for the poor fellow who has to suffer either a curtain-lecture or the attentions of the indigenous *pulex irritans*.

71. Fools are aye fond o flittin
And wise men o sittin.

72. Fools and bairns shouldna see wark half-dune.

73. Fools look to tomorrow ; wise men use tonight.

74. Fools mak feasts and wise men eat them.
The Duke of Lauderdale was making a great feast in London when one of his guests very impudently said the above words. The Duke, who was a great wit, replied, ' Aye, and wise men mak proverbs and fools repeat them.'

75. Forth bridles the wild Hielandman.
The river Forth and the Firth of Forth are so deep that they were said to keep the Highlanders from driving cattle back over them from the rich farms of the Lowlands.

76. Frae the greed o the Campbells,
Frae the ire o the Drummonds,
Frae the pride o the Grahams,
Frae the wind o the Murrays,
Good Lord deliver us !

This was the grace of an eccentric Highland laird, Maxtone of Cultoquey. He was no respector of persons, and it is said that when visiting the Duke of Montrose, who was a Graham, he recited his customary grace, and quickly discovered the truth of his third line.

77. Fry stanes wi butter and the broo will be guid.
Even the most useless things can appear quite good if much is spent on them.

78. Gie a beggar a bed and he'll pay ye wi a loose.

79. Gie your tongue mair holidays than your heid.

80. Giff-gaff maks guid friends.
>Exchange of necessities between neighbours makes for friendship.

81. Guid gear gangs intae sma bouk.
>Valuables are usually small, the analogy being applicable to persons. But some add to the proverb 'and sae does poison.'

82. ' Hame's hamely, quo the deil when he found himsel in the Court o Session.

> Lawyers were associated with devilries.

83. Hang a thief when he's young and he'll no steal when he's auld.

> This is a good sample of the humour of the infamous Lord Braxfield, original of Stevenson's 'Weir of Hermiston.' At the trial, in 1794, of Muir and others for alleged conspiracy, one of the accused referred to Christ as a reformer. Braxfield's reply was, ' Muckle guid he made o that ! He was hangit for it ! '

84. Hauf a tale is eneuch for a wise man.

85. Hawks winna pike oot hawks' een.

86. He canna mak saut to his parritch.

> He cannot earn even the smallest necessity of life.

87. He jumped at it, like a cock at a grosset.

> He accepted the offer greedily.

88. He needs a lang spune that sups kail wi the deil, or a Fifer.

> Few men were considered the equal of these in cunning.

89. He stumbles at a strae, and lowps ower a linn.

> He finds difficulties only where he wants to.

90. He that blaws in the stoor fills his ain een.

> He that stirs up trouble, finds himself in it.

91. He that eats but ae dish seldom needs the doctor.

92. He that has a muckle neb thinks ilka ane speaks o't.

93. He that invented the Maiden first hanselled it.

> The Maiden was a Scottish prototype of the guillo-
> tine, and was so called because it was coarsely said
> that though many men had lain with her, none
> had got the better of her. The truth of the above
> proverb is open to doubt, and seems more to satisfy
> a love of poetic justice than to describe the truth.
> It is supposed that the Earl of Morton, who suffered
> death by the Maiden, had introduced it shortly
> before. The same is often said, without founda-
> tion, of Dr Guillotin.

94. He that looks wi ae ee, and winks wi anither,
    I wouldna believe him, though he was my brither.

> A childish rhyme against winkers.

95. He that strikes my dog would strike mysel, if he daured.

96. He that tholes, overcomes.

97. He that will to Cupar, maun to Cupar.

> If a person is pig-headed, just let him go on.

98. He would skin a loose for the talla.

> No source of gain is beneath his miserly attention.

99. He's as bold as a Lammermuir lion.

> The Lammermuir Hills is an extensive pastoral
> district, not 'rich in lions.'

100. I had a wee sister, they ca'd her Peep-peep ;
She waded the waters sae deep, deep, deep ;
She climbed up the mountains sae hie, hie, hie ;
And puir wee thing she had but yin ee.

     A star is the answer to this children's riddle.

101. I gied him a bonny blue nocht wi a whistle on the
end o't.

     I gave him nothing worth. The Italians have a
similar proverb, ' I paid him with a handful of
flies.'

102. I met a man wha speered at me,
Grow there berries in the sea?
I answered him by speerin again,
Is there skate on Clocknaben?

     This rhyme is a reply to inquisitive persons.
Clocknaben is a mountain.

103. I sat upon my houtie-croutie ;
I lookit ower my rumple-routie ;
And I saw John Heezlum-Peezlum
Playing on Jerusalem pipes.

     A children's rhymed riddle describing someone
sitting looking at the moon between crossed fingers.

104. I will add a stone to his cairn.

     ' I shall testify to the virtues of the departed ' is
the meaning of this Highland proverb. In the Lowlands such an action had exactly the opposite meaning, and only persons abhorred by the populace
were buried under cairns.

105. I, Willie Wastle, stand firm in my castle,
And a' the dogs in your toun
Canna ding Willie Wastle doon.

> This is a Scots form of ' I'm the King of the Castle.'
> It is said that this rhyme was once sent by letter chal-
> lenging Oliver Cromwell when he was in Scotland.
> He immediately ' bent his cannon ' on the challenger
> and reduced him.

106. I wish ye may hae as muckle Scots as tak ye to your bed.

> When drink began to tell, many Scots of old used
> to address the company in a rigmarole of Latin and
> other tongues. The above sarcastic wish expressed
> also a doubt whether or no the wordy one would
> have any coherent language at all before morning.

107. I've made a vow, and I'll keep it true,
That I'll ne'er stang man through guid sheep's woo.

> This is called the Adder's Aith. These reptiles were
> not supposed to be able to bite through woollen
> cloth.

108. I wouldna ken him if I met him in my parritch.

109. I would raither be your Bible than your horse.

> You overwork the latter.

110. If a' things are true, then that's nae lee.

> An elegant periphrasis meaning ' It's a lie.'

111. If a' your hums an haws were hams and haggises, the
pairish would be weel fed.

> Said to those who could not make up their minds.

112. If Candlemas Day be dry and fair
The hauf o winter's to come an mair ;
If Candlemas Day be wet an foul
The hauf o winter's gane at Yule.

> Candlemas Day is 2nd February. The rhyme tells
> of a superstition nearly two thousand years old.

113. If I had a dog as daft as you, I'd shoot him.

114. **If I'm spared.**

> A very common expression among the pious, and thought to be little out of the ordinary.
>
> An old lady, surveying a kirkyaird of pleasant surroundings, remarked 'Eh, I'd like fine to lie there some day, if I'm spared.'
>
> Another, bidding her tea-table friend goodnight, remarked, 'Weel, Janet, I'll see ye again next Tuesday, if I'm spared.' The other replied, a thought acidly, 'And if ye're no, I'll no expect ye.'

115. **If ye dinna see the bottom, dinna wade.**

116. **If ye sell your purse to your wife, gie her your breeks to the bargain.**

> If the wife holds the money, she rules the house.

117. **Ilka blade o gress keps its ain drap o dew.**

> Everybody has his particular business and has enough to do to attend to it.

118. **Ill herds mak fat tods.**

> The careless shepherd allows the foxes to make easy prey of his lambs.

119. **It's better to hear the lark sing than the moose cheep.**

> The outdoor life is the better.

120. **It's a far cry to Lochow.**

> During a battle between the Gordons and the Campbells in 1594, in which the Campbells were

defeated, one of the Campbells betrayed his chief, and, as he did so, made the above remark. His meaning was that, as it was a long way to Lochow, the chief seat of the Clan Campbell, he would be safe from the anger of his people. This proverb was used to mean that it was safe to do something unlawful or sinful because there was little risk of being punished.

121. It's a lang loanin that has nae turnin.
A change of circumstance will come sometime.

122. It's a silly hen that canna scrape for ae bird.

123. It's an ill bird that files its ain nest.
He's a very wicked person that does evil to his own family.

124. It's an ugly lass that's never kissed,
And a silly body that's never missed.
A kindly proverb which our impersonal age might with advantage adopt.

125. It's folly to live poor to dee rich.

126. It's guid to hae your cog oot when it rains kail.
It's a good thing to have even a small share of a universal benefit.

127. It's ill dune to teach the cat the way to the kirn.
From whatever motives we are actuated, we are foolish to put temptation in the way of untrustworthy persons.

128. It's ill makin a blawin horn oot o a tod's lug.

129. It's ill to tak the breeks aff a Hielandman.
For they used to wear kilts only. You cannot take away what is not there to begin with. The forthright and eccentric C.O. of a well-known Highland regiment is said to have given a personal demonstration of the truth of this proverb, before a thousand men, during the First World War, after he had received complaints that several men were wearing trews under the kilt.

130. It's lang or four bare legs gaither heat in a bed.
     There's more to successful marriage than many think.

131. It's no easy to straucht in the aik the crook that grew in the saplin.

132. It's no lost what a friend gets.

133. It would be a hard task to follow a black-dockit soo through a burnt muir this nicht.

134. Jouk and let the jaw gae by.
     Take shelter until the rough shower blows past. This was one of the first things to learn in such wild countryside as comprises much of Scotland. It also means, by easy analogy, that it is foolish to battle against what can't be avoided and will soon be past.

135. Keep a thing seven years and ye'll find a use for't.

136. Keep your ain fish-guts for your ain sea-maws.
     Charity begins at home.

137. Keep your breath to cool your parritch.
     Spoken to those who talked too much and out of their turn.

138. Keep your gab steekit when ye kenna your company.
     Be careful in talking before strangers.

139. Keep your mou shut and your een open.

140. Kindle a candle at baith ends and it'll sune be dune.
     Bed late and rise early and you'll soon be dead.

141. Kindness is like cress-seed: it grows fast.

142. Lady, Lady Landers,
Lady, Lady Landers,
Tak your coats aboot your heid
And flee awa to Flanders.

>Children chanted this as they threw ladybirds into the air. The ladybird would then open out her wings and vanish.

143. Lang-tongued wives gang lang wi bairn.

>Those who tell everyone their plans long beforehand are unwise and invite ridicule.

144. Lasses are like lamb-legs : they'll neither saut nor keep.

>A pastoral version of ' Gather ye rosebuds while ye may,' but in a less elevated strain.

145. Let the bell wether brak the snaw.

>The oldest and most experienced sheep in the flock, which had a bell attached about its neck, was the best to lead the flock over treacherous snow. Tried leaders are best in emergencies.

146. Let that flee stick to the wa ; when it's dry the dirt will rub oot.

>Never mind that point at present, and later we'll forget about it.

147. Lift me up and I'll tell you more.

A stranger came upon this line carved on a great stone in a moor. He gathered a number of local helpers to help him turn over the stone, and, expecting to find a treasure, paid them all handsomely. His helpers laughed knowingly when, on the other side of the stone, there appeared the line :

Lay me doon as I was before.

148. Licht suppers mak lang days.

The Scots were often forced to make a virtue of necessity.

149. Like Moses' breeks—neither shape, form nor fashion.

In the old illustrated Bibles, Moses was often shown dressed in a very extraordinary fashion. The comparison was applied to any oddly-made article.

150. Little's the licht will be seen on a mirk nicht.

151. Macfarlane's Lantern.

>A proverbial name for the moon, which lit the wild Macfarlanes upon their excursions.

152. Macgregor as the rock,
Macdonald as the heather.

>This is the translation of an ancient provocative Gaelic proverb which probably expressed the view that the Macdonalds, as descendants of the Scottish Gaels, were comparative newcomers to the land compared with the Macgregors, who traced their descent (always a touchy matter with the Highlanders) to the aboriginal Picts.

153. Maiden's bairns are weel guided.

>Being of those ' whose habitation is in the air, are the best-condition'd Creatures imaginable.'

154. ' Mair haste, the waur speed,'
Quo the wee tailor to the lang threid.

155. Maist things hae a sma beginnin.

156. Mak a kirk or a mill o't.

>Do as you please with it.

157. Mennans are better than nae fish.

158. Monday's bairn is fair o face ;
Tuesday's bairn is fu o grace ;
Wednesday's bairn is a bairn o wae ;
Thursday's bairn has far to gae ;
Friday's bairn is lovin, forgivin ;
Saturday's bairn warks hard for a livin ;
But the bairn that is born on the Sabbath day
Is lively and bonny and wyce and gay.

159. Moosie, moosie, come to me,
The cat's awa frae hame.
Moosie, moosie, come to me,
I'll use ye kind, and mak ye tame.
  An invitation never accepted by ' moosie.'

160. Multiplication is vexation,
Division is as bad ;
The rule of three it vexes me,
And practice drives me mad.
  This rhyme was commonly printed by school-
  children upon their arithmetic books.
  Another favourite rhyme was :—
—— —— is my name,
Scotland is my nation ;
—— is my hame,
And H—— my destination.
  The blanks were filled in according to the whims of
  the writer.

161. Nae gairdener ever lichtlied his ain leeks.
    No man speaks ill of what he values most.

162. Naething like being stark deid.
    Spoken with malicious satisfaction upon hearing of
    the death of an enemy.

163. Naething to be done in haste but grippin fleas.

164. Ne'er find faut wi my shune, unless ye pay my soutar.
    Don't criticise something outwith your knowledge
    and concern.

165. Ne'er let your feet run faster than your shune.
    Don't outstrip your resources.

166. Ne'er look for a wife until ye hae a hoose and a fire to
    put her in.
    The misplaced phrase suggests that the giver of this
    advice was also ' het at hame,' i.e. on ill terms with
    his wife.

167. Ne'er marry a widow unless her first husband was
    hanged.

168. Ne'er misca a Gordon in the raws of Stra'bogie.
    Don't speak badly of a man among his friends. The
    Gordons were the principal clansmen about Strath-
    bogie, in north-west Aberdeenshire.

169. Ne'er speak ill o them whase breid ye eat.

170. Ne'er tak a stane to brak an egg when ye can dae i
    wi the back o' your knife.
    To bring a great force against a contemptible obstacle
    only invites ridicule.

171. Neevie, neevie, nick, nack,
  Which hand will ye tak?
  Tak the richt, tak the wrang,
  I'll beguile ye if I can.

> Children who have a ' sweetie ' or some other prize
> to dispose of, clench their hands, one of which
> contains the prize, behind their back and chant the
> above rhyme.

O

172. O, wad some power the giftie gie us
  To see oorsels as ithers see us !

> A well-known wish of Burns, which is not likely to
> be granted. It has become proverbial and is one
> of the few Scots proverbs still much used.

P

173. Powder me weel and keep me clean,
  I'll carry a ba' to Peebles Green.

> This was said about Mons Meg, the great cannon
> in Edinburgh Castle. But on one occasion long ago,
> after the cannon had been fired in salute, the ball was
> retrieved from Wardie Moor only two miles away,
> so we are justified in doubting whether Meg could
> have reached Peebles, twenty miles away.

174. Put twa pennies in a purse and they'll creep thegither.

175. Rain, rain, rattlestanes,
Dinna rain on me,
But rain on Johnny Groat's hoose
Far ower the sea.

> Chanted by children during a heavy shower of sleet or hail.

176. Raise nae mair deils than ye can lay.

> This refers to the ancient belief in the power to raise spirits out of the earth by magic, as described in the Odyssey, the Book of Kings, and elsewhere. But the proverb probably means nothing more than, ' Don't start anything you can't stop.'

177. Rattan an moose,
Lea' the puir woman's hoose ;
Gang awa ower to the mill,
And there ane and a' ye'll get your fill.

> Those whose homes were infested by rodents wrote this doggerel on the wall, or on a piece of paper, where the animals could see it and, unless illiterate, read it.

178. Rise when the day daws,
Bed when the nicht fa's.

> This proverb dates from a more Arcadian age than the present.

179. Rodden tree and reid threid
Put the witches to their speed.

> These, among such articles as amber beads and horseshoes, were supposed to prevent the attentions of witches and warlocks.

31

180. Scorn not the bush that bields ye.

181. Seagull, seagull, sit on the sand,
     It's never good weather when you're on the land.
         Yet the black-headed gull spends much of its year
         far inland, nesting and feeding. The common gull,
         or herring-gull, is probably meant in this proverb.

182. Set a stoot hert to a stey brae.
         The harder the task, the more determination is
         needed.

183. Some hae meat that canna eat,
     And some wad eat that want it ;
     But we hae meat, and we can eat,
     For which the Lord be thankit.
         The Covenanters' ' Grace before Meat,' a favourite
         with Burns, and grown proverbial.   ' Want ' in the
         second line means ' lack,' not ' desire.'

184. Sorrow and ill weather come unca'd.
         These two evade all attempts at planning.

185. Speak o the deil and he'll appear.
         Said, as a joke, when someone appears of whom the
         company has been talking.

186. Speak weel o the Hielands, but dwell in the Laigh.
         Those who inhabited the Moray Coast, or Laigh o'
         Moray, were wisely advised neither to invite the
         hostility nor to seek the hospitality of their turbulent
         Highland neighbours.

187. Speer nae questions, and I'll tell ye nae lees.

188. Spunky, Spunky, ye're jumpin licht,
Ye'll ne'er tak hame the schule-bairns richt,
But through the rough moss and ower the hag-pen,
Ye droon the ill anes in your watery den.

> A rhyme to intimidate ill-doers, about the Spunkie,
> or Will o' Wisp.

189. Sticks and stanes may brak my banes,
But names'll never hurt me.

> This chant is still used by school-children as a reply
> to abusive language.

190. Steek your een and open your mou
And see what the King'll send ye.

> This rhyme is spoken in fun to boys and girls when
> someone wishes to put a tasty-bite into their mouth.
> It sometimes ends in a practical joke.

191. Sunny, sunny shooer
Come in for hauf-an-hour,
Gar a' the hens cour,
Gar a' the hares clap,
Gar ilka wife o Lammermuir
Put on her kail-pat.

> A Berwickshire rhyme graphically describing the
> effects of a heavy shower. The shepherd's wife heats
> up the kail, or broth, because she shall soon have
> her husband home, drenched, from the bare hillside.

192. Suppers kill mair than doctors cure.

> But these were the suppers of a Gargantuan age.

193. Tak awa Aiberdeen, and twal mile roond, and faar are ye?

> There would, in the opinion of the Aberdonians, be very little worth in the North if Aberdeen and its fertile hinterland were removed.

194. Tammy Norrie o the Bass,
Canna kiss a bonny lass.

> This rhyme describes the puffins which nest on the Bass Rock. They have a parrot-like beak. But a Tammy Norrie is any shy, awkward fellow.

195. Thanks winna feed the cat.

> This is a boorish speech, and is much on a line with the Highlander's remark when the tourist admired the magnificent scenery, " Maybe aye, but ye canna fatten the coos on't.' The Scots were not fond of bombastic language, and took some delight in deflating it with such unsentimental remarks.

196 That was langsyne, when geese were swine
And turkeys chewed tobacco,
And sparrows bigget in auld men's beards,
And mowdies delved potatoes.

> This was considered a good reply to a scarcely credible statement.

197. The best-laid schemes o mice and men
Gang aft a-gley.

> This is perhaps the most universally quoted of Burns's lines, though not always spoken in Scots.

198. The breath o a fause friend's waur than the fuff o a weasel.

> The most ferocious creature, weight for weight, is the weasel. Before attacking a man it squeals, then fuffs. This was accounted an odious noise, but had the merit of being without deceit.

199. The coo that's first up gets the first o the dew.

200. The corbie says unto the craw,
'Johnny, fling your plaid awa':
The craw says unto the corbie,
'Johnny, draw your plaid aboot ye.'

> If the raven calls first in the morning, the day will be fine; if the carrion crow, then wet. With the present scarcity of ravens, few can benefit by these meteorological portents.

201. The deil's aye guid to his ain.

> A jocular expression nowadays, but in former times it was believed that Auld Nick had power to provide for his adherents.

202. The fish that sooms in a dub will aye taste c mud.

203. The gravest fish is an oyster;
The gravest bird's an owl;
The gravest beast's an ass;
And the gravest man's a fule.

204. The King lies doon,
Yet the warld rins roun.

> No man is indispensable.

205. The loodest bummer's no the best bee.

206. The men o the East
    Are pykin their geese,
    And sendin their feathers here-awa, there-awa.
    > Children used to sing this at the onset of snow.

207. The muirhen has sworn by her teuch skin
    She ne'er shall eat o the carle's win.
    > The waterhen or moorhen was supposed never to
    > eat of field crops.

208. The peesweep aye cries farrest frae its ain nest.
    > Most people, however naive they appear, are cunning
    > enough to mislead those who are trying to get the
    > better of them.

209. The siller penny slays mair souls than the nakit sword
    slays bodies.

210. The proof o the pudden's in the preein o't.

211. The robin and the lintie,
    The laverock and the wren,
    Them that herries their nests
    Will never thrive again.
    > These four sweet singers are the most innocent of
    > birds.

212. The tae hauf the warld thinks the tither hauf daft.

213. The tod ne'er kills the lamb except at a distance frae his ain hole.

> A fox will travel over a parish rather than ki'' near his den, as he knows that this would lead to his destruction. Some persons also do evil far from home and are all innocence to their neighbours. This proverb could have been applied very fittingly to the behaviour of Charles II, who liked everyone to be happy in his Court but caused 18,000 persons to be butchered in Scotland during his reign.

214. The willing horse is aye wrocht to daith.

215. Them that's brocht up like beggars are aye warst to please.

216. There ne'er was a bad, but there micht be a waur.

> It is hard to say whether or not this is a comforting thought.

217. There's aye some water whaur the stirkie droons.

> There must be some cause for a great fault or misfortune, no matter though people may try to explain it away.

218. ' There's baith meat and music here,' quo the dog when he ate the bagpipes.

> This comical proverb was often repeated by those

who were invited to an entertainment and found refreshments as well as musicians.

219. There's nae airn sae hard but rust will fret it;
There's nae cloth sae fine but moths will eat it.
> There seems to be a touch of malice in this proverb,
>
> as if the person quoting it were somehow rejoicing in mortality and, like John Knox, holding up a death's-head for all to see. A similar proverb which I have heard is, " There was naething made yet but it wad brek.' This is the savage spirit of many of the 'Guid and Godlie Ballants' of the 17th century.

220. There's naething got by delay but dirt and lang nails.

221. There's nocht sae queer as folk.
> Even in the days before psycho-analysis, the heart of man was known to be more unfathomable than all other natural phenomena.

222. There's nocht for it but the twa thoombs.
> A unique proverb, made during the war of 1914-18 by a Gordon Highlander. The sanitary authorities having failed to de-louse or de-flea the garments of the battalion, this canny lad made the above remark, referring to the primitive but sure method of killing fleas and lice by crushing them between the thumb-nails.

223. They craw crouse that craw last.

224. They hae need o a canny cook that hae but ae egg to their denner.

225. They wha hae a guid Scots tongue in their heid are fit to gang ower the warld.
> The implication here is that they will always find someone who can understand them, i.e. a fellow-Scot.

226. They wha pay the piper hae a richt to ca' the tune.

227. They wha stey in gless hooses shouldna thraw stanes.

This proverb is attributed to James VI and I, who is said to have replied in these words to Buckingham, who was complaining of the London Scots breaking his windows. It was known to the King that the young Duke had previously, in a frolic, broken the Scots' windows.

228. They're fremit friends that canna be fashed.

They're strange friends who cannot be bothered.

229. They're tarred a' wi ae stick.

It was the habit to mark sheep with tar to distinguish the ownership. The proverb could apply to people who were alike in bearing a common vice, the brand of Auld Nick.

230. Think mair than ye say.

231. Time tries a', as winter tries the kail.

The hardy kail, or borecole, was for long the only vegetable in the Lowlands of Scotland. Indeed, in the Highlands they did not relish the refinement of kail, but ate boiled nettles. The point of the proverb is that the kail was unpalatable until after it had suffered frost, which, however, often killed some of it. So with people : if they could survive the trials of life, without being embittered, they were a great asset to humanity and a credit to their kind.

232. To send round the fiery peat.

This was done on the Borders to summon the clans or family adherents. In che Highlands the expression was ' the fiery cross,' but it was never sent round alight : one end was charred black, the other reddened with blood, to symbolise fire and slaughter.

233. Truth and honesty keep the croon o the causey.

> The 'croon of the causey' was the highest and driest part of the street. When the gutters were so filled with filth, and never flushed until heavy rain came, there was naturally much competition for the 'croon o the causey.' The most respectable citizens generally insisted upon walking there.

234. Truth will stand when a' things failin.

> This noble proverb is found in 'Caller Herrin,' written by Lady Caroline Nairne about the New-haven fisherwomen.

235. Tweed said to Till,
'What gars ye rin sae still?'
Till said to Tweed,
'Though ye rin wi speed,
And I rin slaw,
Yet where ye droon ae man
I droon twa.'

> When the Scots retired in small companies from Flodden Field after their defeat, twice as many were drowned in the Till as in the Tweed : the still waters of the narrow Till deceived many, while the wide and brawling but shallower Tweed claimed few victims.

U

236. Use of hand is father of lear.

> First learn to use your hands ; that opens the way to other knowledge.

237. Want o wit is waur than want o gear.

238. We're to learn while we live.
    Often said in irony.

239. Weel kens the moose that the cat's oot o the hoose.

240. Well saipet is hauf shaven.

241. Wha daur bell the cat?
    This is about the best known of the Scots proverbs.
    At a meeting of mice, where they were discussing
    how to deal with the cat, a young mouse said that
    a bell should be hung round the cat's neck, then
    all might hear him coming. An old mouse rather
    spoiled this clever scheme by asking, ' Who will
    bell the cat? "
    In Scottish history there is a story that, at a meeting
    of nobles to discuss how to deal with Cochrane, the
    favourite of James III, some suggested seizing and
    hanging Cochrane. Lord Gray remarked, ' Well
    said, but who will bell the cat? ' Douglas, Earl
    of Angus, said that he would do it, and soon
    after he hanged Cochrane and a number of the
    King's servants over Lauder Bridge.

242. What fizzes in the mou winna fill the wame.
    Tasty food is not always best, and this principle
    applies to all attractive things.

243. When a' men speak, nae man hears.

41

244. When Cheviot ye see pit on his cap
O rain ye'll hae a wee bit drap;
When Ruberslaw draws on his coul
Wi rain the burns will a' be full.

> A Border proverb of the weather. The lower the
> clouds, the more rain.

245. When Yule comes
Dule comes,
Cauld feet and legs;
When Pasch comes
Grace comes,
Butter, milk and eggs.

> Pasch is Easter, and rhymes with grace.

246. Wise men buy and sell, and fools are bought and sold.

247. Ye breed o the leek, ye hae a white heid and a green tail.

> This was a rebuke to old men who were full of
> bawdy talk.

248. Ye canna gaither berries aff a whinbush.

> Don't go to ill-tempered people for favours.

249. Ye canna hae mair o a soo than a grumph.

250. Ye canna mak a silk purse oot o a soo's lug.

251. Ye canna pit an auld heid on young shouthers.

252. Ye come o the MacTaks, but no o the MacGies.

> These clans are found all over the world; the
> saying means, 'You're greedy.'

253. Ye found it where the Hielandman found the tongs.

    You stole it : the Hielandman had a reputation for thieving, not undeserved.

    This proverb recalls a notice in a certain golf-course, ' Players are requested not to pick up lost balls until they have stopped rolling.'

254. Ye hae gotten to your English.

    When a Highlander, addressing his opponent in argument, wished to satisfy his self-esteem he aspired to grandiloquent though often uncouth English. The above remark, which became proverbial, was judged to be the most aggravating reply that could be readily made, reminding the eloquent one that he was out of his element in attempting the mastery of a foreign tongue.

255. Ye ne'er see green cheese but your een reel.

    Green cheese means cheese newly-made : a great temptation to gourmands.

256. Ye seek grace o a graceless face.

    When Johnny Armstrong, the Border chief, was treacherously captured by James V he pleaded for his life, promising all kinds of service to the King in return for grace, or mercy. In the end, when he saw that his requests were in vain, he changed his manner of speaking and boldly addressed this verse to the King :

> ' To seek het water beneath cauld ice
> Surely it is great folly ;
> I hae socht grace at a graceless face,
> And there's nane for my men and me.'

257. **Ye** shape shune by your ain shauchled feet.

You judge all characters by your own, and it is deformed.

258. **Ye** wad wheedle a laverock frae the lift.

You have a winning way with you.

259. **Ye** was put oot o the oven for nippin the pies.

You can't keep your fingers off other people's property.

260. **Ye'll** be a man afore your mither.

Little boys were often promised this.

261. **Ye** would be a guid piper's bitch ; ye smell oot the weddins.

A scoffing reply to a gossip who envisaged certain matches between couples. The piper's dog had, of course, an interest in finding business for his master, who attended the weddings to provide music, but the gossip had not even that excuse.

262. ' Ye're a liar,' said the dummy ;
' Sae I see," said the blin' man ;
' Weel, dinna shout sae lood,' said the deaf man.

They were all cheats. In olden times, after bad harvests, great numbers of beggars swarmed over Scotland, and many professed to be physically afflicted. ' Sorning,' or begging by force, was heavily punished under the later Jameses. In the 18th century beggars were given licences.

263. **Ye're** feard for the day ye never saw.

You are worrying unnecessarily.

44

264. Ye're like a hen on a het girdle.
     You can't keep still.

265. Ye'll no sell your hen on a wet day.
     On a wet day a hen has little glamour.

266. Your mind's aye chasin mice.
     ' Your wits are wool-gathering ' is the English
     proverb.

267. Your tongue gaes like a lamb's tail.
     You are never done talking.

     Eneuch's eneuch o breid and cheese.

GLOSSARY

Scots.	English.
gaislin	gosling.
gang	go.
gaun	going.
gar	to force.
gear	possessions.
giff-gaff	exchange of goods.
girdle	flat iron plate for baking.
girning	complaining.
grace	mercy.
greet	weep.
grice	young pig.
grosset, grossart	gooseberry.
grumph	grunt.
guid	good.
hag-pen	bog-hole.
hanselled	brought a lucky first gift.
haud doon	to bully.
hauf	half.
herries	robs.
het	hot ; uncomfortable.
houtie-croutie	buttocks.
ilka	each.
ill	bad.
jaw	rough shower.
John Heezlum-Peezlum	Man in the Moon.
jouk	dodge.
kail	broth ; kind of cabbage.
kail-blade	cabbage-leaf.
kebbuck	a cheese.
kenna	know not.
kep	herd ; protect ; keep ; catch.
kirk	church.
kirn	churn ; fireside concert.
kitchen	relish.
Laigh (the)	Lowlands.

Scots.	English.
lang syne	long ago.
laverock	skylark.
lear	learning.
lichtlied	spoke contemptuously.
lichtsome	pleasant.
lift	sky.
linn	a gorge through which a torrent falls.
lintie	linnet.
loaning	country lane.
loose	louse.
lowp	jump.
lug	ear.
maun	must.
mennans	minnows.
mickle	great.
mirk	dark.
mowdies	moles.
neb	nose.
new-come	newly commenced.
nocht	nothing.
oo, or woo	wool.
or	before ; ere.
Pasch	Easter.
peesweep	green plover.
pike	pick.
preein	tasting ; trying.
pykin	plucking.
quo	said.
raip	rope.
rattans	rats.
raws	rows of cottages.
riggin	roof-top.
rumple-routie	nonsense word, perhaps meaning crossed fingers.
saipet	soaped.

47

Scots.	English.	Scots.	English.

sark—chemise; shirt.
saut—salt.
schule—school.
sea-maws—sea-gulls.
shauchled—shapeless; broken-down.
shoon—shoes.
siller—money; silver.
soo—sow.
sooms—swims.
soutar—shoemaker.
speer—ask.
Spunky—Will-o'-Wisp.
stang—sting.
stark-deid—stone-dead.
steekit—shut.
stey—steep.
stirkie—bullock.

stoor—dust.
straucht—straight.
tae and the tither—the one and the other.
teuch—tough.
thole—endure.
tod—fox.
toom—empty.
wae—sad; sorrow.
wame—belly; stomach.
waukrife—unable to sleep.
waur—worse.
whin—gorse; furze.
wispit—wiped with hay.
woo or oo—wool.
wrocht—brought about; worked.
wyce—wise; sensible.
yett—gate.